CASE STUDIES IN WESTERN CIVILIZATION

CASE STUDIES IN WESTERN CIVILIZATION
VOLUME I ANCIENT CIVILIZATIONS

GAVIN LEWIS
JOHN JAY COLLEGE
CITY UNIVERSITY OF NEW YORK

HARCOURT BRACE COLLEGE PUBLISHERS

Fort Worth   Philadelphia   San Diego   New York   Orlando   Austin   San Antonio
Toronto   Montreal   London   Sydney   Tokyo

Publisher	Christopher P. Klein
Senior Acquisitions Editor	David Tatom
Developmental Editor	Susan R. Petty
Project Editor	Catherine Townsend
Production Manager	Cindy Young
Art Director	Peggy Young

Harcourt Brace College Publishers may provide complimentary
instructional aids and supplements or supplement packages to those
adopters qualified under our adoption policy. Please contact your
sales representative for more information. If as an adopter or
potential user you receive supplements you do not need, please
return them to your sales representative or send them to:
Attn: Returns Department, Troy Warehouse, 465 South Lincoln
Drive, Troy, MO 63379.

Address for Editorial Correspondence
Harcourt Brace College Publishers
301 Commerce Street, Suite 3700
Fort Worth, TX 76102

Address for Orders
Harcourt Brace & Company
6277 Sea Harbor Drive
Orlando, FL 32887

1-800-782-4479, or 1-800-433-0001 (in Florida)

ISBN: 0-15-501507-9

Library of Congress Catalog Card Number: 96-77708

Printed in the United States of America

6 7 8 9 0 1 2 3 4 5 067 10 9 8 7 6 5 4 3 2 1

FOR NADIA, MICHAEL, ANNA,
ALEXANDER, AND DOROTHEA

PREFACE

This is the first of a projected seven-volume series intended for use in both Western Civilization and upper-level history survey courses. The series seeks to meet the need for reading that deepens students' knowledge and understanding of historical processes, while also conveying a sense of the concreteness and human reality of the past. *Close-ups of the Past* is based on the idea that this need can best be met by showing students general historical processes at work in particular instances involving specific people, places, events, and artifacts of the past—in other words, by case studies.

Each case study introduces students to a particular person, place, event, or object in such a way as to illuminate a major topic that is likely to be covered in a typical introductory or advanced survey course. In this volume, the appearance of the earliest advanced civilization in the Near East is dealt with in a case study that takes students step by step through the rise of Uruk, the first great city of ancient Mesopotamia. The institutions, procedures, political life, and underlying values of Athenian democracy are revealed through the events of a major scandal that shook Athens in 415 B.C. The story of the making of a famous artifact, the Rosetta Stone, introduces students to the political and religious traditions of Egyptian civilization, and its uneasy coexistence with Greek civilization in the bicultural Egypt of the Hellenistic era. Finally, a separate case study on the decipherment of the Rosetta Stone takes students beyond ancient times, through the historic breaks and continuities between ancient and modern civilization, to end with a feat of discovery by humanistic scholarship as spectacular and brilliant as in any field of knowledge.

The case studies assume no knowledge on the students' part, either of the particular subject matter or of the general topic that it illustrates. Each study is complete and self-contained, but the topics are chosen to complement each other, and points of comparison between case studies are indicated by cross-references to both this and forthcoming volumes. The series is prepared in such a way that breaks between volumes, or pairs of volumes, correspond to breaks between upper-level survey courses—ancient, medieval, early modern, and so forth—while also fitting into the various possible divisions of the Western Civilization sequence. All illustrations and maps are specifically related to material discussed in the text. Lists of further readings concentrate on works for general readers by experts—all available in paperback unless otherwise noted—dealing with more detailed aspects of the topics covered in each case study. On average, each case study is about fifty pages in length.

Lists of sources consulted in the preparation of each case study are also included. The purpose of this is, first of all, to make clear that a wide range of up-to-date scholarly works, as well as original sources, has been used—and perhaps to suggest, to any student who might happen to leaf through a list, the many ingenious ways in which modern scholars seek to understand the past. The lists of sources also fulfill the important duty of acknowledging my indebtedness to the works and authors listed for the facts and interpretations in each case study.

The "modular" structure of the series is intended to make it highly flexible in classroom use. Individual case studies can be read within the narrow time limits available for dealing with each historical period, and the instructor can assign them together with a core text, as well as other types of reading. Because the case studies are self-contained, the instructor can assign as many or as few as desired. For example, a Western Civilization instructor with an interest in, say, the rise of cities and city-states could assign the Uruk and Athens case studies; an instructor wishing to stress the relationship and mutual influence of Western and non-Western civilizations could concentrate on the Rosetta Stone case studies; and an instructor in an ancient history survey course might find a use for all four case studies. And even if fewer case studies are assigned, the moderate price of the volume will still justify the expense to the student.

Needless to say, this series is intended not to replace but to supplement other types of readings, whether core texts, documents, literary works from the past, or secondary books on particular topics. But within the spectrum of available readings, *Close-ups of the Past* does have a combination of advantages all its own. It can make the general concepts and processes of history real and accessible to the student in vivid yet truthful form; and it can do so within the severe constraints of student time, student knowledge, and student budget that apply to the typical history survey course.

ACKNOWLEDGMENTS

It is a pleasure to express my gratitude to all those who in various ways have helped bring this book into being.

The manuscript benefited from careful reading and thoughtful comments by Frederick Crawford, Middle Tennessee State University, Thomas F. X. Noble, University of Virginia, and Richard E. Sullivan, Michigan State University, as reviewers; my friend and partner Thomas H. Greer, Michigan State University, the author of *A Brief History of the Western World*, of which I am coauthor; and my fellow veterans of history survey courses at John Jay College, Eli Faber, Daniel Gasman, and James R. Jacob.

In addition, I owe much to the kindness of specialists. Hans J. Nissen, Ancient Near Eastern Seminar, Free University of Berlin; Denise Schmandt-Besserat, Department of Art History, University of Texas at Austin; P. R. Jeffreys-Powell, R. A. Knox, and Douglas MacDowell, all of the Department of Classics, University of Glasgow; Richard D. Billows, Department of History, Columbia University; and Jennifer R. Houser, Egyptian Section, University Museum, Philadelphia, were good enough to read and comment on case studies that fell within their areas of expertise. I owe a special debt of gratitude to Professors Nissen and Schmandt-Besserat, as it was their friendly reaction to Case Study 1 that convinced me that it would be practicable to write a series of "close-up" studies in areas far from my own academic field. "Like an ox in a wrestling ring" was how the Romans used to describe the efforts of anyone who ventured, without many years of study, into some unfamiliar territory of learning. To the extent that I have managed to avoid being ox-like, that is in good part due to the help of all these scholars. If, anywhere, there should still be found a suggestion of the bovine, the fault is entirely my own.

My path has been smoothed by the efforts of many helpful publishing people. Drake Bush and David Follmer, by their supportive interest in this project at different stages of its development, made its publication possible. David C. Tatom has overseen the publication process with understanding and decisiveness. Charles Naylor, Susan R. Petty, Cathy Townsend, Cindy Young, and Peggy Young have contributed their skills to the development, design, copyediting, and production of this book, and dealt with me with exactly the right combination of sympathy and firmness. I hope the business of getting this book into print has been as pleasurable for them as they have made it for me.

Most of all I thank my wife, Nadezhda Katyk-Lewis. She has kept me going with encouragement and belief in my efforts when I most needed it; she has given me time from her own pursuits to enable me to work on this project; and she has even, on various decisive occasions, been able to restrain me as an author from becoming intoxicated by the exuberance of my own verbosity.

CONTENTS

Detailed tables of contents, as well as lists of illustrations and maps, will be found at the beginning of each case study.

1

CLOSE-UPS OF THE PAST

URUK

THE RISE OF A SUMERIAN CITY

CONTENTS

ILLUSTRATIONS

MAPS

INTRODUCTION

Five thousand years ago, in the ancient Middle Eastern land of Sumer, one of the world's first great civilizations was born. The people of Sumer, whose way of life had up to then been no more advanced than that of many other prehistoric peoples living in the Middle East, suddenly began to produce a whole series of extraordinary innovations. Great cities, powerful governments, large-scale irrigation works, magnificent temples, artistic masterpieces, written documents—over a period of not more than four centuries, from about 3200 to 2800 B.C., all these and many other new developments changed the society and culture of Sumer out of all recognition. And the changes did not stop at the borders of Sumer. Other people, neighboring and distant, also began to forsake their traditional way of life. The achievements of Sumer became the common property of all the peoples of the Middle East, and an inheritance that was passed down through the centuries, all the way to our own time.

As with all such great and lasting changes, one cannot help wondering: How did it happen? What factors, in their own society and culture or in the surrounding environment, caused the Sumerians to make a new way of life for themselves? Was their achievement entirely their own, or in part, at least, the result of outside influences? Were they making a complete break with their more simple life of earlier centuries, or were they building on the foundation of earlier achievements? What kind of civilized society, with what beliefs, values, and institutions, emerged from those four centuries of ferment and turmoil? Questions like these are not only interesting in themselves. Since we are the distant heirs of the ancient Sumerian civilization, its history is our history too. In searching into its origins, we are doing two things at once. We are learning something about the factors that enabled humanity to reach forward, out of many thousands of years of prehistoric existence, to a more advanced and complex way of life. And we are also finding out something about the distant beginnings of the worldwide Western civilization of today.

Of course, questions like these are not easy to answer. We are dealing with a period so ancient that the Sumerians themselves, in later centuries when they began to write down what they knew of their own past, could remember nothing of it but a few half-mythical traditions. But

1. THE RUINS OF URUK   In the foreground, foundations of 5,000-year-old temples. In the background, a mound containing the ruins of another of Uruk's many ancient shrines.

although very few reliable historical records have come down to us, there is another source of information that is just as valuable: the ruins of the ancient cities of Sumer. Some of these date back as far as or even farther than the era of the rise of Sumerian civilization. By excavating and analyzing them, archaeologists have been able to find out a great deal about this very early period. As a result, more is known today about the origins of Sumerian civilization than about those of any other great civilization, including that of ancient Egypt, which developed at about the same time.

Of the cities of Sumer, the greatest and most powerful in the earliest times of advanced civilization—in fact, the first great city in the history of the world—was the city of Uruk.* Like the other great cities of Sumer—Ur, Lagash, Nippur, and a dozen or so others—Uruk was located in the south of present-day Iraq, where the Euphrates and Tigris rivers approach each other and finally join to enter the Persian Gulf.†

---

*The city is also known as Erech, the Hebrew version of its name.

†All places in Sumer and neighboring areas mentioned in this case study are shown in Map 1.

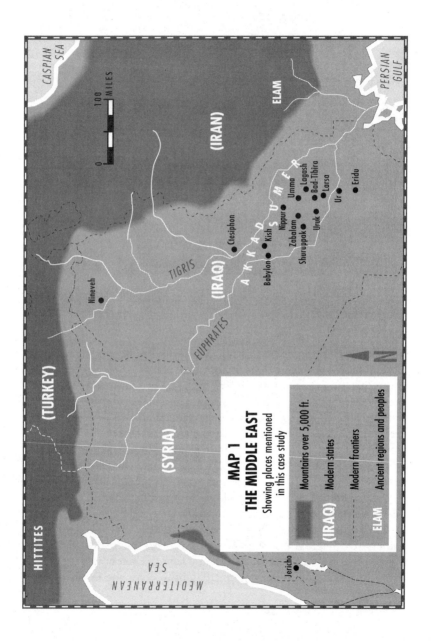

MAP 1
THE MIDDLE EAST
Showing places mentioned
in this case study

Mountains over 5,000 ft.

(IRAQ) Modern states

- - - - Modern frontiers

ELAM Ancient regions and peoples

(The ancient Greeks gave this area, and the whole region between the Euphrates and the Tigris, the name Mesopotamia, "the land between the rivers," and this name is used today to describe both this region and the civilization that began in Sumer.) Today, all that is left of Uruk is a wilderness of ruins, piled into great mounds that stretch for a mile and a half across a flat and arid plain, not far to the north of the present course of the Euphrates River. But since the beginning of this century, teams of archaeologists from Germany have been at work in these ruins. Over decades of patient and careful excavation, they have been able to trace a good part of the story of the rise of Sumerian civilization as it took place in Uruk, almost step by step.

Deep inside the ruin mounds, the archaeologists have found Sumer's earliest known monumental temple buildings, its earliest known masterpieces of sculpture, and also, scratched with reed pens into tablets of clay, its earliest known written documents. They have been able to trace the growth of Uruk itself, from a small town amid undrained and largely uncultivated swamps, into a city of 40,000 people at the center of a flourishing agricultural countryside, nourished by the carefully impounded and distributed waters of the Euphrates River. Study of the art and writings found in the excavations has hinted at the existence of complex religious beliefs and magnificent rituals, at the growth of powerful and highly organized religious and political institutions, and at turbulent rivalries and bitter warfare with neighboring cities, leading to the greatest undertaking of Uruk, the building of the city walls around 2800 B.C. Last but not least, on the basis of these discoveries, the archaeologists have been able to suggest answers to the questions about the rise of the advanced civilization of Sumer that were asked above, and to piece together a convincing story of how this most majestic of human events took place.

It must be admitted that this story lacks two things that most people think of as essential features of history: there are no dates, other than rough estimates,* and there are almost no names of famous people. This is not because Uruk had no famous people or important dates. The city may well have had its equivalents of 1492 or 1776, of Christopher Columbus or George Washington, but nearly all knowledge of them has been lost. Only toward the end of the story do a few named individuals appear. These are rulers of Uruk, who figure as ancient epic heroes in

---

*Since the estimates are rough ones, they are subject to change as research and excavation continue. For this reason, the dates given here may sometimes differ from those given in other books that students may read.

much later Sumerian myths and traditions, but who may really have reigned in the city from about 3000 B.C onward. Otherwise, this story is one not of people who changed the world and their deeds and thoughts, but of buildings and artifacts and what they mean: of temples and fortifications, of sculptured images and pieces of broken pottery, of ancient and enigmatic written documents, and of what these can tell us about the people who made them.

It is no easy matter to puzzle out from such remains the details of the great changes that must have been taking place in the most ancient times of Sumerian civilization. In fact, it is one of the proudest achievements of modern Western civilization that its archaeologists and scholars have been able to reconstruct so much of the achievements of its forerunners of the distant past.* Even so, there is much that remains unknown and mysterious about the earliest days of Sumerian civilization, many questions to which there are no certain and definite answers, but only a balance of probabilities. But mysteries of this kind can only add interest to a story of which the outlines, at least, are fairly clear: the story of the flowering of one of the world's first great civilizations, as seen through the rise of the world's first great city.

---

*For a famous example of a modern civilization reconstructing an achievement of an ancient one, the European decipherment of Egyptian writing, see Case Study 4 in this volume, "Egypt, Greece, Europe: The Rosetta Stone and Three Civilizations, Part 2, Death and Rediscovery of a Civilization."

I
THE TOWN OF URUK, 3200 B.C.

The date when this story begins, about 3200 B.C., is very early in the history of civilization, but it is late in the history of humanity. By this date, at least 20,000 years had passed since human beings of the same type as ourselves had first evolved. Perhaps 4,000 years had passed since the Agricultural Revolution had made farming and stock raising, rather than hunting and gathering, the basis of human society. This was still the "stone age"—to be exact, it was late in the Neolithic or New Stone Age— but in most places, the way of life of the human race was already very different from that of primitive "cavemen." That was true, among others, of the many different peoples who already lived in the Middle East, including the people of Sumer. It was also true of the inhabitants of what was then the small town of Uruk.

In 3200 B.C., the people of Uruk had a way of life that was already many centuries old. They had their traditional crafts and skills, which enabled them to live amid one of the harshest and most hostile environments of the entire region of the Middle East. They had their ancestral religious customs and beliefs, in which they seem to have expressed their awe of and their sense of dependence upon their natural environment. One way or another, their lives were dominated by the forces of their environment. They worshiped these, and at the same time struggled to extract from them what they needed to survive and prosper. In this they succeeded, and in so doing, built the foundations of the Sumerian civilization of later times.

Partly from the results of excavations and geological surveys, and partly by reading back from the conditions of the present day, it is possible to know with reasonable certainty what kind of natural environment the people of Uruk had to contend with 5,000 years ago. It was one in which the climate and the landscape strangely contradicted each other. At that date, the territory around Uruk consisted of a vast flat plain, baking hot and utterly rainless in summer, and chilly but still dry, except for an occasional ferocious cloudburst, in winter. Yet the land was covered for mile after mile with luxuriant, water-loving vegetation. Endlessly, the banks of reeds and tamarisk bushes, the stands of poplars and clumps of oleanders, stretched across the plain. Only occasionally was there a dry and grassy clearing, or rather island. For the immense flat carpet of vegetation, stretching on and on beneath the rainless sky, constituted a single enormous swamp, through which there flowed, in innumerable sluggish, muddy channels, the waters of the Euphrates River.

In the spring and early summer, after the snows had melted in the distant northern mountains where the Euphrates had its headwaters, the river channels would flow swift and high. They would rage through the swamps and spill out onto the islands of dry land, forming ponds and lakes, the edges of which would be lush with green grass. Gradually, through the heat of the summer and on into the relative cool of the fall and winter, the waters would subside, and on the islands, the grass would parch and wither. But even in the driest season, the swamps would remain, an endless tangle of reeds and mud, nourished by the waters of the river. Many creatures, originally at home in rainier yet drier landscapes, had adapted to this rainless yet watery environment: antelopes, wild donkeys, pigs—and also human beings. Strung out along the river channels, across a forty-mile stretch of countryside surveyed by archaeologists to the north and east of Uruk, were a couple of dozen villages.

Inconspicuous though most of these settlements must have been, in this world of wild animals and primeval vegetation, there was one that was already a landmark. It stood on two mounds, a few hundred yards apart, which raised it fifty feet above the surrounding swamps. The houses of the settlement clustered all over the slopes and tops of the mounds, sheltering perhaps as many as a couple of thousand people. Some of the houses were built of yellowish-brown mud bricks, with palm-thatched roofs. Others were ingeniously constructed of reeds, tied tightly together in twenty-foot-long bundles to make the rigid framework members, and woven into matting to form the roofs and walls. On the southern slope of the westernmost of the two mounds stood a larger, more impressive and regularly constructed building, higher than the ordinary houses and probably colored white: the temple of a god, which must have been visible for quite some distance across the plain. The temple of the god, the prominence of the settlement on its two mounds, and the large number of people who lived there made it the most important place in the district. This was Uruk, not long before it began to grow into a city.

Uruk was not only the largest and most important place in the district, but it was also the oldest. The mounds on which it stood were not natural formations, but consisted of the ruins of all the previous houses built on the site—a dozen layers of buildings, dating back to the first founders of the town as much as a thousand years earlier. Who these first founders of Uruk were, or the founders of other early settlements in the land of Sumer, nobody knows. Perhaps they were immigrants from the north or east—the highlands of present-day Syria or Iran—who arrived bringing with them the way of life of settled villagers. Perhaps they had already been living a more primitive, wandering, hunting, and fishing life in the swamps, and had taken to settled village life by imitation from outside. Either way, this particular settlement had been a success from the start. Probably it had begun as a small village, on the site of the western mound. At some point, this village had thrown out an offshoot, a few hundred yards to the east. Later still, perhaps not long before 3200 B.C., the two villages had grown together to form a single town. Over the generations, as Uruk had grown, it had also been more or less continuously occupied, which was unusual for villages and towns in those days. As a result, it had slowly risen above the swamp, as the ruins of its own houses—crumbled, destroyed by floods, perhaps from time to time sacked by enemies—had accumulated beneath it.

Within the endless tangle of mud and reeds and water, one would not have thought that there would be room for such a prominent and old-established town. In fact, to survive in such a place, the townspeople, like the people of other towns and villages throughout Sumer, had had to adjust their whole way of life to their soggy and constricted environment. Skills and techniques that their ancestors had brought with them when they first arrived, or that succeeding generations had learned from neighboring peoples, had had to be adapted to the conditions of the swamps. New skills and techniques had had to be developed to meet the needs of life there. As a result, the citizens of Uruk had not only survived but also modestly prospered, and the skills that enabled them to do so were to be inherited and improved upon by the later advanced civilization of Sumer.

For the townspeople of Uruk, as the remains of their buildings and artifacts indicate, the swamps were a storehouse, bountifully providing them with food and raw materials. They poled their boats up and down the river channels, spreading their nets to haul in catches of fish. They prowled the reeds with bow and arrow, in hopes of ambushing wildfowl. Their sheep and cattle wallowed contentedly in the mud, and grew fat on the lush grass left on the islands of dry land by the subsiding floods. They cut down reeds by the boatload for building and fuel. They dug up the very mud of the swamp to make bricks for buildings, and pottery in every shape and size, from small eating and drinking vessels to huge storage jars, the height of a man. Inside these jars, the townspeople kept the products yielded by one of the most important of the skills that their ancestors had brought with them or learned from neighboring peoples, and adapted to the conditions of the swamps: that of farming.

Scattered, probably, at quite some distance from the foot of the mounds were the fields of Uruk, and its palm groves. They would have had to be widely scattered, because in the mud and water of the swamps, there were only a few spots where cultivated crops could survive—areas on the dry and grassy islands, where river channels flowed close by, but were fairly small and narrow, so that in the flood season they would not be swollen with too much water. The river channels usually ran slightly above the level of the countryside, between levees, or natural embankments, of dried-out mud, left behind by many years of floods. Through these embankments, the farmers of Uruk cut ditches leading out onto the grassy islands that could be blocked and unblocked at will. When the river began to rise in the late fall, fed by the first cloudbursts of the season, the water would gush out through the ditches onto the parched land. Again and again, from the late fall until the spring, when the meltwaters of the northern mountains brought the river to full flood, the waters could be made to gush out, and down onto the fields and groves. Just as important, the waters could be made to stop gushing out when the ground was moist enough for seeds to germinate and plants to grow, but before it became so wet that cultivated plants would "drown." At least in a few favored spots, both the miserliness of the heavens and the too abundant generosity of the river could be made up for by irrigation.

Of course, even in these few favored spots, farming was both difficult and risky. The Uruk farmers had to do a great deal of ditch digging and ditch cleaning, which farmers in regions of the Middle East with more regular rainfall and less floodwater never had to bother with. In addition, the Uruk farmers could never be sure that all this extra work would be rewarded. In the fall—the planting season, when the crops were most in need of at least some reliable watering—the rains might be delayed, and the river might be too low for irrigation. In the spring—the harvest season, when ripening crops could easily be ruined by too much water—the creeks and channels might rise too high for the ditches to handle, and the floods would sweep away six months' toil. All the same, the extra work and the risks were worth it. The floods brought down not only water, but also silt: the soil of many upstream lands, rich in essential plant nutrients. The fields of Uruk were not only watered by the river, but they also received a heavy annual dose of fertilizer. Barley, wheat, lentils, sesame, dates—in good years, all grew in fabulous abundance, by the standards of the time. Comparisons based on present-day farming in the Middle East suggest that the Uruk farmers may have harvested twice as much barley per acre as farmers who had more regular rainfall to depend on, but no irrigation.

In the spring, the townspeople would harvest all this bounty and pack it away into their huge storage jars, sealed at the top with lumps of wet clay that dried out to form a hermetic seal, keeping the produce within cool and safe from vermin. If the harvest had been good, then the Uruk farmers could expect to fill more than enough jars to see them through to the next harvest. The surplus would provide an important reserve against future bad harvests. Just as important, the Uruk farmers must have used the produce from the storage jars to barter with other peoples, neighboring or distant, for products that they lacked.

For the people of Uruk, the most important article of commerce that they obtained in this way would have been a vital raw material, which was unavailable in the swamps but without which they could not survive: stone. The slivers of obsidian, a natural glass of volcanic origin, that the townspeople used as drill bits, came from 800 miles up the Euphrates, in the mountains where the river had its source. Pieces of flint and chert, hard rocks that they used for hoe blades to break up the ground before sowing, had to be imported from the desert plains that lay to the west of the Euphrates swamps. This "stone-age" people, like those of the other towns and villages of the swamps, depended on trade with other peoples—upriver, in the deserts to the west, or in the mountains across the Tigris river—for their very existence. The way of life of the people of the swamps was only possible because there were many other peoples in the Middle East who could supply what they lacked. The achievements of the townspeople of Uruk came from the fact that they formed part of a regional network of trade, contacts, and cultural influences that extended all over the Middle East. That, again, would also be true, on a far larger scale, of the great city that Uruk was to become.

Of course, for the townspeople of Uruk to farm successfully, everything depended on the floods and the rains, the soil of the dry islands, and the heat of the sun coming together in the right proportions to give them a good harvest. But they had a way by which they hoped to ensure this too, or at least make it more likely. This was the worship of their god, and the occasional rebuilding of his shrine.

For a thousand years, as long as Uruk had existed, there had always been a temple in the town, and it had always stood at or near the same spot on the western mound. In later centuries, this spot is known to have been sacred to the chief and father of all the Sumerian gods and goddesses, a god whose name was An, meaning "heaven," in the sense of "sky." Probably, therefore, the people of Uruk were already worshiping this god in 3200 B.C., and had been doing so for many centuries. If their beliefs were similar to those of the Sumerians of later times, then they deemed the sky god to be the first parent, together with the earth goddess, of all the other powers that ruled their lives—the sun, the winter cloudburst, the waters of the river, and many others. They would have regarded these forces of nature not just as blind forces, but also as living, divine beings, with humanlike personalities and humanlike needs. For the townspeople, the worship of these beings would have been essentially a matter of providing for the needs of the gods, so that these would make their dwelling among them, and favor and protect them.

The best evidence that the townspeople held such beliefs is the layout of the temples they built—a layout that had not changed since the earliest days of the original village. At top left in Illustration 2 is the ground plan of the first known temple in Uruk, dating from sometime about 4000 B.C. The plan at bottom left shows a temple that stood on almost exactly the same spot, probably not long after 3200 B.C. Both temples are rectangular buildings about twenty-five yards long, with a long hall on the inside, surrounded by smaller side chambers. This was simply a larger and less higgledy-piggledy version of the layout of private houses. Probably, therefore, the townspeople of 3200 B.C. believed, as their ancestors had done for many generations before them, that the temple was actually the god's house, where he lived. This was not only the best house in town, but it was also the most prominent: it stood on an artificial, brick-built mound, which was heightened and enlarged from time to time, so as to match—or more precisely, to keep ahead of—the "natural" growth of the town mound. Inside the temple, at one end of the long central hall, there would probably have been an object of some kind—a stone, a tree trunk, or perhaps an image in animal or human shape—into which the people believed the god had entered, so that the object and the god were one. In this way the townspeople supplied the god's humanlike need for shelter, respect, and honor. To do so on this scale must have been a great effort. The people of Uruk must have taken a great deal of time off from hunting and fishing, and ditch digging and hoeing to labor on the temple and its mound. But the results were worth it. By doing all this, they ensured that the god was present among them. Themselves, their fields and groves, their flocks and herds, all were under his eye and under his protective power.

This, then, so far as it can be known or pieced together, was the way of life of the townspeople of Uruk about 3200 B.C. In their strange world of mud and reeds under a rainless sky, they had found a way to make a prosperous life for themselves, and worthily to serve their god. Throughout the swamps, the people of other small towns and villages were doing the same. Together, though they were certainly not under a single united government, they formed one people. It is not certain that this people was in fact the same as the later inhabitants of the region whom we call the Sumerians. But there is no doubt that the way of life of these early inhabitants provided the foundation for the advanced civilization of Sumer.

No one at the time, however—if there had been anyone to think of things in this way—could have predicted that out of the life of the people of the swamplands, a great civilization would shortly grow. Remarkable though their way of life was, the people of the swamps were no more advanced and prosperous than many other peoples of the Middle East. Upriver on the Euphrates, in the rolling plains through which it flowed before entering the swamps, or in the mountains across the Tigris, there were towns as large as Uruk, with temples as modestly imposing, and larger retinues of satellite villages. Even if farming in those regions was less productive in per-acre terms, there were far more acres suitable for cultivation than in the swamps. Therefore these upriver societies were just as wealthy as that of Uruk, if not wealthier.

Moreover, the way of life of the swamplands does not seem to have changed very much over the generations. In Uruk, the same small town, and the earlier twin villages, with the same crafts and skills and rituals and beliefs, had existed for perhaps a thousand years. Once in a while, some important technical advance, developed by some more innovative upriver people, had made its way to Uruk—the potter's wheel around 3500 B.C., the small-scale use of copper not much later. But these things do not seem to have made any great difference to the traditional life of the townspeople. Indeed, there was no reason why they should have. The traditional way of life was as successful as could reasonably be hoped for. The people of Uruk had carved themselves a reasonably comfortable, though narrow, niche in their constricted environment. Within that environment, no technical innovations or changes in ways of life could do much to widen the niche. So long as the environment stayed the same, the future would not be different from the past.

But around 3200 B.C. the people of Uruk must have noticed something that had probably already been happening for some time. Perhaps it had already begun to affect their lives. If not, it would shortly begin to do so, with momentous results, not only for themselves, but also for all future generations down to our own time. Their environment was changing.

2
THE CITY OF URUK
3200–2900 B.C.

THE NEW LANDSCAPE

Sometime after 3500 B.C., as analysis of samples of sediment taken from the sea floor indicates, the amount of water discharged yearly by the Euphrates and Tigris rivers into the Persian Gulf began to decrease. Probably this was the result of a minor climatic change, affecting the entire region of the Middle East. Throughout the region, temperatures became a little cooler on the average; and taking one year with another, slightly less rain and snow fell. The change may well have been hardly noticeable in the daily weather, but in the southern swamps, its effect on the landscape was remarkably swift. The level of the Persian Gulf, fed mainly by the two rivers, began to sink. To reach the sea, the rivers had to carve themselves new and lower-lying channels through the swamps. Year by year and decade by decade, the floods covered less of the land, and the network of river channels grew less dense. The carpet of mud and reeds began to shrink, and the islands of dry land began to multiply and grow. As the decades turned into centuries, a new landscape appeared, neither constricted by swamps nor overwhelmed by water, nor yet too dusty and parched for cultivation. This was a landscape that could nurture a civilization.

For the people of Uruk and other towns and villages of the swamps, the new landscape created an extraordinary opportunity—or as they no doubt saw it, the gods of soil, water, and weather who ruled their lives had given them a great gift. All of a sudden, the niche that they occupied in their environment had widened. Using just their familiar traditional skills, the people of the swamps now had access to exploitable resources far greater than those of other Middle Eastern lands.

If the original people of the swamps were in fact the same as the Sumerians of later times, then it must have been they who took advantage of this gift. Or perhaps it was only now that the Sumerians arrived, as immigrants or invaders attracted by the bonanza, conquering or absorbing the original inhabitants while learning their skills. Either way, it is certain that the opportunity was seized. The evidence is that the changes in the landscape were accompanied by an explosive increase in population and a long-continuing agricultural boom.

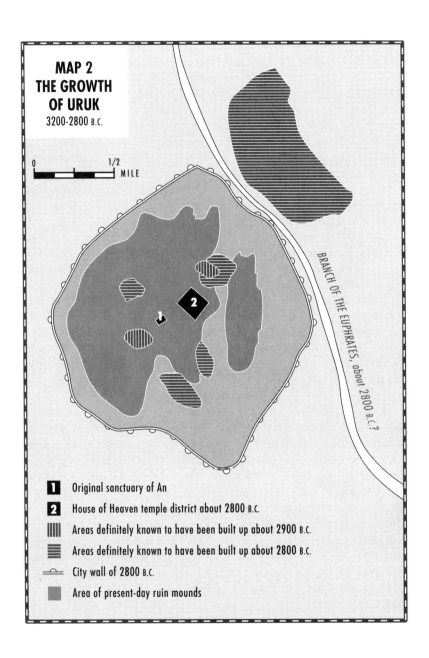

**MAP 2
THE GROWTH
OF URUK**
3200-2800 B.C.

0   1/2
MILE

BRANCH OF THE EUPHRATES, about 2800 B.C.?

1 Original sanctuary of An

2 House of Heaven temple district about 2800 B.C.

||||| Areas definitely known to have been built up about 2900 B.C.

≡ Areas definitely known to have been built up about 2800 B.C.

City wall of 2800 B.C.

Area of present-day ruin mounds

By 2900 B.C. at the latest, the territory around Uruk was no longer the primeval landscape of earlier days. The original carpet of swamp had given way to an intricate patchwork of river channels and side creeks, muddy levees and dry soil, banks of reeds and stretches of grassy plain. In this new landscape, places where water in manageable amounts flowed close to land that was dry enough to cultivate were no longer rare. Now, there were countless such places, where hard work could make water and fertilizing silt gush out onto fields and groves. In fact, groves of date palms and fields of barley and other crops now formed at least as prominent a part of the varied landscape as any natural vegetation; and the overflowing harvest of the irrigated fields and groves supported a population that by the standards of the time was enormous. Every creek and channel of the river was lined with villages and small towns: more than 150 of them, in the forty-mile stretch of countryside surveyed by archaeologists to the north and east of Uruk. Some of these places had mosaic-covered houses of wealthy farmers, and their own modest temples of local gods and goddesses. Throughout the countryside there must have been people and animals to be seen: farmers shoveling out mud from the ditches leading down to the barley and date palms; sheep and cattle grazing on the lush grass of early summer; fishermen punting up and down the river channels in their graceful, high-prowed boats. In only three centuries there had grown up, in this suddenly bountiful territory, a society wealthier and more populous than any the world had yet seen.

There was one part of the territory where the wealth and population were especially densely concentrated. It consisted of a zone about five miles across, where the palm groves and fields of barley lay so close together that there was little if any room for the other, wilder elements in the patchwork of water and vegetation. Nowhere else in the world was there a continuously cultivated area of land that even approached the size of this one. At the center of the ring of fields and groves there stood what to any contemporary visitor must have been an amazing, almost terrifying sight: Uruk itself, swollen to a size far larger than that of any previous human settlement. Beyond the twin mounds of the original town, the mud brick and reed-built houses had spread far out onto the level ground, perhaps as much as half a mile in every direction, though interrupted by gardens, pastures, and claypits.*

---

*The size of Uruk at different dates, and the location of all places in the city mentioned in this case study, are shown in Map 2.

In this vast sea of houses, there lived perhaps 10,000 people. Most of them were probably farmers, and much of Uruk must have resembled an enormous village. The houses were closely packed together, with no straight streets or broad avenues. There must have been as many animals as people in the place: flocks of sheep grazing in the outskirts, goats tethered in the yards of houses, oxen blocking the narrow lanes and alleyways between them. But such things were to remain a prominent feature of the urban scene for thousands of years to come. They made no difference to the fact that Uruk had become a human settlement of a new type, unknown in the past but with a great future before it: a city.

The changes that had taken place in the Uruk region did not stop at its borders. The whole land of the swamps had changed in the same way. Everywhere were villages and small towns, and at fairly frequent intervals there was a place large enough to count as a city. Only thirty miles down the river were two such places, Eridu, and one of the most famous cities of later Sumerian times, Ur. About the same distance upstream was Shuruppak. Beyond it was Nippur, and a hundred miles away, near the northern limit of the land of Sumer, was the city of Kish. Of this line of cities strung out along the lower course of the Euphrates River, none, so far as is known, had been more than a small town or village four centuries earlier. Now, although none was nearly as large as Uruk, they too had grown to unprecedented size. And other cities had sprung up beyond the land of Sumer, upriver in the neighboring land of Akkad, and across the Tigris in Elam. The changes in Sumer were spreading up and down the valleys of the great rivers. Throughout Mesopotamia, a new kind of society, based on intensive farming and large cities, was replacing the old world of scattered villages and small towns.

This new society was not simply bigger and wealthier than the traditional one out of which it had grown. It also seems to have possessed great dynamism and sense of purpose, though to judge from the evidence of Uruk, these were expressed in a way that we today might find strange. Throughout the centuries of population explosion and agricultural boom, the people of Uruk had been committed to a continuing, indeed endless common project. This project must have consumed a good deal of their expanding resources, and the evidence suggests that it stretched their technical abilities to the limit, helping to force the development of many new skills.

The results of this project, so far as it had progressed after three centuries, were easy to see in Uruk itself. At the center of the swollen city, the two mounds of what had been the small town of Uruk were no longer covered by the humble dwellings of farmers. Instead, they were occupied by a group of huge and magnificent public buildings, some completed, some under construction, and still others in the process of being torn down. The chief "occupant" and "owner" of this impressive complex of buildings, construction projects, and demolition sites was a mighty goddess whom the people of Uruk now worshiped, having seemingly turned away from their ancestral sky god. The three centuries in which Uruk had grown from a small town to a city had also been an era of changing traditions, of religious anxiety and hope, and very likely of rivalry and conflict: an age of creative turmoil, out of which a civilization had grown.

THE HOUSE OF HEAVEN

The first evidence that the ancient religious traditions of Uruk were beginning to change dates from some time around the year 3100 B.C. At that date, in an area of the eastern mound of Uruk about a quarter of a mile from the shrine of the sky god on the western mound, a new temple was built. In later centuries, when this eastern district had already grown old as a sacred spot, it was known as "Eanna," meaning "House of Heaven." Perhaps, then, the first temple on the spot was simply a new dwelling place for the sky god—an additional one, in fact, since the old one continued in use. Even so, for the sky god to command a new residence to be built on a spot that, as excavations indicate, had been inhabited for a thousand years by mere farmers and fishermen, was a significant break with tradition. The temple itself represented an even greater break with tradition. On this new site, the builders obeyed a new divine command—to construct a building lavish and magnificent beyond anything the world had yet seen.

Of the very first House of Heaven, nothing has survived but heaps of pieces of clay, colored red, white, and black, of a kind that was used in later temples to form mosaics. Even this is enough to show that it must have been a more imposing building than the white-plastered temples on the eastern mound. But within a few decades, it was replaced by another temple, which the archaeologists have been able to reconstruct in more detail. Its ground plan is shown at right in Illustration 2 next to those of the traditional temples. The most impressive thing about this new building was its enormous size: no less than eighty yards long and thirty yards wide. So far as is known, no one in Sumer, indeed no one else in the world, with the possible exception of the Egyptians, had ever

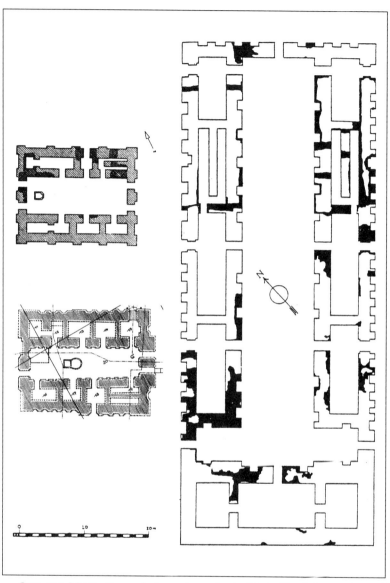

2. OLD AND NEW Ground plans of temples in Uruk. Top left, a traditional temple, dating from perhaps 4000 B.C. Bottom left, a temple that stood on the same spot about 3000 B.C., with dimensions and ground plan very similar to those of the first. Right, one of the first temples on the House of Heaven site, the Temple on the Limestone Base, dating from about 3000 B.C. The darker areas in the plans at top left and right are foundations actually excavated by archaeologists, from which the rest has been reconstructed.

tried to build a building as large as this one—unless, perhaps, the first House of Heaven had already been so large.

The problems simply of designing this building and laying it out must have been enormous. Hundreds of thousands of mud bricks had to be laid in complicated patterns, so as to produce long vertical slits or "niches" as a decorative feature on the outside, and the various suites of halls and chambers on the inside. Yet all of this had to be done in such a way that the walls ran parallel and met at right angles. In addition—if this temple was like the first, and like later ones built on the same spot—many thousands of pieces of mosaic had to be laid in even more complicated patterns, to decorate the exterior wall niches and the inner chambers. Finally, the base on which the temple rested was made of limestone, which had to be quarried in the desert perhaps forty miles to the west, transported in the baking heat over the drifting dust of the plain and through the reeds and mud of the swamp, and finally hauled up the eastern mound to the site of the sanctuary. To build this building needed skills of design, surveying, and craftsmanship such as had never been put forth on this scale before. It needed the labors of brickmakers and bricklayers and stonemasons, of many troops of load-bearing animals, and whole flotillas of riverboats. But the results were worth it. On the western mound there stood, as before, the simple, white-plastered traditional temple of An. On the eastern mound, three times as long and twice as broad, stood the mosaic-encrusted House of Heaven. On one mound stood a modest "chapel," and on the other, a great "cathedral." It was the symbol of a new age.

But the building of the temple on the limestone base was only a beginning. In the decades that followed, two other temples, just as large or even larger, were built alongside it. Other divine beings, it seems, were now considered worthy of equal honor with the first dweller upon the eastern mound. The identity of one of these upstart deities is known for certain. Wall decorations and other objects dating from this period display an emblem known as the "reed bundle": it seems to represent a bundle of reeds, tied together to form the rigid gatepost of a reed-built farm building, decorated with a streamer for some solemn occasion. (The emblem can be seen, depicted twice, at top center in the diagram of the carvings on the Uruk Vase shown in Illustration 5.) From Sumerian records of later times, it is known that this was the emblem of a great goddess, Inanna, whose name meant "Lady of Heaven."

In later Sumerian mythology, Inanna was the most beloved, honored, and feared of goddesses. Among her many powers and attributes, some of the most important were those she was deemed to possess as the goddess of the storehouse. This the Sumerians thought of not just as a building, but also as a bountiful living being: a "womb," teeming with life that it brought forth in due season. Inanna was the bride of Dumuzi, a fertility god who "died" and revived each year with the vegetation.* Every year in the spring following the harvest, Inanna and Dumuzi were believed to perform a mighty and magical act of procreation, so that the storehouse might "conceive" and give birth again the following year.†

It is fairly certain that when Inanna first appeared in Uruk, she was already worshiped in this way. As the landscape changed, and every year the storehouses became more heavily "pregnant" with barley and dates and wheat and sesame, perhaps the goddess of the storehouse seemed ever more worthy of honor. She must have elaborate rituals to serve and influence her, a staff of servants to perform the rituals, and of course a magnificent residence to accommodate her. Dumuzi, too, perhaps, had to have his own lavish dwelling. Vast changes, as it must have seemed to the people of Uruk, were under way amongst the divine powers that ruled the landscape and their lives. They must build not just one huge temple, but three.

Even when the builders had accomplished this feat, they were still dissatisfied—or as they probably believed, the gods and the goddess themselves, speaking through their priests and priestesses, their prophets and prophetesses, were discontented. Indeed, the gods and the goddess turned out to be extremely hard to please. Over the next hundred years, each of the new temples was individually demolished and rebuilt three times over. Each time, the walls were torn down to a few inches above ground level, and the rubble from higher up was shoveled between and over them to make level foundations on which a new temple would be built. Each time, the new temple was just as large and splendid as the old one, or even larger.

But even after a hundred years of constant rebuilding, still there was something wrong. Not long after 3000 B.C., the builders tore down all three temples, together with the entire maze of subsidiary buildings that had grown up around them. The builders carried out rituals of

---

*Inanna and Dumuzi are often known by the names given them by a later people of Mesopotamia, the Babylonians: Ishtar and Tammuz.

†For similar myths of death, life, and fertility among other ancient peoples, see Case Studies 2 and 3 in this volume, "A Political Scandal in Democratic Athens," pp. 90–92 (Demeter and Persephone), and "Egypt, Greece, Europe: The Rosetta Stone and Two Civilizations, Part 1, Two Civilizations in One Land," p. 143 (Isis, Osiris, and Horus).

purification, with flaming sacrifices, throughout the sacred temple precinct. Then they started all over again.

This time, instead of three temples, there was only one. It was placed not at ground level but on a brick-built terrace that raised it above the surrounding buildings. Ritual and other objects dating from this time continue to show the divine emblem of the reed bundle, but there is no evidence that the sky god had a dwelling place in the house that bore his name. A great revolution, it seems, had taken place among the divine beings. Inanna had become the mistress of the House of Heaven.

But even with the new plan of construction, there was still a problem: the terrace on which the new temple stood was not high enough. More and more layers of mud bricks were piled on top of the terrace and on its sides. Again and again the buildings surrounding the terrace were torn down and rebuilt, to accommodate it as it grew. In addition, the service of the goddess required ever more subsidiary buildings around the central temple. Eventually, her holy precinct spread to the western mound of the original town, and swallowed up the buildings there. The sky god, who had been worshiped in Uruk for a thousand years, now had no dwelling to call his own.

It was not until 2000 B.C. that the House of Heaven reached its final form. By that time, the terrace had grown into an artificial mound more than a hundred feet high. It had become a "ziggurat," such as was to be built in honor of the gods and goddesses of the great cities of Mesopotamia—Ur, Babylon, Nineveh, and many others—for thousands of years to come. But already by 2900 B.C., two centuries after the new plan was adopted in Uruk, the high terrace with its holy of holies dominated the temple district and the whole city. It must have been visible for miles across the countryside, as if to proclaim the message "Here lives a mighty goddess, the protectress and owner of this land and all its people."

That, in its barest outlines, is the story of the building and rebuilding of the House of Heaven, in the three centuries that followed the "arrival" of the first divine being on the eastern mound. The story is not simply one of architectural change. It also provides clues to what was going on in the minds of the people of Uruk during the era of the rise of advanced civilization.

For one thing, the long succession of temple ruins is obvious evidence of the overwhelming importance that the people of Uruk attached to serving and honoring the gods. The newly populous and wealthy society of Uruk must have inherited from the prehistoric past a sense of its utter dependence on the gods, and of the absolute necessity of honoring them and serving their needs. It was prepared to use its vastly expanded resources to provide for the gods with unheard-of magnificence. The only problem, it seems, was: which gods?

The people of Uruk must have deemed it essential to the well-being of their city to answer this question aright. But the constant demolition and rebuilding of the temples suggest that they had the greatest difficulty in finding the answer. This perplexity must have been a source of continual excitement, anxiety, and conflict. Perhaps it led to a great crisis of some kind, which was finally resolved by the establishment of Inanna as the mistress of the House of Heaven. Even then, apparently, it took a great deal of rethinking to satisfy her needs. For Uruk, the era of the rise of civilization must have been an age of uncertainty, growing out of a breach with religious tradition.

No doubt these religious changes were connected with other changes that were taking place, political, economic, and social. Possibly, if the original inhabitants of Uruk were not Sumerians, it was now that the Sumerians arrived, whether as immigrants or as conquerors, bringing with them the cult of Inanna. Perhaps the dethronement of the sky god by the fertility goddess was the result of some kind of change of attitudes among the people of Uruk, produced by such factors as the increase in population or the growing productivity of farming. Very likely, the religious changes were connected in some way with the development of new government institutions, and the rise and fall of powerful leaders. But it is impossible to do more than guess at such things. All that can be said for certain is that among people so obsessed with serving the gods as those of Uruk, ferment and turmoil involving the service of the gods were sure signs of ferment and turmoil throughout the entire fabric of society.

All this excitement, taking place in a long-ruined city over the worship of long-forsaken deities, might seem of little importance today. But in fact, it was to be of the greatest significance for the entire future history of civilization, right down to the present. It seems to have been to a large extent their obsession with serving the gods that spurred the people of Uruk to adopt or help pioneer many of the skills and devices that have remained basic to civilized society ever since.

To build and rebuild temples of unexampled size, and to serve the goddess with unexampled magnificence, it was not enough for Uruk to be wealthier and more populous than any earlier society. It also had to become technically more advanced, artistically more skilled, and far better organized. The society of Uruk did indeed develop in this way between 3200 and 2900 B.C., and the leaders in this process seem to have been the priests and priestesses of Inanna. By 2900 B.C. they had built up a highly organized bureaucracy, which itself directly controlled, in the name of the goddess, a sizable share of the vastly increased wealth of Uruk. Presumably it was this bureaucracy that organized and mobilized the resources to build the great temples. Certainly it sponsored many technical and artistic innovations. This is not guesswork, for the bureaucracy left evidence of its activities behind. This evidence was the result of the most notable single innovation of those centuries, an innovation that the priestly bureaucracy itself pioneered: writing.

"ONE — DAY — BEER — BREAD"

The invention of writing is something that has happened several times over in the history of the human race, but the time that it happened in Sumer was perhaps the single most important; for it was from Sumer that the idea of writing spread to the Egyptians and later to other peoples of the Middle East and Europe, to produce the great majority of writing systems used in the present-day world.* In Sumer itself, the invention of writing did not take place once for all, at one particular date in history. It was a long, slow process, taking several centuries to accomplish, and was no doubt pioneered in other cities besides Uruk. Still, the fact is that most of the earliest surviving Sumerian written documents come from in or near the ruins of the House of Heaven. There are about 4,000 of them—clay tablets originating from various dates between about 3000 and 2900 B.C., roughly the same period when Inanna was becoming the supreme goddess of Uruk. The earliest of these tablets must date from a time very close to that at which the gradual development of Sumerian writing first began.

By working backward from the better understood Sumerian writing of later times, modern scholars have been able to decipher the meaning of more than 500 out of a total of roughly 700 signs used by Inanna's scribes. This is enough to reveal the enormous importance of the tablets as historical documents. They tell of the earliest stages in the development of writing, a truly world-changing innovation in the history of humanity; and they bear witness to the appearance of other innovations of equal import.

---

*For the subsequent development of writing in Egypt, the Middle East, and Europe, see below, Case Study 3, "Egypt, Greece, Europe: The Rosetta Stone and Three Civilizations, Part 1, Two Civilizations in One Land," pp. 158–74.

3. THE EARLIEST WRITING   This 5,000-year-old clay tablet records one day's allocations of beer and bread to the temple staff of the goddess Inanna.

This is not because the scribes deliberately set out to record what they were doing, or the happenings in the city around them. They felt no need to write the history of their own times, or to express their thoughts and feelings, or even to set down the revelations delivered by the priests and priestesses of the goddess. These were all later uses to which writing was put. What Inanna's scribes wanted to do was something more practical and everyday: to keep track of supplies entering and leaving the goddess's storehouses. Nearly all the Uruk tablets are simply account-keeping documents, the equivalent of today's invoices and inventories and purchasing orders. The development of Sumerian writing seems to have taken place rather in the same way as the data-processing revolution of our own day and age. It began as a record-keeping convenience, made necessary by a society that was producing more of everything, including information.

In fact, even the earliest writing was not a completely new invention, but an improvement upon an already existing record-keeping system. For thousands of years, people all over the Middle East had been keeping records by means of small clay counters, many with pictures and other signs on them, representing farm produce, animals, clothing, and other goods. But the system of counters had weaknesses. It was difficult to see at a glance, by looking at a pile of counters, how much or what kind of goods one had on hand. Also, it was hard to make a pile of counters into a permanent record. This might not have mattered to the townspeople of prehistoric Uruk, with their comparatively small number of storage jars and other items to be recorded. But by the time the great temple on the limestone platform came to be built, with its hundreds of laborers and vast quantities of materials and other supplies, things must have been very different. One can imagine a whole team of clerks, sitting in some sweaty reed-built site office, muttering as they shifted counters from one pile to another, cursing as they lost count and had to start over, always frustrated and often in a panic—especially when the high priest walked in with an awkward question like "How many days' supply of bricks do we have on hand?" Probably, working as they would have been before 3000 B.C., they had no other way of operating. But over the next 200 years, their successors devised a radically new system.

How the new system worked, after it had already been growing and developing for about a century, can best be shown by a tablet dating from about the same time as the sketch of the city and the countryside given previously, roughly 2900 B.C. The tablet, which is shown in Illustration 3, is a piece of clay, about four inches by four, and an inch thick. The signs at the left of the broad strip at the bottom of the tablet are a "heading," explaining what the rest of the tablet is about. Reading from right to left, the first sign—the dark mark more or less in the middle of the strip—is most likely the remains of a bullet-shaped hole, $\bigcup$, made by pushing the blunt top end of a piece of dried reed at an angle into the wet clay. It means "one." Then comes a picture of a rising sun, $\bigvee\!\!\!\vee$, which stands for "day." Next is a pitcher with lines across it, $\boxminus$. The scribes used pictures of pitchers to indicate the liquids they contained, and one with horizontal lines across it meant "beer." Finally comes a sign that is broken off but should look like this: $\bigtriangledown$.

It seems to be a depiction of a clay bowl of a type that was manufactured in large numbers about this time, probably as a standard-capacity container for rations; and it means "bread." As in the old counter system, all of these signs—and all the other ones that can be understood—stand for whole words. The signs for both "one" and for "bread" have been taken over from the counter system. The most important innovation is that instead of appearing on separate little pieces of clay, the signs have all been put together on one large piece, to make a single, easily read message:

> One—Day—Beer—Bread

But the tablet contains much more information than this. Above the "heading" are about fifty boxes, all with signs in them, some of which, in every case, are number symbols: in some boxes "ten," in others "twenty," in one case (the fourth row from the top, the third box from the right), as many as "thirty-four." What are the numbers for, and what do the other signs mean? The heading, bald and telegraphic as it is by present-day standards, makes this reasonably clear. The numbers are quantities of rations of beer and bread that have been issued for one day, or that are supposed to be issued daily; and the other signs must be the names of people who have received, or are entitled to these rations. From the tablet, the scribe can see at a glance exactly who has received, or is entitled to how much. He can deal with queries and complaints. If the high priest should walk in with any awkward questions, the scribe can pull out the tablet and give him an answer on the spot. And in order to make sure that he will have no trouble reading the entries on the tablet for as long as necessary, as soon as the scribe has finished writing with his reed pen on the soft, wet clay, he has put the tablet aside in a well-ventilated place to dry and harden—a procedure which in this case has been so successful that his entries can still be read after 5,000 years.

As the tablet suggests, by 2900 B.C. the scribes had perfected a system of writing that enabled them to express everything they needed in the day-to-day running of the temple—quantities, time periods, goods and supplies of all kinds, names, professions, and official positions. But they must have sensed that the new invention had far wider possibilities of expression. The scribe who wrote the "One—Day—Beer—Bread" tablet may already have been aware of a radical new idea, which must have caused a great deal of discussion, some enthusiastic, and some no doubt headshaking, among his colleagues: the idea of using signs to represent, not words as such, but the spoken sounds that make up words.

In another century, by 2800 B.C., signs representing sounds were already fairly common, in tablets found in neighbor cities of Uruk. As a result, fewer signs needed to be used, and they were becoming easier to draw: instead of being true pictures or complicated diagrams, they were made up of small, straight, wedge-shaped strokes. This wedge-shaped or "cuneiform" system of writing lasted in Mesopotamia, serving many different peoples, with many different languages, for thousands of years. Even in the fully developed cuneiform system of writing, the more convenient sound-signs never completely replaced word-signs. All the same, the system made it possible to write down any word, no matter how complicated or abstract its meaning. From mere record keeping, writing had become a true means of communication.

But even these early record-keeping tablets can tell us some important things about the changes that were taking place in Uruk during the centuries when it was becoming a great city. The tablets are records of what must have been the city's leading institution at the time, the temple of the goddess, and they show something of how it was run and what it did. The temple, it seems, was not only a place of worship. It was also the seat of a large organization, with many employees. In addition, the organization was wealthy and innovative. It controlled a large share of the resources of the city and the surrounding countryside, using the latest technology to exploit these resources.

A suggestion of how large and complex the temple organization must have been is given by the "One—Day—Beer—Bread" tablet. Some of the fifty or so boxes above the heading are hard to read, and others are missing, but the total of all the numbers in the separate entries seems to be about 500. Why should fifty people be receiving 500 rations, some getting 10, others 20, and one lucky person as many as 34? They must be receiving rations, not only for themselves, but also for their underlings. Perhaps they are the foremen of laborers working on some building project—500 workers, divided into fifty gangs, each with its separate task. Or perhaps they are temple officials, performing administrative or religious duties with the help of their staff—500 employees, working in fifty separate departments. Either way, the temple is operating on a large scale, which needs a great deal of organization and coordination—and a large amount of resources to keep it going.

That there were plenty of resources is suggested by signs that appear frequently in other tablets. The goddess's storage chambers contained "barley," "grain," "wheat," and "fish." There were fruit and vegetables from the "gardens," dates from the "palm trees," and game brought down by the temple "hunting dogs." In the "stalls," there were more than thirty different kinds of "sheep" and "goats," as well as "cattle." All these animals were moved into and out of the stalls in herds of "ten," "sixty," and "one hundred." The produce moved in and out of the storage chambers in loads of "six hundred," "twelve hundred," and "thirty-six hundred." If Inanna's temple organization operated in the same way as the better-documented Sumerian temple bureaucracies of later centuries, then all this produce was the harvest of the goddess's own gardens and groves and fields. This must have been a substantial proportion of the entire harvest of Uruk and its region, and much of the belt of intensively cultivated countryside surrounding the city must have belonged directly to her. There is no way of knowing how much she owned, but estimates based on the more detailed records of later centuries suggest that as much as one-fifth of the land controlled by a Sumerian city could have been the property of its god or goddess. The harvest of this land not only supported the temple organization, but also formed a reserve for the whole community, to be drawn on—or as it was no doubt believed, to be vouchsafed by the god or goddess—in time of need. If this was the way that Inanna's temple organization worked in 2900 B.C., then she must have dominated the economy of Uruk, just as she had come to dominate the thoughts and hopes of its citizens.

In addition to managing and controlling the goddess's vast wealth, the temple bureaucracy of Uruk increased her wealth still further by making use of the latest "high-technology" devices and materials. This, too, is revealed by signs appearing in the temple documents. The fields that grew the wheat and barley in the goddess's store-chambers were no longer prepared for sowing by the traditional method of hacking laboriously at the earth with stone-bladed hoes. Instead, the farmers turned the soil over faster and more thoroughly by using ox-drawn "plows." The heavy loads of produce, moving constantly from field to storage chamber and out again, were carried not only on the backs of people and animals, but also on "sledges" and "wheeled wagons." Besides produce, the wagons carried frequent consignments of an advanced material, which was beginning to replace obsidian, flint, and other types of stone in tool-making and weapon-making applications: "copper."

This is not to say that the plow, the wheel, or metalworking were actually invented in the House of Heaven, in Uruk, or even in Sumer. In ancient times, civilized peoples had no monopoly on technical progress, and Inanna's priests most likely adopted these innovations directly or indirectly from foreigners whose ways of life were in most other respects less advanced than their own. Metalworking probably came to them from the inhabitants of the ore-bearing mountains that fringed Mesopotamia; wheeled vehicles from nomadic peoples of the Asiatic grasslands that lay beyond the mountains; and the plow, perhaps, from distant Europe, where traces of furrowed soil have been found beneath the graves of chieftains who were buried several hundred years before the priests of Inanna listed the implement in their tablets.*

But the tablets do provide the first known indication of all these innovations being used on a relatively large scale, in the same place, and at the same time. That itself is a significant fact. It suggests that the newly wealthy society of Sumer was better able than any other at the time to adopt and use innovations, wherever they originated. Moreover, it was most likely the priestly bureaucracies such as that of Uruk that took the lead in this process, for it would have been they, more than anyone else in the early days of Sumerian civilization, who felt the need and possessed the resources to innovate.

Technical progress is always a matter of adopting new devices and processes to meet new problems—and often the problems are ones that arise from growing wealth. Precisely because Inanna dominated the economy of Uruk, problems of this kind would have been particularly troublesome for her servants. Their documents suggest, for instance, that they were constantly moving heavy loads of produce from remote fields and groves to central storehouses, and out again to many different consumers. One can imagine how much easier this would have become once they began using, instead of the backs of people and animals, wagons with wheels.

Likewise, technical progress always requires investment of resources, and if anyone in Uruk had resources to invest, it was the servants of the goddess. It was they more than anyone else who had jars of produce available, beyond what they immediately needed to consume, the contents of which could be bartered with the upriver peoples for copper

---

*On a later period in the history of plows and agriculture, that of preindustrial Europe, see Case Study 17, in Volume 5 of this series, "Peasant and Emperor: An Enlightened Despot Plows a Field."

and other metals. Out of the same extra storage jars, the servants of the goddess could feed specialist craftsmen, relieving them of the tasks of farming so that they could experiment and improve their skills. Within the complex network of trade and cultural influence among the peoples of the Middle East and more distant regions, the House of Heaven and the many other shrines of Sumer must have acted like magnets, attracting innovations and innovators from nearby and far away. In this way, the combination of growing wealth and religious dynamism also brought technical progress.

In the same way, the need to serve the goddess stimulated the city of Uruk not only to technical progress, but also to notable cultural and artistic achievements. This is suggested by the works of art that have been found in the ruins of Inanna's temple district—objects that are more magnificent, and more vividly expressive of complex beliefs and ideas, than any previously known. In addition, because they are capable of expressing complex ideas, the works of art also give information about another side of Uruk in the era of the growth of advanced civilization: its rulers, its government institutions, and its wars.

THE SACRED VASE

Sometime around 2900 B.C., the priests and priestesses of Inanna buried within the precinct of the House of Heaven a large collection of objects that had presumably been made obsolete by changes in ritual and ceremony. Many of the items thus entombed were both beautiful and precious. A good deal of the goddess's vast wealth had probably been spent on importing costly materials from distant lands, and on supporting specialist craftsmen while they perfected their skills. In making these objects, the craftsmen had given of their best. There were beakers, inlaid with pieces of seashell resembling mother-of-pearl, for pouring out offerings of beer, sheep's milk, or date wine. There were seals for marking the stoppers of the goddess's storage jars, made of gold, lapis lazuli,* and other precious materials, and delicately engraved with microscopically detailed scenes of sheep herding and hunting, worship and warfare (see Illustration 6). There were realistically carved stone animals—sitting sheep, crouching lions, and so on—which were perhaps intended as magical substitutes for the real beasts. Above all, there was a great

---

*Lapis lazuli is a semiprecious stone, deep blue in color and flecked with spots of metal resembling gold, that was much prized by the Sumerians. The nearest known sources of the stone were a thousand miles away in the mountains of what is today Afghanistan.

4. THE URUK VASE Alabaster ritual vase, about three feet high and carved with scenes of a harvest procession, which stood in the House of Heaven sometime before 2700 B.C.

ritual vase, about three feet high. It was made of a costly imported stone, alabaster, and carved on the outside with scenes of the most solemn and holy import.

Once entombed, the objects remained in their place of burial for 5,000 years, until finally the archaeologists found them. For us today, they no longer possess ritual and magical power, but still they are worthy of reverence. They are a treasure trove of works of art from the earliest days of civilization.

Among all these works, the most impressive is the Uruk Vase, as it is called. No one knows what it was used for, and parts of the scenes are missing, for the vase was found broken in pieces—crushed, probably, by the weight of ruins above it. But it must have been a very holy object. Even with gaps, the scenes on the vase clearly depict the most important event in the mythology of Uruk: the coming of Dumuzi, at

5. THE HARVEST PROCESSION   Diagram showing the carvings on the Uruk Vase as they would look if rolled out flat.

the head of a solemn procession bearing gifts of harvest bounty, to wed Inanna and fill her storehouse-womb with "the kindly fruits of the earth."

The procession begins at the water's edge, amid fields, groves, and flocks: the wavy lines at bottom left in Illustration 5 represent the Euphrates River, the alternating plants above the waters are barley and date palms, and the animals are rams and ewes. The bearers in the procession carry the produce of fields and groves: dates, probably, in the big jars, grain in the shallow bowls, and date wine, milk, or beer in the spouted pitcher. The bearers are naked, not because they are slaves, but because the Sumerians deemed nakedness to be fitting for a holy ritual.

In the topmost scene, the procession has reached its destination. A piece of this scene is broken off, but enough is left to show that an important person is standing at the head of the procession, with a servant behind him holding his train. This would be the giver of the gifts, Dumuzi himself. In front of him, a naked bearer presents a jar of dates to a person whose costume, to judge by later Sumerian depictions, is that of a woman. Behind the woman are gifts that have already been delivered, and other people and objects. Dominating the scenes are two great reed bundles. We are in the holy storehouse, and the woman is probably a handmaiden-goddess, receiving the gifts on behalf of the divine bride within.

To make the viewer witness all these things, the maker of the vase had to possess many kinds of artistic skills. Naturally, he had to be an expert stone carver, to make all these complicated scenes on the rounded surface of the vase. In addition, he had to be a close observer and student of the appearance of natural objects and living creatures, including the naked male body, of whose more or less realistic depiction this is a very early example. But the carver's greatest artistic breakthrough is the fact that he has managed to create the sense that all the scenes, carved in their endless parallel bands on the rounded surface of the vase, belong together. To achieve this effect, he has used artistic devices that seem simple enough now, but were probably revolutionary at the time. Within their respective bands, the plants, animals, and bearers are all the same size, and they alternate in a regular pattern: barley and palms, ewes and rams, pairs of bearers. Between different bands, the sheep face one way, the bearers the opposite way, and the people at the head of the procession the opposite way again: this sets up a rhythm among the three separate bands, which is then dramatically broken by the woman, who faces the foremost bearer. Only in the temple itself, with its jumble of people and objects, does the rhythm of the depiction break down. Apart from this, the carver has arranged all the details so that they create a serene and orderly whole.

By doing all this, the maker of the vase has also succeeded in communicating something of the beliefs of the early Sumerians about the world they lived in, their own place in it, and the powers they deemed to rule it. The world depicted on the Uruk Vase is a bountiful one, with abundance of barley and dates and flocks of sheep springing from life-giving waters. It is an ordered, hierarchical world, in which everything has its place and its function. Water nourishes barley, dates, and sheep; a higher race of beings, the humans, reaps the produce of the lower ones—the bearers are depicted larger than the plants and animals—and brings it in tribute to the highest beings of all, the gods, who are depicted larger still. In the world of the Uruk Vase, everything exists, ultimately, to serve the gods. But by serving the gods, the human race raises itself to a higher state of holiness: in the topmost scene, the naked bearer is shown just as large as the divine beings.

In later centuries, Sumerian religion is known to have been grim and pessimistic, regarding the human race as mere slaves and playthings of capricious gods and goddesses. The evidence of the Uruk Vase suggests that in the earliest days of Sumerian civilization, this was not so. True, the gods were all-powerful rulers and owners of everything, but the world they ruled and owned was an orderly one of joyful abundance, in which the human race had an assured and honorable place. This was a fitting religion for a society to which soil, water, and weather had suddenly become generous, and that had used these gifts to achieve things never before imagined.

But fertility and abundance were not the only things that early Sumerian religion rejoiced in. Other works of art from Uruk, dating from about the same time as the vase, indicate that along with fertility, war and victory were also considered holy, and that Uruk's great goddess of the storehouse also showered her blessings on "mighty men of valor," who made victorious war.

THE MAN IN THE NET SKIRT

The works of art that provide this evidence are objects known as cylinder seals. These are small cylinders of stone, carved on their surfaces so that they would produce an impression when rolled across the lumps of soft clay that were used to seal the goddess's storage jars. These seals, made of costly materials and carved with impressive skill, were

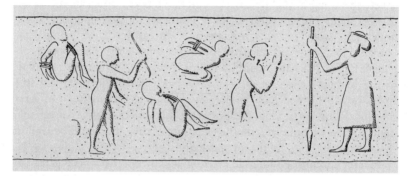

6. WORSHIP AND WAR   Impressions made by seals used to mark storage jars in the House of Heaven, about 2800–2700 B.C. Top, a ritual takes place on a boat (modern impression); at right, the cylinder seal that made the impression. The cylinder is carved from lapis lazuli, a semiprecious stone, and the knob is of gold, cast in the shape of a bull. Bottom, drawing of an indistinct impression on a fragment of an actual jar stopper: victorious commander and naked prisoners.

obviously important objects, and the scenes that were carved on them presumably represented things that mattered a great deal to their makers and users. The carvings on seals of about 2900 B.C. depict many different activities, but a great many of these involve one and the same person. The top picture in Illustration 6, an impression taken by archaeologists from a cylinder seal, shows a man wearing a transparent skirtlike garment riding in a boat. Next to him, carried on the back of an animal, is what seems to be a box or shrine, bearing the reed-bundle emblem of Inanna and perhaps containing objects sacred to her. The diagram at bottom, a drawing of an impression found on an actual ancient jar stopper, seems to show a victorious soldier in front of crouching captives. The shape of his garment, and of his beard and headdress, suggest that he is the same person as the passenger in the boat, who is also depicted on many other seals: the "Man in the Net Skirt," as the archaeologists call him.

Obviously, if the Man in the Net Skirt was a winner of battles and was entitled to ride in the same boat with Inanna's holy things, he must have been a very important person in Uruk. Most likely he was none other than Dumuzi himself. Sumerian myths, written down in later centuries, portray him as being both a warrior and a guardian of things that were sacred to Inanna. But generally the activities of gods, as portrayed in myth, are modeled on the activities of actual human beings. If the people of Uruk depicted their god as a warrior, standing spear in hand, while his enemies cowered in fetters before him, then it is certain that in Uruk there must have been real warriors, captains and mighty men, who did exactly the same. If the people of Uruk depicted their warrior god as one who guarded what belonged to Inanna and rode in boats with her sacred objects, the chances are that the mighty men of Uruk did these things too.

It is also possible that such a mighty man might bring gifts to the goddess and even "marry" her, as depicted on the Uruk Vase. The scenes on the vase may well depict not only an event from mythology, but also an actual ritual intended to reenact such an event. The procession may actually be taking place in Uruk; the giver of the gifts could well be a victorious warrior, who by spells and enchantments has "become" Dumuzi; inside the House of Heaven, he will actually perform, with a priestess who has magically "become" the goddess, the act of procreation on which the welfare of Uruk depends. Such rituals and enchantments are known from later Sumerian times. Obviously, a captain of warriors who had "become" Dumuzi and wedded Inanna in this way would be all the more mighty for being holy.

Later Sumerian traditions, myths, and epics, mostly written down toward the year 2000 B.C., seem to preserve the memory of these mighty men of early times. Several of these later works tell of heroes whom they depict as ancient rulers of Uruk, as doers of great deeds, and as favorites of Uruk's goddess. The great ruler Enmerkar, for instance, is described as "the lord chosen by Inanna," and he speaks to her as "my sister"—the name by which a Mesopotamian husband would call a beloved wife. To decorate her shrine, so says one of the epic poems about him, he obtained gold, silver, and lapis lazuli from the ruler of a distant mountain land by a combination of barter and threats. He defended Uruk against marauding nomads—"the Martu, who know not grain"—he drained the Euphrates swamps, invented writing, and magnificently enlarged the city: "Fifty years did I build, fifty years did I build!" If Enmerkar really existed, it is perfectly possible that he did all of these things—except, of course, for personally inventing writing—

and the epics about him and the other hero-rulers of early Uruk may well contain an important truth: that side by side with the priestly bureaucracy, Uruk had developed an elite of warriors, who directed the city's activities in peace as well as war, and whose power was based also on their role in the rituals of the goddess.

These rulers probably did not have total power. They must have been much beholden to the priestly bureaucracy, and later Sumerian traditions indicate that they had to rule together with an assembly composed of "elders" and "men of the people," as if there were some kind of popular and participatory government institutions in Uruk.* Still, the hero-rulers must have been strong and successful leaders to leave such a vivid memory in the tales and epics of later times. Insofar as Uruk now had such a powerful leadership, active in peace and war, sharing in the holy rituals on which the city's welfare depended, backed by the priests and able to win the consent of the citizens through popular assemblies, the city was more than an unprecedentedly large human settlement, or even a community organized around its goddess. It was a state—to be precise, a city-state, a type of small but highly organized and effective political entity with a long history before it, stretching from Athens and Sparta through Rome and Carthage to Venice and Florence.

Uruk's rise to statehood came only just in time, for shortly after 2900 B.C., it had to face new and serious problems. At some point not long after that date, the forces of soil, water, and weather, which had been so kind to Uruk for so long, began to turn against it. This was not because of any further climatic changes. On the contrary, the long-lasting "dry spell" simply continued; and just as it had brought a new and bountiful landscape in the first place, so it eventually destroyed what it had created. The waters went on retreating, and the swamps continued to shrink. In place of the patchwork landscape that had nurtured a civilization, there grew up one in which dry land predominated and much of the countryside was far from the life-giving river channels. The townspeople of prehistoric Uruk had been hemmed in by floods; for a couple of centuries, water and dry land had balanced each other, and the town had grown into a city and a center of civilization; now, the rulers of the state of Uruk had to confront the threat of drought.

---

*For later examples of assemblies and how they operated, see Case Studies 2 and 3, "A Political Scandal in Democratic Athens," pp. 67–68, 89–95 (Athenian democracy); "Egypt, Greece, Europe: The Rosetta Stone and Three Civilizations, Part 1, Two Civilizations in One Land," pp. 134–35, 139–40 (Egyptian priests); and Case Study 10, in Volume 3 of this series, "Debates, Petitions, and Impeachments: A Crisis Session of the English Parliament" (medieval representative institutions).

3
The State of Uruk, 2800 b.c.

By the year 2800 B.C., much which had once been a continuous carpet of swamp, was a dry and dusty plain. The swamps had not entirely disappeared. At in- of the territory around Uruk, tinuous carpet of swamp, The swamps had not entervals of five or ten miles, belts of mud and reeds, tamarisk bushes, poplars, and oleanders straggled from north to south across the countryside. Sometimes these belts of swamp were broader, sometimes they were narrower, sometimes they joined to form larger patches of wetland and then separated again; but always they clung closely to the few broad channels, with hardly any smaller side creeks, in which the Euphrates now flowed across the plain.

In the spring and early summer the river still inundated what was left of the swamps, and even spilled out onto the dry plain, bringing renewal of life and vegetation wherever its waters spread. But much of the plain was no longer within reach of the waters. On these dry stretches, the winter cloudbursts might nourish a few patches of grass, but over the rainless months of summer they would turn to harsh and lifeless desert; and the dust of the desert covered the ruins of many once-thriving villages. In a hundred years, as the archaeological surveys of the Uruk region indicate, nearly half of the 150 settlements of the boom centuries had been abandoned. Where barley had ripened and palm trees had put forth heavy clusters of dates, there were empty badlands where wandering herders counted themselves lucky to find a little rough grazing for their goats.

But the appearance of emptiness was deceptive. The people had not abandoned the territory. They had simply adjusted their way of life to the changes in their environment. They had learned to exploit the resources of the region more efficiently, and to compete for them more fiercely. To do so, they had strengthened the power of the institutions that had grown up in the boom centuries. The years of drought had forced the development of large-scale, centrally coordinated irrigation systems; of intensive, highly organized warfare; and of powerful, competitive states.

In spite of the harsher landscape, the more centralized and highly organized society of 2800 B.C. was probably more populous and wealthier than the society of a hundred years before. Nearly all of the settlements that had been abandoned during those hundred years had been

outlying villages, presumably situated on remote creeks and side channels that had dried up. What was left were larger villages and small
towns, located—to judge by the patterns left by their ruins on the
map—on three or four broad main channels of the river. Far from declining, these large settlements had actually grown over the past century, so that their combined built-up area was greater than that of the
more numerous settlements of 2900 B.C.

Of the large, concentrated settlements in the Uruk region, at least
half a dozen were big enough to count as cities in their own right. The
names of most of these are known from later Sumerian records.
Shuruppak, Umma, Zabalam, Bad-Tibira, Larsa, Eridu, Ur—they were
ranged around Uruk, in a rough half-circle to the north, east, and south
of the city, at distances between ten and thirty miles. Each of these large
centers was surrounded by groups of less important settlements, in a
manner that suggests that they were subject to it. Some of the cities, in
turn, may have been satellites of Uruk itself. Others, undoubtedly, were
its rivals.

In the immediate neighborhood of these cities, the landscape must
have been just as flourishing and full of people as it had been a century
before. But in addition to fields and groves and farmers and fishermen,
there was now another sight to be seen: massive engineering works to
conserve and distribute the waters of the river. Wide canals led the water away from the river channels, and branched into a network of
smaller dikes and ditches to reach the fields and groves and of farmers
far from the river: one group of settlements to the east of Uruk was
strung out in a dead-straight line more than ten miles long, as if they
had all been situated on the banks of an artificial waterway of that
length. In the weeks before the river rose, gangs of laborers must have
been everywhere at work on the canals and dikes, shoveling the mud
out of them so that the water would not back up, and piling more earth
onto their embankments—for they had to run, like the river channels
with which they were connected, above the level of the fields and groves
they nourished. But the effort could not be avoided. Without the natural patchwork of swamp and water that had nurtured it in the first
place, the civilized society of Sumer depended on its more concentrated
network of artificial waterways to survive.

As large as many of the settlements in the region had become, they
were all of them dwarfed by the gigantic size of Uruk itself. In a hundred years, it had grown to a city of perhaps 40,000 people. From the
central mounds, with the temple of the fertility goddess on its high terrace and the surrounding sacred district, the close-packed houses now

stretched for perhaps a mile across the level ground. On the other side of the Euphrates channel that probably ran to the east of Uruk, there was a "suburb" not much smaller than the main city. Within the city there were potteries, workshops for making the traditional but still much-used stone products, and smithies where newer "high-technology" metal goods were cast. For the most part, however, Uruk must have been a vast encampment of farmers, "commuting" to work in the surrounding zone of fields and groves, which was now perhaps ten miles across. To enlarge an area of cultivated land to such a size, in the face of growing drought, was an extraordinary achievement. It must have taken a sophisticated knowledge of hydraulic engineering, mobilization of labor on a massive scale, and detailed supervision of the use of water by individual farmers. It must also have taken a very powerful central authority, to enforce the cooperation and obedience necessary to put engineering plans into effect, recruit the laborers, and see that regulations on the use of water were obeyed.

This was not the only thing that this powerful central authority had done. It had also provided Uruk itself with a new architectural landmark. This new feature was not as prominent at a distance as the House of Heaven, but from close up one would have been able to see that it was far larger. It was a great defensive wall, running all the way around the city.

Defensive walls surrounding cities were nothing new in themselves. Far away to the west, in the lands bordering the Mediterranean Sea, the town of Jericho had had such a wall as early as 7000 B.C. Uruk itself probably already had a wall enclosing a much smaller area than that of the enormously enlarged city, since there is a sign meaning "city wall" on written tablets dating from before 2900 B.C.

All the same, this wall was something special, both on account of its sheer size, and on account of the thoroughness with which the builders had used every possible device to make sure that it was utterly impregnable. The wall was six miles long, so as to enclose all of the enlarged city, and probably allowed ample extra room for sheep and cattle to be driven in from the countryside in time of danger. It was perhaps thirty feet high—the ruins still rise to above twenty feet in some places—so that an enemy would have the greatest difficulty clambering over it. It was fifteen feet thick, so that even though, like everything else in the land of Sumer, it was built of soft and crumbly mud brick, an enemy would never be able to smash through it. At ten-yard intervals throughout its length, towers projected forward from it—nearly a thousand of them—so that the defenders could see and shoot at attackers, even if they were right up against the wall. Finally, to make absolutely sure that the city was impregnably protected, another wall was built ten yards in front of the first—nine feet thick, also with projecting towers, and also, of course, running right around the city.

This, then, was the wall to end all walls—unquestionably, in its time, the mightiest work of fortification ever built. It must have taken many years to build, and the labors of many thousands of people—far more years, and more laborers, than any temple in Inanna's sacred district. For such a vast and lengthy project to have been undertaken at all, there must have been the most urgent reasons—great military dangers to be overcome, boundless possibilities of conquest to be attained. And to be able to commit the resources of the city for so many years, whoever was responsible for building the wall must have been a man of bold imagination, iron determination, and great political power.

Later Sumerian traditions, which most modern scholars believe are based on fact, have handed down to us the name of this remarkable leader. He was Gilgamesh, the most famous of all the early hero-rulers of Uruk. His reasons for building the walls were no doubt as many and urgent as his reasons for fighting wars—and it seems likely that the newly civilized society of Uruk had more numerous and compelling reasons for fighting wars than its prehistoric forerunner. As the tales about Gilgamesh's predecessor Enmerkar suggest, there were nomadic peoples against whom the farmers of Uruk had to be defended, and mountain peoples to be intimidated so that they would yield their stone and metals to Uruk's craftsmen on favorable terms. In addition there were probably other Sumerian city-states that competed with Uruk for control of the Euphrates channels that provided irrigation water and access to foreign lands upstream. The gradual retreat of the waters may well have made this competition for control of resources all the fiercer. As the Sumerian cities became artificial "oases" in an otherwise arid landscape, they perhaps became all the more tempting to covetous foreign peoples; as the waters that nourished these "oases" continued to retreat, the rivalry for control of the life-giving river channels must have become all the more intense. Presumably, then, it was vital interests of this kind that were at stake for Gilgamesh when he built the walls of Uruk.

But he probably had something else at stake that was bigger and more ambitious than simply ensuring Uruk's survival in an increasingly competitive world. The Sumerian traditions relating to these early times all indicate that the warfare among the city-states was a struggle not only for resources but also for something that is usually translated as "kingship." How much actual power belonged to the kingship is unknown. But it does seem that whoever possessed it could claim to hold some kind of dominance over the other city-states, not just by force, but as of right. In addition, it seems that the kingship was recognized not only throughout Sumer, but also throughout the territories to which civilization on the Sumerian model had spread, especially Sumer's northern neighbor, the land of Akkad.

Furthermore, it seems that the kingship could also be won or lost by force of arms, without affecting its validity. One of the earliest halfway reliable traditions about Uruk says that in Gilgamesh's time, the city was involved in a struggle for the kingship with the neighboring city of Ur and the more distant northern city of Kish—a struggle that Uruk eventually won. If there is anything to this tradition at all, then it suggests that when Gilgamesh built the walls of Uruk, his ultimate purpose was to win, and even more important, to keep, the kingship for the city he ruled. After all, Uruk could not expect to enjoy the kingship undisturbed. Restive Sumerian city-states would certainly contest Uruk's possession of it, and Gilgamesh must be free to move away from Uruk with his army, to overawe or punish them, or even to enforce recognition of Uruk's kingship on more distant communities. For this, the city, in its enormously enlarged state, must be completely secure. Now was the time to make Uruk impregnable, so as to keep for all time the kingship over Sumer, and Akkad too, and perhaps more distant, outlying territories. Whatever the exact power and status of the kingship, in gaining and keeping it, Gilgamesh was probably responding to the first stirrings of the urge to empire.

That was how far Uruk had come in four centuries. Before the first temple had been built on the eastern mound, it had been no more than a small town and a center of worship for a small surrounding district. Now it had been fitted out as a capital city from which to wield power over many lands and peoples of the Middle East. And that was how far civilization had advanced in four hundred years: from a world of modestly prosperous villages and small towns to a world of wealth and war, where powerful rulers could contemplate building empires.

But the time of empires had not yet arrived, and even the great walls could not keep the kingship in Uruk forever. The Sumerian traditions record that after Gilgamesh's time, toward the year 2500 B.C., Uruk was "smitten with weapons," and its kingship was "carried" to its neighbor and rival, Ur. For another five centuries, the struggle for kingship among the Sumerian cities would continue. Four times, in those five centuries, Uruk would win it back. Four times, again, it would be "smitten." Apart from this, not much is known about the history of Uruk during these later Sumerian times. Other Sumerian cities, notably Ur, Lagash, and Nippur, have left many more buildings, works of art, and written records from these centuries for archaeologists to discover. But Uruk certainly remained one of the leading cities of Sumer down to 2000 B.C.

Around that date, however, the cities of Sumer were overwhelmed by foreign invaders and immigrants. They lost their independence, and even their language ceased to be spoken, except in religious ritual. In the next 2,000 years, a succession of peoples—Babylonians, Assyrians, Persians, Greeks, Parthians—built a succession of empires in Mesopotamia and the surrounding regions, most of them larger and longer-lived than anything the Sumerians had been able to create. Uruk itself lived on for all of those 2,000 years as a backwater—a local center in a succession of empires ruled from other, upstart cities: Babylon, Nineveh, Persepolis, Ctesiphon.

Even so, for all of this time, the early greatness of Uruk was never forgotten. The walls alone were an almost indestructible reminder of what the city once had been. "Ramparted Uruk"—that was what the city was called in the most famous literary work of ancient Mesopotamian civilization, composed by Babylonian scribes on the basis of Sumerian poems and traditions: the Epic of Gilgamesh. Two thousand years after Gilgamesh's time, in Babylon, in Nineveh, even far away among the Hittites in present-day Turkey, people still read of the great ruler and his works:

> *Of ramparted Uruk the wall he built,*
> *Of hallowed Eanna, the pure sanctuary . . .*
> *Draw near to Eanna, the dwelling of Ishtar,*
> *Which no future king, no man, can equal.*
> *Go up and walk on the walls of Uruk,*
> *Inspect the base terrace, examine the brickwork:*
> *Is not its brickwork of burnt brick?**

---

*"Burnt brick" means bricks made of clay that has been hardened by firing in a kiln. In fact, the walls of Uruk, like all early Sumerian structures, were made of bricks that had been hardened by exposure to the air and the sun.

Ishtar was the Babylonian name of Inanna, and it was under this name, or variations of it, that the great goddess of Uruk came to be worshiped throughout Mesopotamia and in many more distant regions for thousands of years after the Sumerian cities had fallen. The Greeks called her Astarte, and believed that she was the same goddess as their own Aphrodite, or Venus. The Old Testament prophets knew her as Ashtoreth, and called her an "abomination," because her rites, with their spells and enchantments and unbridled sexuality, tempted some of the Hebrews to turn aside from the God of Israel. But it was not only the worship of Inanna, and the other Sumerian gods and goddesses, that survived the downfall of the Sumerian cities. Their writing, their methods of building, their irrigation farming and astronomy and arithmetic—all these and many others of their beliefs, customs, and inventions formed the basis of Mesopotamian civilization so long as it endured. Eventually, of course, new religions, new customs, and new systems of writing developed, and Mesopotamian civilization died. But the Greeks and the Hebrews both knew it well, and were heavily influenced by it; and through them, its achievements have come to form part of the basis of present-day Western civilization.

Uruk itself was abandoned at last—swallowed up by swamps, probably, about 200 B.C., when the ever-changing balance between the waters and the dry land shifted in favor of the waters. Over further centuries, the balance shifted yet again, and left the ruins of Uruk high and dry, in the midst of an empty desert. So they remained until the beginning of this century, when the archaeologists came. Today, as a result of their work, we know far more about the most ancient times of Uruk even than the writer of the Epic of Gilgamesh did. No single place in the world, perhaps, can tell us more about the earliest origins of advanced civilization than Uruk.

What it tells us, first of all, is that the rise of the civilization of Sumer was not a sudden leap out of the world of the "caveman." Instead, it was a change that took place in a society that had already reached a respectable level of prosperity and culture, and was already very old. This society had its skills of building and agriculture, and its traditional religious beliefs. Perhaps just as important, there were many other peoples in the Middle East with their own skills and religious beliefs, who by way of trade and cultural influence, could supply the people of Sumer with many things that they lacked. Without this "springboard" provided by the traditional society and the neighboring peoples, the leap to an advanced civilization could never have been made.

But when this traditional society began to change, it did so with dramatic speed. The four centuries that separate the prehistoric town of Uruk from the great walled city are not a long span of time, as history goes. They are not much longer than the period that separates the English colonization of North America from the United States of the present day, and the changes between the small town of Uruk and the ramparted city were just as great as those between the time of the Pilgrim Fathers and our own.

In Uruk, and presumably in the rest of Sumer, those changes seem to have been set in motion by a change in the natural environment, which created a window of opportunity for civilization to grow. The suddenly fertile landscape enabled the traditional society to grow much larger and wealthier, and at least to start with, this could be done fairly easily, using the tried and true methods of small-scale irrigation farming. But this initial change, once it was under way, led to other changes: a break with religious tradition, massive building projects, rapid technical progress, a flowering of artistic creativity, deliberate and organized warfare, and the rise of powerful political institutions led by warrior-kings.

Once these changes started, they all seem to have pushed each other forward, like different constituents in a complicated chemical reaction. The service of the goddess required great temples, costly materials, and many priests, administrators, and laborers; growing population, increased wealth, and the expansion of trade enabled Uruk to satisfy these needs. As the temple organization grew wealthier and more complicated, the goddess's servants ran into problems of growth that could only be solved by innovation: they pioneered writing, and adopted the plow and wheeled transportation. Prosperity created reasons for war, wealth and organization enabled armies to be equipped and sent into battle, victory increased the power of army commanders, and the goddess gave them legitimacy; as a result, the community of Uruk grew into a state. Everywhere new abilities created new needs, and new needs called forth new abilities. In this way, Mesopotamian civilization was born.

Eventually, the environment turned hostile again, and the window of opportunity closed. But the civilization that had grown up in the boom centuries was strong and adaptable enough to survive this change. It grew more systematic and efficient in its use of scarcer resources, and out of the competition for these resources came the beginnings of the great empires of the Middle East. The changes that had taken place in the boom centuries were irreversible. They had survived drought and war, and they would survive even the disappearance of the Sumerians themselves. Mesopotamian civilization would endure for more than two thousand years, and when it finally died, it would leave an inheritance for other civilizations that it had helped to create.

The birth of a great civilization out of an earlier, simpler society, without massive outside influences, peaceful or warlike, from other already existing advanced civilizations to help bring it about, is a very rare event in world history. Sumer was probably the first time it happened, though very soon followed by Egypt. In the thousands of years since then, only four other peoples, or groups of peoples, seem to have followed on their own the path from a prehistoric society to an advanced civilization: the Indians of the Indus River Valley, the Chinese of the Huang Ho River Valley, and the native Americans of Central America and the Andes Mountains. Even in some of these cases, there were perhaps outside influences at work—of Sumer upon Egypt, for example—but with these civilizations as against all others, there is no reason to suppose that outside influences were decisive.

Wherever the independent rise of an advanced civilization has happened, researchers have found the same kind of factors at work, though in different ways and in different combinations, as at Uruk: an advanced prehistoric society, the presence of several different peoples who influenced each other, the wealth created by unusually productive agriculture, the inspiring force of religion, and some kind of self-sustaining process of change in which new abilities and new needs reinforce each other.* In this way, there is something to be learned from Uruk not only about the earliest beginnings of Sumerian civilization, but also about all the independently arisen civilizations of the world.

Modern Western civilization is not one of these. It has developed out of an enormously lengthy and complicated process of change and interaction, involving several different advanced civilizations as well as many prehistoric peoples, that stretches all the way back to Sumer. This

---

*For an example of agriculture, religion, and other factors combining to spread an existing civilization, see Case Study 9, in Volume 3 of this series, "New Farms and New Cities: The Land Rush in Mecklenburg" (spread of medieval European civilization into a frontier zone).

case study has focused on a place and time that are particularly significant for understanding how the process began. Subsequent case studies will focus on themes that are similarly significant for understanding some of the twists and turns of the process, down through the centuries to the present day.

FURTHER READING

Ancient Sumer is one of the most difficult and technical of subjects, but also one in which many leading experts have taken the trouble to share their discoveries with the general public. The works listed here are not only authoritative, but clear and readable as well.

Crawford, Harriet. *Sumer and the Sumerians* (Cambridge, 1991). Brief, up-to-date, and well-illustrated general account.

Jacobsen, Thorkild. *The Treasures of Darkness: A History of Mesopotamian Religion* (New Haven, CT, 1976). A standard work that is also a fine piece of literature.

Kramer, Samuel Noah. *The Sumerians: Their History, Culture, and Character* (Chicago, 1963). General account that stresses mythology and literature; the work of a distinguished scholar and entertaining writer.

Lloyd, Seton. *Foundations in the Dust* (London, 1947). An expert and entertaining account of the excavation of the cities of Mesopotamia from the 1840s to the 1940s.

Nissen, Hans J. *The Early History of the Ancient Near East, 9000–2000 B.C.* (Chicago, 1988). Outline of the prehistory and early history of Mesopotamia by Germany's leading authority; impressively presents archaeological evidence for social, economic, and environmental factors.

Sandars, N. K. *The Epic of Gilgamesh* (Harmondsworth, 1978). Readable English version of the famous epic, with introduction and explanations for the nonspecialist reader.

Schmandt-Besserat, Denise. "An Ancient Token System: The Precursor to Numerals and Writing" (*Archaeology*, November/December 1986). Nontechnical account of the token system and its relationship to writing, by the scholar who discovered the link between them.

SOURCES

The main source for this case study is the excavation reports of the German archaeologists who have been digging in Uruk for most of this century. In addition, standard works by leading scholars on Sumerian agriculture and settlement, art and architecture, government, religion, and writing, as well as on the rise of Sumerian civilization in general, have been used.

The abbreviation *UVB* designates the Uruk excavation reports: *Vorläufige Berichte über die . . . Ausgrabungen in Uruk-Warka* [Preliminary reports on the excavations in Uruk-Warka] (Berlin, 1929–   ).

Adams, Robert McC., and Hans J. Nissen. *The Uruk Countryside: The Natural Setting of Urban Societies.* Chicago, 1972.

Damerow, Peter, Robert K. Englund, and Hans J. Nissen. "Die Entstehung der Schrift" [The origin of writing]. *Spektrum der Wissenschaft* [Spectrum of science], February 1988, pp. 74–85.

Falkenstein, Adam. *Archaische Texte aus Uruk* [Archaic texts from Uruk]. Berlin, 1936.

Haller, A. von. "Die Stadtmauer" [The city wall]. *UVB* 7 (1935): 41–45.

Haller, A. von, and Heinrich Lenzen. "Eanna: Überblick über die Entwicklung des Tempelbezirks von der Djemdet-Nasr-Zeit bis in die achämenidische Zeit" [Eanna: Survey of the development of the temple district from the Jamdat Nasr period to the Achaemenid period]. *UVB* 9 (1937): 5–10.

Heinrich, Ernst. *Kleinfunde aus den archaischen Tempelschichten in Uruk* [Small finds from the archaic temple levels in Uruk]. Berlin, 1936.

———. "Grabungen im Gebiet des Anu-Antum-Tempels" [Excavations in the area of the Anu-Antum temple]. *UVB* 10 (1939): 21–39.

———. "Die Stellung der Uruktempel in der Baugeschichte" [The place of the Uruk temples in the history of architecture]. *Zeitschrift für Assyriologie* [Journal of Assyriology], n.s. 15 (1950): 21–44.

Jacobsen, Thorkild. *The Sumerian King List.* Chicago, 1939.

———. "Early Political Development in Mesopotamia." In *Toward the Image of Tammuz and Other Essays in Mesopotamian History and Culture,* edited by William T. Moran. Cambridge, MA, 1970.

———. "Primitive Democracy in Mesopotamia." Ibid.

———. *The Treasures of Darkness: A History of Mesopotamian Religion.* New Haven, CT, 1976.

Jordan, Julius. "Die archaischen Schichten von Eanna" [The archaic levels of Eanna]. *UVB* 2 (1930): 12–55.

———. "Die archaischen Perioden I bis V" [Archaic periods I to V]. *UVB* 3 (1932): 5–18.

———. "Die prähistorischen Perioden der Tiefgrabung in Eanna" [The prehistoric periods of the deep sounding in Eanna]. Ibid., pp. 29–31.

———. "Zusammenfassung" [Summary]. Ibid., pp. 35–37.

Kramer, Samuel Noah. *The Sumerians: Their History, Culture, and Character.* Chicago, 1963.

Lenzen, Heinrich. "Die archaischen Schichten von Eanna" [The archaic levels of Eanna]. *UVB* 8 (1936): 8–19.

———. "Uruk IV" [Uruk level IV]. *UVB* 20 (1964): 8–10.

———. "Uruk III" [Uruk level III]. Ibid., pp. 11–18.

———. "Uruk IV" [Uruk level IV]. *UVB* 21 (1965): 16–21.

Moortgat, Anton. *Die Entstehung der sumerischen Hochkultur* [The rise of Sumerian high civilization]. Leipzig, 1945.

Nissen, Hans Jörg. "The City Wall of Uruk." In *Man, Settlement, and Urbanism,* edited by Peter J. Ucko. Cambridge, MA, 1972.

———. *Grundzüge einer Geschichte der Frühzeit des Vorderen Orients* [Foundations of a history of the early Near East]. Darmstadt, 1983.

———. *Mesopotamia before 5000 Years.* Rome, 1987.

Nissen, Hans J., Peter Damerow, and Robert K. Englund. *Archaic Bookkeeping: Early Writing and Techniques of Economic Administration in the Ancient Near East.* Chicago, 1993.

Oates, David, and Joan Oates. "Early Irrigation Agriculture in Mesopotamia." In *Problems in Economic and Social Archaeology,* edited by G. de G. Sieveking. London, 1976.

Schmandt-Besserat, Denise. "The Earliest Precursor of Writing." *Scientific American,* June 1978.

———. *Before Writing: From Counting to Cuneiform.* 2 vols. Austin, TX, 1992.

Schmidt, Jürgen. "Grabung im Gebiet der Anu-Antum-Zikkurat: 1. Tempel der Obed-Zeit in K XVII" [Excavation in the area of the zigurrat of Anu-Antum: 1. Temples of the Ubaidian period in grid square K XVII]. *UVB* 31 (1983): 9–19.

A POLITICAL SCANDAL
IN DEMOCRATIC ATHENS

CONTENTS

ILLUSTRATIONS

MAPS

INTRODUCTION

The Greeks, as everyone knows, invented democracy. Along with democracy, there also appeared in Greece, for the first time in history, a typically democratic form of real-life drama: the political scandal. Every really serious political scandal takes the form of a drama, with great issues at stake, leaders of power and reputation dishonored, and secret wickedness publicly revealed. But for the drama to be truly effective, it has to have an audience—preferably one that itself takes part in the action, clamoring for the truth to be found out, and sharing in the punishment of the guilty. This happens best in societies where it is possible to expose to the public the misdeeds of the powerful, and where public opinion can make or break politicians; and that is why the juiciest scandals always take place in democracies.* In fact, the first such scandal of which we have any detailed knowledge took place in the most famous of ancient democratic states, Athens in the fifth century B.C.

The scandal in question certainly had all the ingredients to make it juicy. It began with a series of spectacular crimes, carried out in 415 B.C. by unknown perpetrators, which appeared to threaten the most vital interests of the Athenian people: their position as a "great power" among the Greeks, the stability of their democratic system of government, and the customs and values that held their community together. As it unfolded, the scandal showed all those features that lend interest and excitement to the scandals of the present day. There were boards of inquiry, grants of immunity, and public denunciations. There were categorical denials, fresh revelations, and counter-revelations. There were complex maneuvers by politicians, steering the scandal in the direction they wanted it to go. There were mass arrests, confiscations of property, and public executions. In addition, there was a historic personal destiny at stake. At the center of the scandal stood the most widely admired yet deeply distrusted Athenian political leader of the time, Alcibiades: a man whose reputation has lasted down the centuries for courage and resourcefulness unchecked by conscience, for spiritual yearnings corrupted by ambition, and for charm and beauty misused in the service of ruthless egotism.

---

*A scandal that took place in a nondemocratic, though still fairly open political system, that of medieval representative government, is discussed in Case Study 10, in Volume 3 of this series, "Debates, Petitions, and Impeachments: A Crisis Session of the English Parliament."

As for the ordinary citizens of Athens, of course they could not read about the scandal in the newspapers or watch the proceedings on television, but they did not have to. They could take part in it themselves, since much of the scandal was thrashed out in the Assembly, the chief deliberative, legislative, judicial, and executive decision-making body of the democracy, to which every free and native-born male Athenian citizen had access as a speaking and voting member.

But a great scandal, however dramatic, is not just a form of free public entertainment. At the time it takes place, it is a shattering event—a kind of political earthquake, in which the underlying faults and stresses of the system release their pent-up force, shaking and sometimes destroying long-established political habits and institutions. And just as an earthquake reveals the hidden geology of a landscape, so a major scandal can tell us a great deal about the workings of the political system under which it takes place.

All this was true of the scandal of 415 B.C. It took place at a time when both the power and glory, yet also the problems and inner tensions, of Athens had reached their height. At that date, the Athenians constituted an independent, self-governing community with its own laws, traditions, and way of life—a city-state, or as the Greeks called it, a *polis*.* They were one among a couple of hundred similar communities—in effect, small sovereign states—among which Greece was divided, together with many other areas of the Mediterranean where Greeks had settled. In the course of a century of historic military, political, intellectual, and artistic achievement, the Athenians had come to outshine all the others; but as so often happens, great achievements had brought great problems. The Athenians had grasped successfully at power and empire, yet this had provoked the jealousy and fear of many other Greek city-states, and involved them in a major war that they had been unable to win. Their system of government had evolved into the world's first full-scale democracy, but the very completeness of democracy's triumph had alienated an influential minority of citizens. In Athens and elsewhere, Greek thinkers had brought about an intellectual revolution, yet the new ideas threatened to undermine the traditional customs and values that held the community together. In many ways, Athens was ripe for a crisis.

---

*There was nothing new about city-states, nor were they exclusive to the Greeks. The Phoenicians, a trading and seagoing people of the Middle East, also lived in city-states scattered around the Mediterranean, and this type of political entity already had a 2,500-year history behind it, going back to the dawn of civilization in ancient Sumer. For an example of a Sumerian city-state, see Case Study 1 in this volume, "Uruk: The Rise of a Sumerian City," pp. 37–45.

The crisis, when it came, was one that tested the political system to the uttermost, and is therefore highly revealing of its workings. Why should a series of crimes, however spectacular, have been seen by the Athenians as a deadly threat to their democracy and their power? Granted that they were right, what institutions and procedures did they have with which to meet the danger? How did the political leaders cope with the crisis, and how did they use it to further their own policies and ambitions? Why did the powerful Alcibiades fall victim to the scandal?

The answers to these questions can tell us much about Athenian democracy, and about the deeper problems that it faced: how to defend itself against internal threats and compete successfully against external adversaries, while maintaining a free way of life; how to admit ordinary citizens to government while preserving the power and effectiveness of the state; how to pursue prudent and consistent policies, in circumstances where every political decision was the outcome of rivalries among ambitious politicians, acting upon changeable public opinion. All these problems, common to democracy from the time of the ancient Greeks to the present day, were involved in the scandal of 415 B.C. Ultimately, the story of the scandal is the story of how far the Athenians succeeded in solving these problems, and how far they failed.

Besides all this, the scandal is also revealing of another, vitally important aspect of the political life of ancient Athens: the community values that its citizens held dear, and that they expected to be observed in public life. At the bottom of every great scandal, ancient or modern, there is always a breach of these values. For instance, in a society where the honor of the nation is felt to be bound up with the honor of its armed forces, deceit on the part of military officers can be politically explosive. In France a hundred years ago, when leading generals covered up the imprisonment of a junior officer, Captain Dreyfus, on false charges of espionage, this led to one of the greatest scandals of modern times, which shook the French republic to its foundations. In a society where obedience to law is held to be the supreme civic virtue, it is the most disgraceful of misdeeds for a public official to approve the commission of illegal acts for political advantage. That was what led to the Watergate scandal, which certainly shook the presidency as a leading institution of the American republic.

Likewise in Athens in 415 B.C., the crimes with which the scandal began constituted a supreme breach of civic values. The values in question, however, were very different from those of nineteenth-century France or twentieth-century America. Collectively, the crimes of 415 B.C. constituted a monstrous act of sacrilege: an impious deed that, if unsolved and unpunished, would bring down upon the Athenians, or so most of them believed, the wrath of a formidable god.

I
GLORIOUS HERMES

Throughout the ancient city of Athens, there stood hundreds of statues of the god Hermes, the son of Zeus and his father's swift-traveling messenger to the human race. These statues did not look like what we are accustomed to think of as the image of a Greek god. They did not show him as an ideally handsome, larger-than-lifesize human being, majestically clothed or splendidly naked. Instead, they consisted of square-cut pillars of stone, wood, or bronze, anything up to nine feet high, with only two humanlike features. On top was the head of the god, with heavy, braided locks and beard, sometimes with smiling face, and sometimes with grave and firm-set mouth. In front, sometimes jutting stiffly upward from a realistically depicted cluster of testicles and pubic hair, or sometimes bunched together with them in dignified repose, was a phallus.

These statues, or *herms* as they are called in English, were an Athenian specialty. The city was full of them. They stood at the doors of private houses, where men, women, and children brushed past them on their way in and out. They guarded the entrances of temples of other gods and goddesses. Worshipers on their way up to the Acropolis, the ancient citadel of Athens with its magnificent temples, among them the newly finished Parthenon, must first pass by the herm that stood guard at the Propylaea, the ceremonial gateway of the sacred precinct.* The Agora, the central town square and marketplace just below the Acropolis, was thickly dotted with herms, among which the citizens strolled and gossiped, argued over politics, and bargained for provisions; or they freshened up in the open-air barbershop that did business right next to one of the familiar statues. Herms watched over the sons of solid citizens and the upper class, as they wrestled and raced and did arms drill with shield and spear in the gymnasia, or schools of athletic and military training, on the outskirts of town. Herms guided travelers along the country roads leading to the villages and townships of Attica, the territory about the size of a couple of American counties of which Athens was the capital city. Wherever one was in the land of

---

*All places and buildings in Athens mentioned in this case study are shown in Map 1.

1. GLORIOUS HERMES Herm from the Aegean island of Siphnos, about two feet high, with the head of Hermes on top and carved phallus in front. Images such as this one, dating from about 500 B.C., were an everyday feature of the street scene in Athens of the fifth century B.C.

the Athenians, one could not miss the herms—especially as they were painted in bright and surrealistic colors. The herm shown in Illustration 1, for instance, has traces of light blue hair and a red supporting pillar; and no doubt the other features were picked out in suitable contrasting hues.

For the Athenians, the herms were venerable images of deep religious and moral significance. Often, carved on their front panels, they carried maxims for the conduct of life . The herm at the gateway of the Acropolis bore one of the most famous pieces of Greek proverbial wisdom.* "Know thyself," it admonished the worshipers on the way up to the Parthenon. The roadside herms of the countryside often combined moral instruction with useful information. "Don't cheat your friends," they might say on one side of their front panels, or "As you walk on, think righteous thoughts"; and on the other side, "Here, halfway between the township of Cephale and the city of Athens, stands glorious Hermes."

Often, too, a herm would bear the name of the person responsible for setting it up—usually in order to commemorate some notable deed of his own and to give thanks to the god for enabling him to do it. In the Agora, there was a group of three such herms, commemorating an important victory, the capture from the Persians in 476 B.C. of the northern Greek city of Eion; carved into the front panels of the statues were words in praise of the army of ordinary Athenian citizens that had taken the city. These herms were the most revered monument in Athens of the Persian Wars, the forty-year struggle (490–449 B.C.) of the Greeks against the mighty neighboring empire of Persia.† Of all the Greek city-states, the Athenians had contributed the most to the common victory in the conflict; they had suffered the most in the course of it; and they had gained the most from its successful outcome. The Persian Wars were to them what the Revolution is to the Americans, the defeat of the Spanish Armada to the English, or the Great Patriotic War of 1941–45 to the Russians. What more fitting way to commemorate this supreme moment of their history than with these three effigies, with their democratic words in praise of Athenian citizen-soldiers, their powerful, godlike faces, and their massively upstanding erections?

---

*The importance of proverbs among the Greeks and Romans, and the way in which the humanists of the European Renaissance used ancient proverbs as a key to understanding ancient civilization, are discussed in Case Study 11, in Volume 4 of this series, "Library without Walls: A Humanist Classic Gets into Print."

†All places outside of Athens mentioned in this case study are shown in Map 2.

From the point of view of the Athenians, this made perfect sense. The god atop the herms was "the Friend of Man," ever ready to help the human race in difficult undertakings. As a traveler himself, Hermes guided and helped, not only travelers, but also anyone with business that required persistence, courage, and cunning: the merchant, wheeling and dealing in the marketplace; the lover, sneaking past angry fathers and husbands; the city-capturing warrior, patiently outlasting the defenders, boldly storming the walls, or slyly dealing with a traitor among the garrison. So strong was the interest that Hermes took in the human race that he even lived among them. He guarded the doorways of private houses, or of temples where more pretentious gods and goddesses resided. He oversaw the arduous training in the gymnasia; and on the country roads, he waited for travelers to tell them how far they had to go. The Athenians, in their language, called the statues by the name of the god: the *Hermai* or "Hermeses." Whoever stood in front of one of them was standing before the god himself.

As if the presence of the god were not awesome enough, the herms also displayed a sacred object, hallowed by tradition and ritual, and also possessing more than human power. Even if erect, the phallus was not supposed to mean that the god was sexually aroused; in fact, it did not belong to him at all. In the religion of the Athenians, and of the Greeks in general, the phallus was far more than just a piece of male anatomy. It was a symbol on its own, with the magical power to bring about the things it stood for.

These things were all connected in one way and another with male sexuality. One of them was riotous and aggressive sexual frenzy—but also the beneficent results of such frenzy: fertility, prosperity, and power. The phallus brought good luck and warded off evil influences, whether for the benefit of merchants or travelers, householders or warriors. In addition, it stood for the praiseworthy aspects of "manliness," in general—once again, the kind of qualities that enabled an army to capture a well-defended city from a determined foe. But of course, to bring about all these desirable things, like any magical symbol the phallus had to be publicly displayed, whether at roadside or doorway, in the marketplace or on war memorials. What more natural than to display it together with Hermes—whose presence was so desirable in exactly the same places—and get double protection?

No doubt for this reason, phallic images of Hermes were very ancient. The actual herms, with their particular form and arrangement, were only about a century old, but that did not make them less beloved. The century since the herms had first appeared on the streets of Athens was that of the Persian Wars; of the coming of democracy; of the dramas of Aeschylus and Sophocles, Aristophanes and Euripides; and of the building of the Parthenon. All the while, individuals and groups of men had been building and venerating herms throughout the city and the surrounding countryside. Collectively, the herms amounted to a formidable concentration of divine and magical powers, protecting and furthering the undertakings not just of their builders, but of the Athenian democratic community as a whole.

One morning in the early summer of 415 B.C., the Athenians awoke to find that the herms had been massively vandalized overnight. Wherever they looked, in the doorways of houses, at the gates of temples, among the historic monuments of the Agora, they saw the same thing. Everywhere, the face of the god had been hacked and scarred and mutilated. Everywhere, the phallus had been savagely lopped off.

2
STATE OF EMERGENCY

The first reaction of the Athenians to this sight must have been one of confusion and fear. As more and more of them left their homes and saw what had happened, crowds of men would have collected in the streets and then, probably, headed for the Agora. One can imagine some of them simply staring at the mutilated images in horrified disbelief; others, perhaps, pointlessly trying to make themselves useful by picking up broken pieces of Hermes for future reassembly; and screaming quarrels starting up among nervous groups of citizens, arguing over the as yet unanswerable questions of who had done this deed and how they might be brought to justice. It must have been a scene of confusion bordering on panic of the kind that today would be brought to an end by the news that the proper authorities were taking appropriate measures to bring the situation under control, and that meanwhile everyone should stay calm, report any troublemakers, and go home.

But under the Athenian democracy, that could not happen. Here, the proper authorities, whose duty it was to bring the situation under control, were none other than the people themselves—the very same crowds of perplexed and frightened men who were presumably milling around in the Agora. No other agency of government could take more than provisional measures until the people, meeting together in the Assembly, had decided what these measures were to be. The task of other agencies of government at this moment was not to persuade the citizens to disperse, but to bring them together in large numbers as quickly as possible, and to help them take the necessary decisions.

Accordingly, what would have put an end to the confusion would have been the news that one particular government agency, the board of "presidents," had set in motion the machinery to assemble the citizens. Not that the presidents had any power or discretion in the matter. On the contrary, the constitution of the democracy ensured that neither they nor any other executive agency could ever vie for power with the assembled people. There were no less than fifty presidents, serving mere six-week terms—far too many of them, and with far too short a time in office, ever to develop a collective will of their own. What they actually presided over was a larger body, to which they themselves belonged: the Council of

2. THE AGORA View of the remains of the government, business, and social center of ancient Athens. The circular structure at lower left is the ruins of the Round House, where the fifty presidents resided. At right center are the ruins of the Council House, the executive headquarters of the democracy. Further to the right, somewhere beneath the modern buildings, would have been the Eion victory monument. The flat area to the right of the Round House and the Council House was in the fifth century an open space, dotted with herms and other monuments, and used as a meeting place, market, and parade ground for civic and religious ceremonies.

Five Hundred, whose members were chosen by lot for a one-year term. In this way, no one could ever plan on being councilman or president, and there were no elections to be bought; and once having served a maximum of two terms, no citizen could ever be a councilman again.

Still, in this emergency, it was up to the presidents to act. They would not have taken long to do so. The presidency building, known from its shape as the Round House, where the presidents resided in shifts for twenty-four hours a day during their term of office, was located right on the Agora. To find out what had happened, all they had to do was to look out the door. No doubt there were citizens collected outside, urging them to hurry up, until the word filtered through the crowd that the presidents had summoned the Council of Five Hundred into session, in their meeting hall right next to the Round House. Many of the councilmen would have already been waiting in the crowd, or even have made their way over to the Council House in anticipation of being summoned. Thus, the council, in turn, would not have taken long to do its duty and call the citizens into assembly. Pretty soon, the "archers"—tough government-owned slaves from warrior-nomad peoples living to the north of the Black Sea—would have fanned out across the Agora, carrying the long red rope with which they were accustomed to round up the sometimes reluctant citizens for Assembly meetings. This time, there can have been little unwillingness, but even so it would have taken several hours for the citizens to stream from the Agora and else-where in the city to the Pnyx, the open hillside a few minutes from the Agora that was their meeting place.

Meanwhile, the Five Hundred, as they were called, would have be-gun deliberating, to consider what measures they would propose to the citizens, to accept, amend, or reject in the Assembly. In this way, the people would have something specific to discuss, and not waste their time in mere formless arguing; but the actual decisions would still be up to them.

Perhaps it would have taken the council most of the morning be-fore they had agreed on a set of proposals, and were ready to troop over to the Pnyx. By that time, the citizens would also have assem-bled. In an emergency such as this, the Pnyx would have been crammed with all the citizens it could hold—about 6,000 out of the 40,000 male citizens of Athens. At the latest by early afternoon, the "herald" or state announcer would have been striding forward, ready to strike his staff upon the ground and call out, "Who wishes to speak?" Seated on the gentle slope of the hillside, the citizens in

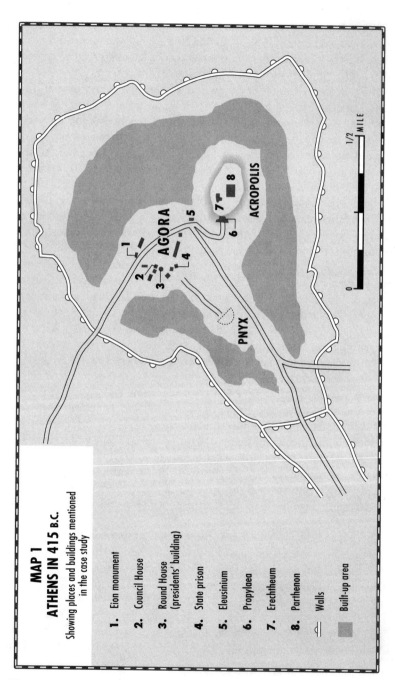

MAP 1
ATHENS IN 415 B.C.

Showing places and buildings mentioned
in the case study

1. Eion monument
2. Council House
3. Round House (presidents' building)
4. State prison
5. Eleusinium
6. Propylaea
7. Erechtheum
8. Parthenon

⚏ Walls
▨ Built-up area

AGORA

PNYX

ACROPOLIS

0   1/2
▭▭▭▭ MILE

their thousands could all see, and quite a few of them could no doubt also hear, as one by one the speakers came forward, to give their opinions on the meaning of this vicious attack upon the Friend of Man, and what should be done about it.

What they said, and what proposals the Five Hundred made to the citizens, are unknown. But the actual measures that the people took can be pieced together from two accounts written not long afterward: one by the historian Thucydides, and another by an Athenian citizen, Andocides, who was himself deeply involved in the scandal. The decisions of the citizens show that they considered this to be a major crisis, which must be resolved with the utmost speed. They elected a board of investigators, probably from among the members of the council, charged with bringing the culprits to justice. This was a highly unusual procedure, for under the Athenian legal system there were no public prosecuting or investigative agencies, and the normal procedure for discovering and prosecuting criminals was for private citizens on their own initiative to prosecute any offense they happened to be aware of.

To help the investigators with their work, the citizens offered a reward of 100 minae—about 100 pounds' weight of silver, or half a lifetime's wages for a skilled worker—to anyone coming forward with information about the perpetrators. They also granted immunity from prosecution, and a reward of 1,000 drachmae—about ten pounds of silver, but a 100-mina reward seems to have been added later—to anyone, free or slave, Athenian or foreign, who would come forward with information concerning any other acts dishonoring a god or goddess. The enormous rewards, and the offer of immunity even to rightless slaves, who must also be expected to be impious scoundrels of the worst sort, suggests how little the investigators had to go on at this point; and the extension of the investigation beyond the immediate deed of the mutilation of the herms is testimony to the mood of general terror and suspicion that had taken hold of the citizens.

Finally the Assembly gave the council full powers to take any measures that it deemed necessary to bring the culprits to justice. In effect, the citizens handed over to the Five Hundred some of their own sovereign power, which the whole normal functioning of the constitution was designed jealously to protect against subordinate agencies. From now on, the Athenians would be living under a state of emergency—one that they had imposed upon themselves.

Evidently, when faced with a major crisis, the Athenian democracy could act fast and decisively to resolve it. But why did the Athenians consider this a major crisis? Thucydides and Plutarch—a writer whose account dates from about five centuries later, but is based in part upon near-contemporary sources that are now lost—both describe how the Athenians in general interpreted the meaning of what had happened. Most of them, it seems, were agreed upon one thing: whoever had done this deed intended to achieve some deep and evil purpose by it. True, there were some citizens who argued that this was simply a case of a few young men on their way back from a drinking party, taking out their high spirits on the street furniture. But would a party of drunks have gone to work so systematically, smashing nearly every herm in the city? Most Athenians thought not. Surely this attack upon a beloved god and a revered symbol must be the work of an organized conspiracy. If so, the conspiracy must be not only against the god and the phallus, but also against the Athenians themselves.

But exactly what was it that the "Hermes-choppers," as they soon came to be called, intended to do? How did they intend to do it? Above all, who were they? Among the citizens, there were three main schools of thought, each with its own answers to these questions. The first believed that this was an act of sabotage by foreign agents, intended to undermine the naval and military plans of the Athenians. According to the second school of thought, it was an act of terrorism by internal subversives, intended to lead to the overthrow of democracy. The third school declared that it was an act of impiety committed by unbelievers, which must lead to a general disruption of good relations with the gods. All of these surmises were frightening. Given the general situation in which the Athenians found themselves in 415 B.C., any, or indeed all, of them could well be true.

3
SABOTAGE, SUBVERSION, AND UNBELIEF

THE SICILIAN EXPEDITION

The mutilation of the herms did not come at a time that was otherwise lacking in strain and suspense. On the contrary, it happened at the exact moment when the Athenians were readying themselves for one of the greatest undertakings of their entire history. Five miles west of Athens, in the harbor of the Piraeus, there lay at anchor a fleet of a hundred triremes—big galley-like warships with three banks of oars—manned by 20,000 rowers and sailors and carrying an assault force of 6,000 infantry. This armada, amounting to about a third of the total military and naval strength of Athens, and including many of the citizens among the crews and the soldiers, was about to be launched at the distant western city of Syracuse, 600 miles away in the island of Sicily.

Already in the east, the Athenians were masters of a far-flung, recently acquired empire comprising many subject city-states. Most of these were scattered through the coastlines of the Aegean Sea and the islands with which it was dotted; nearly all of them were Greek in language and culture. Among them were wealthy and important places that had played a leading part in the rise of Greek civilization: Miletus and Ephesus in Asia Minor, for instance, or Lesbos and Samos among the islands. When they had first associated themselves with the Athenians, it had been as allies in the Delian League, as later historians came to call it, formed in 478 B.C. so as to liberate them from subjection to Persia. Uniting their fleets and armies under Athenian leadership, "the allies of the Athenians," as they were then called in official edicts and proclamations, had won their freedom—but soon lost it again, to their Athenian leaders. More or less voluntarily, the allies gave up their armed forces. Instead, they began paying tribute to the Athenians, who used the proceeds to maintain a single enormous navy under their direct control and savagely to crush allied revolts.

The tribute of the allies also helped pay for the Parthenon and other new temples on the Acropolis, built to replace earlier ones destroyed by

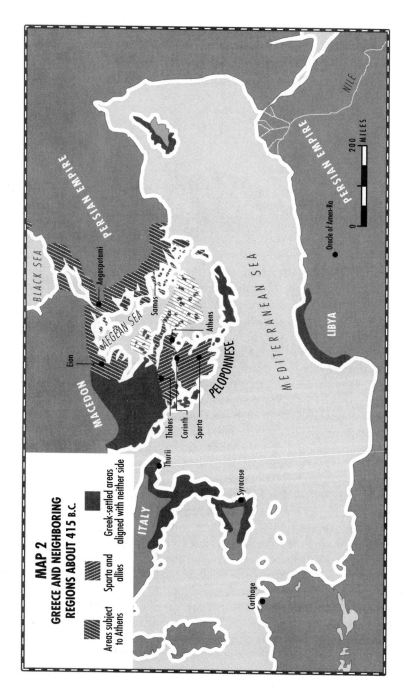

MAP 2
GREECE AND NEIGHBORING
REGIONS ABOUT 415 B.C.

Areas subject
to Athens

Sparta and
allies

Greek-settled areas
aligned with neither side

BLACK SEA

PERSIAN EMPIRE

NILE

MEDITERRANEAN SEA

LIBYA

Oracle of Amen-Ra

200   MILES

0

Aegospotami

Samos

Athens

AEGEAN SEA

Eion

Thebes

Corinth

Sparta

PELOPONNESE

MACEDON

Thurii

Syracuse

ITALY

Carthage

72

the Persians. Imported foodstuffs and naval stores, luxuries and delicacies, and thousands of talented and hardworking immigrants—many coming by choice, and many more as slaves—enabled Athens to grow into a cosmopolitan metropolis of about 150,000 inhabitants, with a total population including the countryside of perhaps 300,000. The greatness and power of Athens, and much of its extraordinary cultural achievement, were built upon the contributions of what the edicts and proclamations now unabashedly called "the states that the Athenians rule."*

But the Athenians were not satisfied with the empire they had already won in the east. With the conquest of Syracuse, they intended to win one in the west as well. Syracuse, too, was a Greek city-state, one of many that were scattered along the coasts of Italy and Sicily, as well as elsewhere in the western Mediterranean. Of all these western settlements, Syracuse was the single most important. In two centuries, it had grown from a pioneer outpost to a center of wealth and civilization almost on the scale of Athens itself. With Syracuse in their power, the Athenians would be well on their way to dominating the entire Greek-settled Mediterranean.

In addition, so the Athenians hoped, the conquest of Syracuse would finally give them the one benefit that their empire had so far failed to provide: security. Rather than making them safe, the growth of their power had actually brought them into danger, for it had exposed them to the suspicion and hostility of those city-states they could not dominate. Above all, it had brought them into conflict with what had traditionally been the strongest state in mainland Greece, Sparta.

A rigidly controlled society in which a military elite held power over a subject peasantry known as the helots, Sparta possessed the most formidable army in Greece. The sudden rise of the Athenian empire, controlled by an enterprising and self-confident democracy, was a threat to Spartan security and to the Spartan social order. Spartan unwillingness to accept Athens as a "great power" was a provocation to the Athenians, and Sparta, together with its many Greek allies, was an obstacle to Athenian plans of further expansion. For decades, the two rivals had wavered between conflict and détente. In 431 B.C., the final struggle had begun: a conflict that later historians called the Peloponnesian War (from the Peloponnese, the southern peninsula of Greece, joined to the rest by a narrow isthmus, in which Sparta and many of its allies were located). The fundamental cause of the conflict, in a famous phrase of

---

*For an earlier example of a city-state ruling over others of its kind, see Case Study 1, "Uruk: The Rise of a Sumerian City," pp. 44–45.

Thucydides, was none other than the fact that "the Athenians had grown great and inspired fear in the Spartans, thereby compelling them to war."

In 415 B.C. the war had been going on for sixteen years, without either side being able to win a decisive victory. This had not been for want of trying. Year in, year out, the Spartans had devastated the countryside of Attica, while the Athenians had hunkered down behind the vast complex of fortifications that linked Athens with the Piraeus, and received their food and supplies by sea. Year in, year out, Athenian seaborne raiders had ravaged the coastlands of the Peloponnese, without coming to grips with the main body of the Spartan army. In 421 B.C., the two sides had made a peace that was still officially in effect in 415, but in practice the struggle had continued unabated, though fought mainly through proxies. The Spartans had fomented revolts among the subject states of Asia Minor and the Aegean islands, and Athenian fleets had swooped down and crushed them. The Athenians had sponsored an alliance of anti-Spartan city-states in the Peloponnese, and their armies had fled before the onset of the Spartan heavy infantry. The war had brought even more suffering and devastation to mainland Greece than the Persian invasions, precisely because, as between what contemporaries called "the rulers of the land" and "the rulers of the sea," it was so hard to reach a decision.

But now the Athenians reckoned that they had at last found a war-winning strategy. They would project their seapower across 600 miles of water to destroy Syracuse, and the other Greek city-states of Sicily would submit. They would attack the Peloponnese from both east and west, and Sparta would be crushed. They would be the masters of the entire Greek world, and there would be nothing to stop them extending their reach beyond it—to Carthage in North Africa, or even to Cadiz, on the great ocean that was known to lie beyond the Pillars of Hercules.

In addition, the great expedition could be expected to bring further glory to the politician and military leader who had done most to persuade the Athenians to undertake it, and was now to be one of its commanders: Alcibiades.

As in all other democracies, when it came to participation in politics the citizens of Athens could be classed in one or other of two groups. The first, and much the largest, consisted of those with a more or less casual interest in politics or none at all, unless the random choice should fall on them to become public servants for a limited term. The second group, which included Alcibiades, was a small minority of leaders and would-be leaders who competed fiercely for influence over the less active majority. In this competition, Alcibiades had been highly successful at an unusually early age. This was partly because of his background. He was the offspring of a family that had been prominent in Athens for at least two centuries. Wealthy, well-educated, devastatingly handsome—a quality much prized in Athens—and profiting from his family connections, Alcibiades had all the inherited advantages necessary to rise to the top in Athenians politics.

But in Athens—again, as in all other democratic communities—it was also necessary for a successful leader to have a record of his own. Alcibiades' record included three items that were highly valued in a community one of whose main activities was making war: he was personally brave, he was willing to spend his own wealth in the military service of the state, and he was a bold and imaginative strategist. He had been honorably wounded, when only eighteen, in the very first land battle of the Peloponnesian War. He had equipped warships for the Athenian navy at his own expense. In 420 B.C., at the exceptionally youthful age of about thirty, he had been elected as one of the ten "generals" who commanded the Athenian army and navy. Both because it involved command of the armed forces and because it was an elective office—with no limit on reelection—the generalcy was the most powerful single position in the state.

Shortly before Alcibiades became general, the Athenians and Spartans had made peace. But the peace was shaky, and disapproved by many on both sides; and Alcibiades had used his position as general to push ingenious diplomatic combinations and military stratagems to undermine the Spartans without being officially at war with them. As it happened, these had all come to nothing, but Alcibiades had been able convincingly to blame others for their failure. At some point, probably around 417, he had survived an effort by rival politicians to have him ostracized—that is, banished from Athens for ten years in case he might become a danger to democracy. The choice of those to be ostracized—which did not require evidence to be produced that they had actually done anything to undermine democracy—was made, like the choice of generals, by vote of the people. Alcibiades' regular success in the generalship elections, as well as his "loss" of the ostracism vote, showed that he had an unshakeable core of support among the citizens.

Finally, Alcibiades had come up with the most daring war-winning strategy of all, the expedition to Sicily. He had maneuvered the project through the Assembly over the protests of a rival leader, the experienced general, influential politician, and advocate of peace with Sparta, Nicias. The people had nevertheless appointed Nicias, together with a

3. ALCIBIADES ON THE BALLOT This broken-off piece of pot (an *ostrakon* or potsherd) has scratched into it the name *Alkibiades Kleinio,* "Alcibiades the son of Cleinias." It was used sometime between 417 and 415 B.C. as a ballot in a vote that Alcibiades worked hard and successfully to lose: a meeting held once a year in the Agora, at which the people chose a citizen to be ostracized (literally, "pot-sherded")—banished for ten years in case he might turn out to be a threat to democracy.

third, less political general, to share command of the expedition. Probably they hoped that Nicias's caution would balance Alcibiades' boldness—or that Nicias would make less mischief as a commander on the spot than as a skeptical politician in Athens. If the expedition succeeded, however, there would be little doubt about who would get the credit for the triumph.

But would the expedition succeed? The Athenians had done everything they could, by way of meticulous preparation and massive commitment of resources, to make sure that it would. Still, there was one fact that clouded their hopes. Not having war games, computer simulations, and think tanks to help them predict the outcome of military operations, they relied instead on oracles and omens; and these had not been entirely satisfactory. True, the mighty Egyptian god Amen-Ra had shown what was known in the technical language of his soothsayer-priests as "strong approval," to an Athenian delegation that went to question him in his shrine, far away in an oasis in the middle of the Libyan desert.* On the other hand, by some oversight, an important Assembly meeting to prepare for the expedition had been held at the time of the festival of the death of Adonis, a Middle Eastern god who had become popular in cosmopolitan Athens.† While the citizens discussed tribute payments and recruitment lists, the voices of the women of Athens drifted over the Pnyx from the rooftops of the city, wailing funeral dirges. It was not exactly an encouraging sign of the favor of the gods for the great undertaking.

Yet now, on top of these conflicting indications, the expedition would be setting sail with a great many of the herms in the city, commemorating and protecting great undertakings, smashed and ruined. Was this not a sign that the great undertaking of the expedition itself would also be smashed and ruined?

The fact that the portent was, so to speak, artificial made no difference. It was perfectly possible to "make" a bad omen by doing or saying something inauspicious. It was this, in fact, that constituted the suspected sabotage, and it probably made the portent all the more terrifying. Somewhere among the Athenians was a group of men so determined to bring the expedition to defeat that they were prepared to challenge the wrath of a beloved and powerful god.

And who were these enemies? According to the sabotage school of thought, they were most likely agents in the pay of Corinth, the city-state from which the founders of Syracuse had set out as colonists two centuries earlier and a commercial and naval rival of Athens and ally of Sparta. But there was another possibility that was even more alarming. The Hermes-choppers must know that by their atrocious act they would spread confusion and terror among the people. In the turbulent politics of the Greek city-states, atrocious acts, calculated to spread confusion and terror, were often a sign that someone was planning to take advantage of the panic to seize power. According to this scenario, then, the mutilation of the herms was not only an act of sabotage. It must also be the prelude to a revolution.

---

*On Amen-Ra, see Case Study 3 in this volume, "Egypt, Greece, Europe: The Rosetta Stone and Three Civilizations, Part 1, Two Civilizations in One Land," p. 137.

†Adonis was the most recent version of the ancient Sumerian god Dumuzi; see Case Study 1, "Uruk: The Rise of a Sumerian City," p. 23.

But this revolution, if it came, would be very different from those of the present day. It would not come from below, from the deprived and disadvantaged, nor from revolutionary organizers, constituting themselves the representatives of the victims of society. Instead, it would be a revolution of the upper classes, in which the wealthy and wellborn elite of Athens would try to overthrow the power of the people.

THE UPPER-CLASS REVOLUTIONARIES

"Under our constitution, the power of government rests not with a few but with the majority; and therefore it is called a democracy." That was the proud boast of Pericles, the most famous of Athenian democratic statesmen, according to Thucydides' version of his oration delivered in 430 B.C. at the state funeral of those who had given their lives in the first year of the war against the Spartans.* It was not the only thing that Pericles found to boast of about the Athenian community. "We are free citizens in our public life, and also toward each other in our daily affairs, living together without mutual suspicion and surveillance . . . our courage in warfare springs more from our way of life than from the compulsion of laws . . . our love of beauty does not lead to extravagance, and our love of the things of the mind does not make us soft . . . even those of us who attend mainly to their private business have no mean understanding of public affairs . . . in a word, I say that in every aspect, our community is an education to all of Greece." For Pericles and for Athens, democracy was more than a system of government. It was a way of life.

In 415 B.C., this way of life was relatively new. Three hundred years before, Athens had been a citadel of warrior chieftains, fitfully enforcing their dominion over other chieftains in the territory of Attica, and providing for themselves out of what they managed to extract from a more or less obedient peasantry. Since then, Athens had grown into a great city surrounded by a prosperous agricultural countryside, enriched by commerce, tribute, and war. It was during this same period that Athens had become a democracy, as a result of a gradual though turbulent evolution that had not been fully completed until as late as the middle of the fifth century.

Strangely enough, one of the main reasons why this evolution had taken place was that the traditional upper-class rulers of Athens,

---

*Most scholars believe that the words of the oration are those of Thucydides rather than Pericles; but the historian was an Athenian who had heard the statesman speak many times, and probably reproduced his ideas if not his actual words.

descended from the chieftains and landowners of earlier days, had allowed it to happen. Partly this was by default, because the upper classes had failed to maintain control of the state in an era of rapid social and economic change. As the lower-class citizens—the *dēmos*, as they were called—increased in numbers, diversity, and sophistication, the upper classes would have needed to maintain their unity if they were to preserve their dominance. Instead, they had been constantly riven by factional disputes, social rivalries, and bloody vendettas. Particularly during the fifth century, it had become a recognized option for an upper-class political leader, hard pressed by his rivals or wishing to strike a decisive blow against them, to set himself up as "protector of the people," introduce democratic constitutional reforms, and rely on the gratitude of newly enfranchised citizens to build his personal power. Even Pericles, who himself came from what was referred to as a "fine and noble" family, had launched his career in this way.

For men like Pericles, however, the building of democracy was not just a means to power. It was also a statesmanlike policy: a way to strengthen the power of the state by involving the people in its destinies, and to liberate the creative energies of the large and diverse community that Athens had become. It could even be argued that it was in the interests of the upper classes themselves. No constitutional reforms, after all, could legislate away the fact that those who had wealth, leisure, and education were better able to lead the state than those who did not. Throughout most of the fifth century B.C., the politically active minority came almost entirely from the "fine and noble" class; and it was the lower-class citizens who constituted the less active majority. True, everything that the leaders now did was at the behest and under the control of the people. But it certainly brought just as much honor, and far more profit, for the upper classes to be the servants of a powerful imperial democracy rather than the rulers of the simple peasant society that Athens once had been.

There were, however, always some among the upper classes who could not bring themselves to accept the new democratic Athens. Unlike present-day critics of democracy, they never claimed that the system was a sham. They never objected to the facts that 40,000 or so female citizens were completely excluded from political life; that there were 30,000 permanent resident aliens who were liable to all the duties of citizenship but had next to no chance of becoming naturalized and enjoying its rights; or that the whole system depended on the labors of perhaps 100,000 slaves. In the Greece of those days, facts of this kind were part of the natural order of things. What the critics of democracy objected to was that as between the few hundred families of the elite and the 40,000 male, freeborn, and native-born citizens, the system worked only too well. It functioned, they complained, with smooth efficiency in the interests of the "useless," the "penniless," and the "base," and against those of the "valuable," "best," and "virtuous" citizens. But so long as democracy brought leadership, wealth, and power to the "fine and noble" ones, most of them probably ignored the critics, and followed the command of Pericles to "fix your gaze upon the power of Athens, and become her lovers."

As for the people, they, too, had every reason to love Athens. No undertaking, from the Persian Wars to the building of the Parthenon, could be embarked on without their consent, and from every undertaking they received a share of the benefit. They got paid employment as oarsmen in the triremes, and land of their own as settlers in the territory of the subject city-states; they shared in the magnificent rituals and festivities of imperial Athens; and they could justly feel that the achievements of Athens were their achievements too. In this way, the Athenian democratic community amounted to a partnership between the upper classes and the *dēmos* that benefited both sides; and both sides, therefore, were ready to put themselves at the disposal of the community in its great undertakings. The growth of Athenian power had made democracy work, and democracy, in turn, had made possible the growth of Athenian power.

But since the beginning of the war with the Spartans, neither the people nor the elite had been getting what they wanted out of their partnership. The people, for their part—those of them, at least, who lived in Athens and could come regularly to the Assembly meetings where decisions were taken—were willing to make the same efforts, and expected the same rewards, as in earlier wars. But this time, the elite could not meet these expectations. Athens and Sparta were so closely matched that even the greatest efforts and sacrifices had not brought decisive victory. Besides, the estates of the upper classes in Attica were exposed to continual devastating Spartan raids, and in their heart of hearts, many of the "fine and noble ones" nourished a fellow feeling with the aristocratic elite of Sparta. Both the strategic realities and their own interests seemed to call for a defensive war, leading to a compromise peace with the Spartans.

Since the upper classes could not or would not deliver what the Athenians wanted, these had for the first time begun to reject their guidance. Instead, they had turned to new leaders, who often called themselves, appropriately enough, "the friends of the people." The "friends of the people" stood for ruthless waging of war, decisive victory over the Spartans, and the maximum expansion of Athenian power— the very things that the Sicilian expedition was intended to achieve.

In addition, their dispute with the traditional elite involved more than questions of strategy, important as these were. It was also a conflict over the question who was to lead the community. The new leaders were far from being mere ordinary citizens. They seem mostly to have been members of a growing new class of "industrialists"—that is, owners of workshops staffed by a dozen or so slaves—that had sprung up with the growing prosperity of imperial Athens. But this did not make their conflict with the traditional elite any less bitter. Like any new elite knocking at the doors of power, the "friends of the people" were brash, aggressive, and insecure. They treated any opposition to themselves as a conspiracy against democracy itself, and in favor of what to the Athenians was the most despised and detested form of government, one-man dictatorship, or tyranny. As a result, they contributed to a rising sense of insecurity and suspicion in Athens during the years of war. A character in Aristophanes' comedy *The Wasps*, which was first performed in 422 B.C. and was full of topical satire, berates a group of Athenians: "With you, everything is 'Tyranny!' and 'Conspiracy!' . . . I hadn't heard the word 'tyranny' in fifty years, but these days it's cheaper than smoked fish!"

As for the "fine and noble" ones, like any old elite wishing to bar the doors against newcomers, they felt nothing but contempt for their upstart rivals. In his tragedy *The Suppliant Women*, first performed sometime between 420 and 416 B.C., and also full of topical allusions, Euripides makes a herald from the aristocratic city-state of Thebes say of democratic Athens:

> *When a wretch, a nothing*
> *Obtains respect and power from the people*
> *By talk, his betters sicken at the sight.*

For those among the upper classes who were sickened by the rise of the "friends of the people," the issue in the political struggle was not just the Sicilian expedition, or even the question of who was to lead the democracy. It was democracy itself.

Intense though the rivalry was between the traditional and the new leaders, there was one politician who had managed to beat both sides at their own games. Alcibiades belonged, by birth, to the "fine and noble" class, and in many ways he followed the traditional rules of the game of Athenian politics as it had been played under the leadership of the elite—only he played it more flamboyantly than any of them. He had spread his wealth around with exceptional lavishness so as to win the gratitude of the humbler citizens. Not only had he equipped warships, but also he had paid for the staging of plays at the public drama festivals, and the training of contestants in the great pan-Hellenic athletic contests, the Pythian, Nemean, and Olympic games. Only recently, in 416 B.C., he had entered no less than seven teams—just one was a luxury of the very richest—in the most important and aristocratic Olympic event, the four-horse chariot race. According to the victory ode composed in his honor by none other than Euripides, he had swept the field with first, second, and third place. (The unpoetic Thucydides says it was only first, third, and fourth.) In any case this was an unprecedented triumph, bringing the Athenians great honor among the Greeks, and Alcibiades much gratitude among the Athenians.

In addition to his family connections, Alcibiades had taken care to follow the advice of the proverb, much quoted among the Greeks, to "Provide yourself with friends as well as kin." In the absence of political parties or patronage of the modern kind, the proverb applied to politics just as much as to life in general. Every successful Athenian political leader relied heavily on his "companions" or his "entourage," as they were called, to spread his influence and bolster his power—a tendency encouraged by the way of life of the upper class, for whom male companionship was among the most important values. Alcibiades' entourage was a particularly formidable group. It consisted of men his own age—thirty-five or thereabouts—and younger, whom he could deploy to make speeches in the Assembly, start applause or catcalling as appropriate, or simply canvass uncommitted citizens alongside them, so as to swing Assembly votes in his favor—and swinging Assembly votes was what Athenian politics was all about.

With the rise of the "friends of the people," however, the rules of the game were changing; and Alcibiades had shown himself equal to this challenge, too. The "friends of the people" had taught the Athenians to want daring strategies against the Spartans, leading to total victory. Ever since his election as general, this was what Alcibiades had tried to give them; and though he had not been entirely successful, still he could claim that when it came to war and diplomacy, the "friends of the people" were great talkers, but he had acted. Now, with the Sicilian expedition, he had outbid the advocates of total victory yet again.

It was true that by outbidding both sides, Alcibiades had made many enemies among his fellow politicians. He had separated himself from the upper-class advocates of defensive war and compromise peace, and indeed helped sabotage their policies, yet he was not beloved by the "friends of the people" either, whose strategy of total victory he had taken over and conducted more effectively than any of them. Still, by 415 B.C. he had built up exceptional standing in the eyes of the citizens in general. If the Sicilian expedition succeeded, he could expect to out-top every other Athenian politician, whether "fine and noble" or a "friend of the people."

Right now, however, the ordinary Athenian citizens had something else to think about. The herms, the most democratic of objects of worship, lay in ruin throughout the city. The Hermes-choppers, living in a democratic community whose way of life they must hate, had done more than merely feel sickened, as Euripides had put it, at the challenge to the power of the upper class: they had released their feelings in a vicious and violent act. Perhaps the "friends of the people" had been right all along. Perhaps Athens really was on the brink of an upper-class revolution, in which a group of "fine and noble" malcontents would seek to replace democracy with the tyranny of one man. Who was the would-be tyrant? Were he and his supporters perhaps in league with the Spartans, who had always viewed Athenian democracy with distaste, and who in earlier days, before Athens had grown great, had more than once intervened in its internal affairs? No one knew, and no doubt that made the possibilities all the more terrifying.

Whether they were saboteurs or revolutionaries or both, it was clear that the Hermes-choppers would stop at nothing to achieve their aims. The offense they had committed was not merely one against property or public order, as it would be today. Under Athenian law, it constituted an aggravated case of *impiety*, or dishonoring a god. If they were caught, the penalty would be death. If they escaped, so most Athenians believed, the results would be even worse: disaster for the community, and a miserable fate for themselves. And the fact that the Hermes-choppers had risked all this raised a further appalling possibility. Could these men be so deaf to all natural awe and reverence that they did not fear the wrath of the gods? Were they so abandoned to all sense of modesty that for them the phallus, the symbol of manly virtue, was nothing but an excuse for an obscene act? Had they set themselves so arrogantly above the community they belonged to that they despised not only its constitution and its citizens, but also its gods?

THE DENIERS OF THE GODS

In Athens, the responsibility for serving the gods was borne, not by a church or a professional clergy, but by the citizens themselves. At the ordinary everyday level, the members of the household tended to Hermes who stood at their door, cleaning him and decking him with garlands on the fourth day of every month, his sacred day, and sharing their food with him in the form of offerings of figs—treating him, in fact, as one of the family. With more sublime deities, it was not much different, except that the gods were more magnificently served, and by the community as a whole. It was the Athenian community that built the Parthenon as a worthy dwelling place for Athena, the great goddess of the state, that set aside lands and revenues for her support, and stamped the image of an owl, the goddess's familiar bird, upon its coins. Likewise, it was the community as a whole, or citizens fulfilling their duty to the community, that provided the animals for endless public sacrifices, at which hundreds of victims were ritually slaughtered and

4. THE FRIEND OF MAN   This painting, on a wine-mixing bowl dating from about 475 B.C., shows a family religious ritual being performed before a herm. Hermes is garlanded for the occasion; devoutly and with dignity, a bearded father and his clean-shaven sons sacrifice a piece of meat to the Friend of Man. After the meat has been roasted on the altar, it will be shared among the men, women, and children of the household, and the god.

butchered, and the cuts of meat distributed to all, so that even the humblest citizen could share with the great gods the fellowship of feasting. In these and countless other ways, the Athenians provided for the humanlike needs of the gods, and were united with each other in fellowship with the divine beings. By doing all this, they hoped to ensure that the gods would in turn favor and protect their community. But, as they also believed, it was only their common service to and fellowship with the gods that made them a community at all.

These patterns of collective human behavior toward the gods were far from being peculiar to Athens. They were the basic patterns of behavior of pagan religion as a whole, which the Athenians shared with all the Greeks and with a multitude of other peoples, both neighboring and distant. They were an inheritance from the prehistoric past, which had inspired the Sumerians who built the first great temples at the dawn of civilization, and which was still alive twenty-five centuries later for the builders of the Parthenon.* But in Athens, one thing had changed. Here, there was an articulate minority of citizens who questioned the ancient inheritance of pagan religion.

That such a thing could happen was the result of the work of several generations of Greek thinkers, observing and reflecting upon the gods, humans, and the natural world in a new way—a way that undermined the traditional explanations of these things that had satisfied the Greeks themselves for many generations. Today, these criticisms of the traditional beliefs count among the greatest achievements of Greek thought. The criticisms came from the yearning for some divinity more worthy of reverence than, for example, Hermes with his all-too-human tricks, and for some object of veneration more idealistically awe-inspiring than the male genitals; and from the desire for some explanation of the universe and human events that would be more orderly, and more in accord with observation and experience, than the needs and desires, the whims and caprices, of the dwellers on Olympus. Out of the meditations of the early Greek thinkers came a new age of scientific discovery, understanding of the human race, and religious belief. But at the time, the new ways of thinking, and those who pioneered them, were thoroughly unpopular with all true-believing Greeks.

In Athens in particular, which as a wealthy imperial metropolis naturally attracted many thinkers and educators, the spread of the new ways of thinking was by the later fifth century B.C. giving cause for

---

*On the relationship of a Sumerian city-state with its goddess, see Case Study 1, "Uruk: The Rise of a Sumerian City," pp. 20–25.

serious public alarm. In 432 B.C. a law was passed—not by some religious authority jealous of its power, but by the democratic assembly of the people—which made it an offense "to deny the gods, or disseminate teachings about the things that take place in the heavens." The law was directed against the philosopher Anaxagoras, who taught that the sun was not a god but a white-hot stone, and it was probably also intended to embarrass Anaxagoras's freethinking friend Pericles. A few years later, in 420 B.C., the playwright Aristophanes made fun of the new ideas in his comedy *The Clouds*, where he made no less a thinker than Socrates explain to the simpleminded hero of the play, Strepsiades, that Zeus does not exist. "Then who makes thunder?" asks Strepsiades, and gets a lecture explaining how science has proved that thunder, far from being the work of Zeus, is in fact a kind of large-scale, upper-atmosphere farting.

The real-life Socrates certainly did not believe that the progress of knowledge had made religion obsolete, but that certainly was a conclusion that could be drawn from the new ways of thinking. It was a conclusion that some of the professional teachers of rhetoric and philosophy, the Sophists, who were becoming increasingly fashionable as educators of the young men of the Athenian upper class, did in fact draw. Some at least of the next generation of the elite were indeed growing up in the belief that the gods were a fake, invented by crafty lawgivers as bogeymen to make the citizens behave themselves; that the community that served the gods was a collection of simpleminded dupes; and that its laws and traditions concerning the gods and all other matters were therefore mere artificial conventions that one could obey or not at one's convenience.

If that was what the "fine and noble" ones were now being taught, believing Athenians might well ask, what would happen to the community and its all-important relationship with the gods? At the end of *The Clouds*, disillusioned with Socrates' newfangled ideas and uncertain how he can make it up to the gods for having doubted them, Strepsiades does what any ordinary Athenian might do when he had a problem on his hands: he turns to Hermes, standing at his doorway, and asks his advice. The Friend of Man is helpful as ever. Opposite Strepsiades' house is the "Thinkery," where Socrates lives with his disciples. "Burn the loudmouths' house down," says the god, "and be quick about it!" There must have been many in Aristophanes' audience who found this good advice.

In fact, the Athenians valued their freedom too much, and the free-thinking elite was probably too powerful, for any systematic persecution to take place. Still, many ordinary Athenians seem to have felt a real dislike and suspicion of those among the upper classes who despised the religious and other traditions of the community—and among those who were vulnerable to these feelings was the very same politician whom they otherwise most admired, Alcibiades. After all, he was known to have been associated with the religiously untrustworthy Socrates. Though the association had long since ended—according to Plato, because of Socrates' disapproval of his friend's overweening ambition—this did not end the doubts about Alcibiades.

About the very things he had done to attract and impress the people there clustered all sorts of suspicions. Why, in a dispute with the sponsor of a competing group in a singing contest, had he publicly beaten up his wealthy rival, and how had he managed, in spite of catcalls from the audience, to extort a first prize from the judges all the same? Was it true that his wealthy and childless brother-in-law was so afraid of what Alcibiades might do to get his hands on his property that in order to remove temptation, he had bequeathed it all to the people of Athens? And what about the team of horses that Alcibiades was said to have purchased for a friend, using the friend's money, and then entered in the Olympics under his own name, alongside his other teams, so as to maximize his chances of winning?

Facts and rumors of this kind all suggested a man without loyalties other than to himself, for whom individuals and the community were mere objects to satisfy his own desires and ambitions. But of course, the rumors might not be true, and since Alcibiades was so popular, who wanted to believe them? And even if the rumors were true, should Alcibiades return to Athens as the conqueror of Sicily, this would certainly be enough to quell them.

Now, however, it seemed that the democracy was paying the price for its ill-judged tolerance of unbelievers. It had neglected the advice of Aristophanes' play-acting Hermes, to smoke them out; and they had turned on Hermes, in an atrocious act that was all too real. This was what denial of the gods led to: arrogant men, for their own evil purposes, showing their contempt of the gods and the community that worshiped them, with cynical and violent deeds. Now was the time to hold a general reckoning with all who put themselves above the community and its laws, and endangered its relationship with the gods.

An attack on the Sicilian expedition by would-be saboteurs, an attack on the democracy by upper-class revolutionaries, an attack on the gods and the community by unbelievers—however the Athenians looked at it, the mutilation of the herms was a menacing event. Given their military, political, and religious situation in 415 B.C., all their suspicions were perfectly reasonable. No doubt that was why they took the measures they did, appointing a special board of investigators, offering enormous rewards to informers, enlarging the powers of the Council of Five Hundred, and starting a general hunt for those who might have dishonored any and every deity.

But in Athens as in any other democracy, the people did not make up its mind what to do without help. Whatever the exact details of the Assembly meeting that voted the emergency measures, one thing is certain: the people would not have approved them unless many of the prominent political leaders of the time had spoken in favor of them. Unless the political leaders of the time were different from those of all other times, what they had in mind when they spoke was not just the good of the people, but also the good of themselves: how best to further their own policies and careers against those of their rivals. And of course, at this time the rivalries among the politicians were unusually bitter. This does not necessarily mean that the politicians gave conflicting advice. The mutilation of the herms was just the kind of incident that would have led all the rival leaders to outdo each other in their eagerness to solve it. One can imagine "friends of the people" making tough speeches full of "I told you so"s and calls for the harshest possible measures, while "fine and noble" leaders scrambled for cover by joining in the call for swift and ruthless action.

Besides, special boards of investigators and special powers for the Five Hundred created all sorts of enticing possibilities of power, prominence, and public acclaim. Before the eyes of those politicians who had friends among the investigators or the Five Hundred, or were perhaps lucky enough to be investigators or councilmen themselves, there must have floated visions of gold crowns voted by the people, or public banquets held in their honor in the Round House—typical rewards of the democracy for those who deserved well of it.

As for the general hunt for all dishonorers of gods, this created an even more enticing opportunity, as those who proposed it were probably well aware: it made the scandal open-ended. Supposing that there was some powerful leader with many rivals; supposing, too, that his enemies had evidence, true or false, that he was a denier of the gods, but that they had not produced this evidence earlier for fear that it would not be believed; supposing, finally, that this leader was on the brink of a triumph so great that it would make him proof against any evidence;

now, in the climate of religious suspicion and dread created by the mutilation of the herms, his enemies would find their opportunity. Now they would be able to steer the juggernaut of aroused public opinion against him, and it would crush him.

Needless to say, there was indeed such a powerful but vulnerable leader.

4
THE SCANDAL AND THE POLITICIANS

THE SCANDAL WIDENS

Omen or no omen, the Athenians were too far committed to the Sicilian expedition to draw back now. In the week or so that followed the mutilation of the herms, the Assembly met daily, on the Pnyx or down by the docks of the Piraeus, to review the preparations for the expedition and issue final orders to the commanders who would lead it. Meanwhile, other less publicized preparations must also have been under way. Men who were in the know about certain things must have been getting together, comparing what they knew, finding someone who was willing to talk, and deciding how to reveal everything in such a way as to do the maximum damage. They must have been as busy as the Assembly itself. For them, too, the sailing of the fleet was a deadline.

Finally, in what may have been the very last session of the Assembly before the expedition sailed, they sprang their trap. In the middle of the proceedings, a citizen named Pythonicus, otherwise unknown to history, stepped to the rostrum—not to bring up further last-minute details about the expedition, but to deliver an "announcement" against a fellow citizen. Behind this innocent-sounding word lay one of the most formidable prosecutorial procedures known to Athenian law, which enabled a citizen to bring exceptionally serious crimes, or acts harmful to the community that might not even be specifically forbidden by any existing law, directly before the Assembly or the council for the swiftest possible action. Certainly the crime that Pythonicus announced was no ordinary crime, and the citizen against whom he announced it was no ordinary citizen. According to Andocides' account, which dates from sixteen years afterward and probably contains the gist of Pythonicus's statement, if not the actual words, what he said was as follows.

> Athenians, you are sending off this army and fleet with all their equipment and supplies, and you are ready to undergo great risks. But I shall prove to you that your

commander, Alcibiades, has been performing the Mysteries in a private house, together with his friends, and if you will vote immunity to the man I indicate, a slave and personal attendant of someone who is present in this assembly, then this man will describe to you, though he is not initiated, what happens in the Mysteries. If he does not, then do with me whatever you decide, if I am not telling the truth.

Actually, in cases of false announcements, the penalty was already fixed by law: it was death. This alone made it unlikely that Pythonicus was wasting the Assembly's time with frivolous accusations. But if the accusation was not frivolous, then what was now coming out was so horrifying that the citizens might almost have wished they had never been persuaded to hold a general reckoning with the deniers of the gods. This was no mere aftershock of the emergency caused by the mutilation of the herms. This was a whole new emergency. The Mysteries themselves, one of the holiest rituals of the Athenian community, sacred to two of its greatest goddesses, had been mocked and defiled—and by a man who was well on the way to becoming the community's leading warrior and statesman.

The Mysteries were secret rites, celebrated in the fall of every year at the town of Eleusis, about fifteen miles west of Athens. The rites took place on the exact spot where, according to ancient tradition, the goddess Demeter, the "Divine Mother," had received back her daughter Persephone, "the Maiden," from Hades, the dreadful ruler of the underworld and the dead, who had kidnapped and wed her. Though the Mysteries were secret, that did not mean that knowledge of or participation in them was confined to a few. On the contrary, they were perhaps the single most democratic institution of the Athenian state, open to men and women, children and slaves, Greeks and non-Greeks, so long as they understood the Greek language in which the Mysteries were celebrated. But all who participated had to be made worthy to do so by undergoing a ritual purification, and those who had not been thus initiated could not take part or even know what happened.

Such was the awe in which the Mysteries were held, that although they were celebrated for more than a thousand years from about 800 B.C. on, and during that time many hundreds of thousands of people must have learned their secret, it was never once reliably written down, and today we do not know what it was. All that is certain is that the worshipers were led through an elaborate series of experiences, proceeding

5. THE TWO GODDESSES Temple frieze from Eleusis, dating from the fifth century B.C., and conveying something of the solemn and holy spirit of the Mysteries. At left is the goddess Demeter, at right her daughter Persephone. Between them is Triptolemus, a lesser god whom, according to Athenian tradition, the Two Goddesses sent on a mission round the world to reveal to the human race the life-transforming secret of the cultivation of grain.

in stages from "Things Enacted," through "Things Spoken," to a supreme moment when, at night in a great columned hall, a blaze of light shone forth and thousands of people, citizens of Athens and pilgrims from all over the Greek world, beheld the "Things Seen."

It is a reasonable guess that all the rituals expressed in one way or another the ancient beliefs and yearnings that lay behind the myth of the Two Goddesses: the life-giving power of motherhood, the "death" of the seed in the underground storage chamber before it is broadcast upon the surface of the earth and bursts into life, and the hope that after every death, life will be renewed. This female principle of fertility and renewal, like the aggressive sexuality of the phallus, was something upon which the ordered life of civilized communities was deemed to depend. Accordingly, the celebration of the Mysteries, and the whole cult of the Two Goddesses, was for the Athenians an important matter of state.*

But for the thousands who came to Eleusis and heard and saw, the effect was also that of a life-renewing individual experience. It obliged the individual person to live a better life, so that he or she might be "worthy of the Mysteries." It also conveyed a great hope: that beyond death there lay, not the near-nothingness of the underworld that was all the Greeks otherwise believed in, but a new and more blessed life. This was the promise and the hope of Eleusis, which echoed across the world and down the centuries. In the words of the fifth-century poet Pindar, "Happy is he who, having seen these rites, goes beneath the hollow earth; for he knows the end of life, and he knows its god-sent beginning."

Such were the holy rites that **Alcibiades was accused of mocking**, by **performing them in a private house**, and of defiling, by doing so in front of people who had not been ritually purified. No accusation could have been better calculated to destroy him in the eyes of the ordinary Athenian citizens than this one. With the prosperity of the community and the individual's hope of life after death both at stake, the Athenians felt very strongly about anything that might offend the Two Goddesses. Fifty years earlier, when the playwright Aeschylus had presented a tragedy with a scene in it that had too closely resembled the sacred rituals of Eleusis, there had been a riot in the theatre, and Aeschylus was very nearly lynched. This time, if the charges were true, then the insult to the Two Goddesses had been far worse. The man who had done such

---

*For similar myths of life, death, and fertility among other ancient peoples that were also an important matter of state, see Case Study 1, "Uruk: The Rise of a Sumerian City," pp. 22–23 (Inanna and Dumuzi), and Case Study 3, "Egypt, Greece, Europe: The Rosetta Stone and Three Civilizations, Part 1, Two Civilizations in One Land," p. 143 (Isis, Osiris, and Horus).

a thing would not just be finished as a politician. He would certainly be put to death.

For Alcibiades, Pythonicus's announcement must have come as a total surprise. No doubt Alcibiades had been basking in the role of great commander, explaining to his fellow citizens the final details of their and his great undertaking. Now, from one minute to the next, he found himself a suspect, accused of a horrible crime. Of course, if Pythonicus had been acting on his own, then perhaps Alcibiades could have responded by treating him as a jealous and irresponsible nobody. But no sooner had Pythonicus finished than many leading politicians came forward to back his charges. Chief among them was a "friend of the people," Androcles, of whom little is known other than that he was a powerful man and a bitter rival of Alcibiades. One after another, these speakers not only seconded Pythonicus, but also added other charges of their own. One who was impious enough to defile the holy rituals of the Two Goddesses, they said, would also be vicious and godless enough to take a chopper to Hermes; one who by his whole way of life had shown his contempt for the community must intend by this wickedness to subvert its democratic government. Not only did Alcibiades face the dreadful accusation concerning the Mysteries, but the equally dreadful fears and suspicions aroused in the citizens by the mutilation of the herms were also to be turned against him. Evidently, this was a planned maneuver by Alcibiades' enemies. He had fallen into a deadly ambush.

Not even Alcibiades' worst enemy could have denied that he was at his best in a tight spot. Immediately he began to try to extricate himself. According to Andocides' account, "he spent a long time denying the truth of the allegations and arguing against them." Perhaps he pointed out that it was utterly absurd to suppose that he had had anything to do with the mutilation of the herms. Why should he, whose whole future depended on the success of the Sicilian expedition, have done anything to disorganize it?

But the accusations concerning the Mysteries could not be fended off with mere arguments and denials. Eventually the presidents cut the debate short, ordered all those who had not been initiated into the Mysteries to withdraw—probably only a handful of the thousands present had to get up and go—and themselves departed to fetch the slave of whom Pythonicus had spoken. After hearing his story, the people would have to decide whether Alcibiades should stand his trial—a trial that could well end in a death sentence.

The pause that followed cannot have been long. No doubt Androcles and his allies had seen to it that the witness was ready and waiting, dressed in his best clothes. Presently the presidents returned, bringing with them a boy in his teens: Andromachus, the slave and personal attendant of Alcibiades himself. Reassured by a grant of immunity voted by the people for his own personal benefit, Andromachus told what seems to have been a detailed and circumstantial story: how he had been present with his master at a gathering in the house of Pulytion, a wealthy non-Athenian resident in the city; how several other slaves, including a pipe player, had been there too—which indicated that this had been a typical upper-class dinner party, with wine and music; how Alcibiades and two of his friends had acted out rituals of the Mysteries; and how the others present—Andromachus named eleven men, apart from the slaves—had seen and heard the holy rituals, presumably amid drunken belches and guffaws. For Alcibiades, his own slave boy's detailed testimony must have been even more daunting than the wild accusations of his foes.

A less resourceful politician might have tried to prolong the whole business so as to delay the people's decision, but not Alcibiades. According to Thucydides, "he denied the testimony on the spot, and was ready to stand his trial before the fleet sailed . . . he urged them [the people] to put him to death at once, if he were guilty, and insisted that it would be wiser not to send him out in command of such a large force, and with the accusations still unresolved." This was not just bravado. The summer, the only season of the year when the unwieldy triremes could make the passage to Sicily, was passing rapidly. The fleet must sail no matter what. Faced with the choice of sending off the fleet without Alcibiades, the citizens might decide that there was no case to answer; faced with the possibility of sailing without him as commander, the citizens among the soldiers and sailors would very likely cast their votes in his favor; and if he were condemned, various contingents of noncitizens, recruited from the Peloponnese and elsewhere by Alcibiades personally, might decide to go home. Alcibiades must have sensed that if he came out fighting and confronted the charges without delay, he might actually be exonerated.

But his enemies knew this too, and they had had more time to plan their moves. Presumably they had decided to confront Alcibiades with the charges while he was still present to answer them, because it would not look good to bring them up after he had left for Sicily. But the last thing they wanted was for the people actually to decide immediately what to do with him. Instead, Alcibiades must go to Sicily with the charges still hanging over him, and taking with him all the sailors and soldiers who might vote in his favor. Then an excuse must be found to recall him from Sicily. Only at that point, with the expedition underway and his strongest supporters absent, should the people decide Alcibiades' fate.

That, according to Thucydides, was what Alcibiades' foes wanted, and they now put into operation a planned maneuver to achieve this aim. For this purpose, they used the circles of friends and companions that they, like Alcibiades and all leading Athenian politicians, had at their disposal to help them influence the decisions of the people. One by one, there came to the rostrum citizens who would have been recognizable to those in the know as friends of Androcles and others who had just been leading the hue and cry against Alcibiades. One by one, these citizens all made essentially the same speech—earnestly advising the people, for the sake of the Sicilian expedition, not to grant Alcibiades' request for immediate trial. To put one of the commanders of the expedition on trial now, they said, would hold up its departure and endanger its success. There would be time enough to try Alcibiades when he returned. Meanwhile, let him and the fleet sail as planned. In this way, the very factors that Alcibiades must have been counting on to get him out of this trap—the impatience of the citizens to get on with the expedition and the confidence of the sailors and soldiers in himself—were turned against him.

Against this tactic, Alcibiades had no riposte, and the people decided as his enemies intended. All the others denounced by Andromachus were to stand trial. (They all fled and were condemned to death as fugitives, except for one, who was caught, tried, and put to death.) As for Alcibiades, he was to sail with the fleet and stand trial upon his return.

A few days, or at most a week or so afterward, with saying of prayers, pouring out of offerings of wine, and singing of anthems to the gods, in the presence of almost the entire population of Athens, the great fleet put to sea. For the tens of thousands of men aboard the endless line of ships pulling away to the south for the voyage round the Peloponnese, it was the beginning of a great undertaking. But for the many more tens of thousands of Athenians who streamed back into the city that evening, it meant that all the months of preparation and arrangements and decision making were over, and for the time being at least, Sicily was finished with. There was nothing more to worry about, as far as the great expedition was concerned; instead, all suspicions, fears, and anxieties could be focused on the twin scandals. There would be no more hectic Assembly sessions; instead, the decisions on what was now the dominating political issue in Athens would be taken, under the grant of full powers in the matter of the herms—formally extended or informally stretched to cover the Mysteries—by the Council of Five Hundred. And whatever decisions were arrived at, regarding the herms or the Mysteries, this would happen in the absence of the man who had so suddenly become the central figure in both scandals.

Not that Alcibiades' enemies could now crush him at their leisure. By this time, there were too many forces driving the scandal forward—too many denouncers tempted by the huge rewards, too many politicians on the lookout for publicity, too many groups with different interests in its outcome—for the scandal to be fully controllable by any one group. It would still need skill and luck to bring Alcibiades down. In fact, for some time after the departure of the fleet, it may even have seemed as if the heat was off Alcibiades, as new revelations and allegations surfaced that did not involve him, even though they enormously increased the anxiety and alarm of the Athenians.

REVELATIONS AND COUNTER-REVELATIONS

Not long after the fleet set sail, or perhaps just before its departure, the Council of Five Hundred received a message from a non-Athenian resident in the city, by the name of Teucer. This man—possibly a stonemason employed in the building of the new temples on the Acropolis—admitted having taken part in a second defilement of the Mysteries, and claimed to know something about the mutilation of the herms: if granted immunity, he would name names. The Five Hundred, exercising under their full powers a prerogative normally reserved to the people, voted the immunity, and a delegation sought out Teucer in the western neighboring state of Megara, a day's journey away, to which he had cannily withdrawn before making his offer. The delegation returned with Teucer, and two lists of names: twelve more defilers of the Mysteries, and eighteen Hermes-choppers.

The Hermes-choppers all belonged to a club or brotherhood, of which there were many among the Athenian upper class, and which operated to a varying extent as social clubs, mutual assistance societies, political action groups, and gangs of highborn delinquents. The leader of this particular club was named Euphiletus; another of its members had already been denounced by Andromachus as a defiler of the Mysteries. As for the new crop of Mystery defilers, they had presumably been guests at a second after-dinner entertainment; they included the brother of Alcibiades' rival commander Nicias, and another suspect who was known to be a good friend of Socrates. How Teucer got all these names is unknown, but his information, as events were to show, was good.

Teucer's two lists, with their suggestion of a widespread, intertwining network of sacrilegious dinner parties and godless young upper-class desperadoes, must have been far from reassuring to the Athenians. If they could at least have accepted his list of Hermes-choppers as solving that particular emergency, perhaps this might have calmed them. But that was against their expectations, and also against the interests of many politicians—both those who wanted the mutilation of the herms to be part of a conspiracy against democracy led by Alcibiades, and those who perhaps simply wanted to get the maximum mileage out of the scandal for themselves.

In any case, as the arrests and trials and executions got under way, together with condemnations in absence of those who managed to escape, Athens grew tense with expectation of further revelations, and fear of who might be next to be denounced. "Such was the atmosphere in the city," says Andocides, "that when the herald summoned the council into session and the signal-flag was lowered, at one and the same signal the council chamber filled with councilmen, and the Agora emptied rapidly of citizens, each of them fearing that he would be arrested."

Finally, after perhaps a couple of weeks of this almost unbearable tension, a citizen was bold enough to present himself before one of the dreaded council sessions, with the great denunciation that everyone was expecting. His name was Dioclides, and his story was detailed, circumstantial, and—what no doubt made it especially convincing—not at all creditable to himself.

Dioclides testified that on the night of the mutilation of the herms, he had risen well before daybreak to go on a business trip—he had had to walk to Laurium, twenty miles south of Athens, to collect the rental due on a slave of his who worked for a silver mine operator there. Passing through the center of Athens, he had seen about 300 men, coming down from the lower slopes of the Acropolis, and standing around in groups of fifteen or twenty. Later, in Laurium, he had heard of the attack on Hermes, and on returning to Athens, of the 100-mina reward. He had gone to the leaders of the men he had seen (whose faces he said he had recognized by the light of the moon) and informed them that rather than receiving 100 minae from the state for telling what he knew, he would prefer to receive two talents (120 minae) from them for keeping his mouth shut. They had agreed, but not paid; and that, Dioclides explained to the councilmen, was why he was now standing before them.

Dioclides then formally "announced" before the council forty-two men whose faces he said he had recognized. There was the ringleader,

Leogoras, a man of "fine and noble" family whose forefathers had been among the wealthiest citizens of Athens for at least 150 years. He himself was famous for his pheasant breeding, his luxurious dinner parties, and his love of the beautiful and expensive woman of the world Myrrhina. There was a group of close relatives of Leogoras, including his son Andocides—who later wrote the story of the scandal—and a well-known denier of the gods and enemy of democracy, Critias. There were also, among the other conspirators whom Dioclides named, two members of the very council before which he was standing.

Here, it seemed, was the detailed and extensive information that the council needed. It fitted in only too well with other reports that the Five Hundred had received, of military movements among Athens's enemies: armies of unfriendly states to the north advancing toward the frontier, and a Spartan force moving from the Peloponnese to join them. At last, the outlines of the conspiracy were emerging: a large and well-organized group of Hermes-choppers inside the city was about to start an upper-class revolution, with the help of foreign intervention. The council had very little time, it seemed, to decide what to do.

Its first decision, taken amid roars of savage approval, was to rescind the legislation forbidding the torture of Athenian citizens, so that at the latest by nightfall, the names of all 300 conspirators could be extracted from the 42 known suspects. This decision did not sit well with the two councilmen among the suspects, who signified their disagreement by making a dash from their seats for the altar of Zeus and Athena that stood in the middle of the council chamber, and sitting down on it. There was a long delay, with the suspect councilmen refusing to leave the sanctuary of the altar until it was agreed that they should not be tortured but stand trial in the ordinary way, on condition of finding friends who would guarantee their appearance and suffer death in their place if they fled. The guarantors came forward, and the councilmen were allowed to leave the building. Outside, their horses were tethered. They jumped on them, galloped off, and kept on going until they were safely out of Attica; the fate of their guarantors is unknown.

All this must have wasted a good deal of time, but after the suspect councilmen were out of the way, the Five Hundred acted quickly and effectively. They decided on unannounced mass arrests of all those denounced by Dioclides, and then dispersed to carry out the sweep themselves, so as to guarantee maximum secrecy and speed. They summoned those of the ten generals who were not away in Sicily, and ordered them to mobilize all arms-bearing citizens. At nightfall, they transferred their headquarters to the Acropolis, which reverted for once to its original role as citadel and military observation point. Below them in the city, in the fortifications leading down to the sea, and in the Piraeus, thousands of armed Athenians stood-to in the darkness, ready to repel a night assault by the Spartans, a coup d'état by the Hermes-choppers, or both. From the Round House on the Agora came the sound of music and laughter. The presidents were holding a banquet for the public benefactor and hero of the hour, Dioclides.

Not a minute's walk from where Dioclides was sitting, crowned with flowers, the tiny Athenian state prison was overflowing with suspects he had denounced, their feet jammed into the stocks, together with their mothers and sisters, wives and howling children; and in the midst of this crowd of unfortunates was a man who could prove that Dioclides had lied.

The man was Leogoras's son, Andocides, and the reason he could prove this was that he had himself been one of the Hermes-chopping gang, though he may not have taken part in the actual attack. Why Andocides had not spoken is unclear. As he himself described it sixteen years later, he had to argue with himself, and be convinced by a cousin who was also a prisoner, that it was all right to break his word to a few guilty friends for the sake of saving so many innocent men, and restoring peace and tranquility to the city.

But with so many of the guilty already dead or fugitives, and so many innocent lives at stake, it is hard to see why Andocides should have agonized over breaking his word. More likely he was afraid to speak up for fear that the aroused Athenians would not grant him immunity as promised to denouncers; and what his cousin had to convince him of was that his present situation was so grim that he might as well take the risk. Or perhaps it was just that in the general excitement and confusion, Andocides could not get anyone to listen to him. In any case, sometime during the night or early the following morning, he came before the Five Hundred and told his tale.

What he told them was that there was no conspiracy of 300, and that the attack on Hermes was the work of a small group: the very same upper-class gang that Teucer had denounced, together with a few extra members whose names he could supply, having been one of the gang members himself. "One day when we were drinking," he told the councilmen, "Euphiletus suggested this plan," by way of a pledge—that is to say, to reinforce the solidarity of the gang by associating its members in some dreadful deed. As Andocides told it, he himself had opposed the idea, but the others had taken advantage of his being laid up with an injury to carry it out without him. Whether or not the Five Hundred believed this part of his story, they certainly found the rest of it convincing. Off went the presidents to the house from which Andocides said the conspirators had departed to do their deed, and interrogated the slaves there, who confirmed his story. Then they called in Dioclides.

Perhaps still hungover from the banquet in his honor, Dioclides could not cope with the suddenly hostile council. Pretty soon he admitted to having lied; and being now in deadly danger himself, he named some more names—this time, of those who had put him up to making his false "announcement." This did not save him from trial and death, but once again, the new revelation altered the direction in which the scandal was going—bringing it back, this time, onto the track it had been following before Teucer had spoken up. Of the two men Dioclides now named, one is not otherwise known. But the other, Alcibiades of Phegous, was a cousin of Alcibiades the general.

THE DOWNFALL OF ALCIBIADES

Why should Alcibiades' cousin have invented the conspiracy of the 300? The most likely explanation is that he was trying to get Alcibiades off the hook. The Athenians had been led to expect spectacular revelations of a great conspiracy, and Androcles and other "friends of the people" had been trying to pin the conspiracy on Alcibiades; his cousin had therefore arranged for the Athenians to have their spectacular revelations, but leading away from Alcibiades.

But the cousin's choice of a substitute target—perhaps made without Alcibiades' knowledge and advice—had been most unwise. By selecting a group of prominent high-life victims for Dioclides to denounce, he had tried to steer the scandal against the "fine and noble" citizens as a whole; and now that Andocides' testimony had cleared them, they prepared to take their revenge.

From the point of view of the upper classes, Alcibiades was expendable. He had long opposed the policies they favored, and now he, or one of his entourage, had tried to get some of them put to death. In any case, the scandal had put the upper-class citizens under pressure to demonstrate their loyalty to democracy, the community, and the gods. Sacrificing Alcibiades would certainly be a most convincing gesture. The question was, how to do it?

Obviously, there was nothing more to be done with the mutilation of the herms. By accepting Euphiletus and his gang as the Hermes-choppers, the council had in effect cleared Alcibiades of involvement in that crime. But there were still the Mysteries, and if anyone had information about them that could be used to bring Alcibiades home for trial, it would be the people he mixed with socially. Alcibiades had raised against himself the unlikeliest and most dangerous of alliances. What the "friends of the people" had begun, the "fine and noble" would now finish.

None of this is known for certain, but it does seem the best explanation of what happened next. As the hue and cry after the Hermeschoppers died down, three more announcements came in concerning the Mysteries. The first was against Alcibiades, accusing him of another defilement of the Mysteries with a different group of friends; it was brought by a highborn lady who was probably a relative of the man she accused. The next was against Leogoras and some of his friends, and was brought by a slave. It was as if Alcibiades' enemies and his friends were throwing dirt at each other, and most of the dirt seems to have stuck: all those accused by both sides, except for the fortunate Leogoras personally, were eventually found guilty.

But nothing, now, could hold back the scandal from crushing its main victim. The third announcement against Alcibiades came from one of the finest and noblest of citizens. The facts he had to tell, for all that they had been heard several times in recent weeks, must have been shocking enough, even in the dry legal language of the formal accusation:

> Thessalus son of Cimon, of the township of Laciadae, announces against Alcibiades son of Cleinias, of the ward of Scambonidae, that he wronged the goddesses of Eleusis, Demeter and Persephone, by mimicking the Mysteries and showing them forth to his companions in his own house, wearing a robe such as the Displayer of the Sacred Things wears when he reveals the Things Shown to the initiates, calling Pulytion the Torchbearer, and Theodorus, of the township of Phegea, the Herald; and hailing the rest of his companions as initiates and beholders, in violation of the laws and institutions of the Children of Eumolpus, the Heralds, and the priests of Eleusis.*

---

*The Displayer of the Sacred Things, the Torchbearer, and the Herald were the chief officiants in the celebration of the Mysteries; the Children of Eumolpus and the Heralds were two clans that supplied these and the other priests and priestesses of the Two Goddesses.

But the accusation also gained weight from the name and family of the accuser. Thessalus's father Cimon had been one of the greatest Athenian commanders in the Persian Wars, leading them to many victories including the capture of Eion which was commemorated by the now faceless and emasculated herms in the Agora. Probably on the basis of this announcement, the Five Hundred decided to send out the Athenian official trireme, the *Salaminia*, with orders for Alcibiades' recall.

Once arrived in Sicily, the members of the delegation bearing the orders politely requested Alcibiades to return with them, in his own ship. They had been instructed not to arrest him, for fear of causing a mutiny among the soldiers and sailors of the expedition. Politely, Alcibiades consented, perhaps still in the hope that, once on the spot, he could get an acquittal. But as he sailed, in company with the *Salaminia*, back toward Athens, he must have had second thoughts. When the two ships put in at the town of Thurii in southern Italy, he disappeared. After spending some time looking for him, the delegation sailed home alone.

For Alcibiades' enemies in Athens, his disappearance was not necessarily a misfortune. It could be regarded as a confession of guilt, and certainly, without him to slow them down, the wheels of justice turned smoothly to destroy him. He was condemned to death in his absence, his property was confiscated, and a bounty of one talent (about sixty pounds of silver) was offered to anyone who might kill him. In addition, there was a religious punishment. At the orders of the people, the priests and priestesses of Demeter and Persephone, and perhaps of every other deity as well, solemnly cursed him. Finally the people ordered a bronze pillar to be placed on the Acropolis, recording for all time the wickedness and punishment of Alcibiades and all the other defilers of the Mysteries, as well as the Hermes-choppers. With that, probably in the fall of 415 B.C. or about three months after it began, the great scandal came to an end.

Of course, there was still a good deal of legal, political, and administrative tidying up to be done. For one thing, there was the important question of who should get the rewards. In the case of the Hermes-choppers, the people's decision is not known, but over the Mysteries, there was an argument. Pythonicus claimed the money for himself, as the citizen who had made the first announcement, while Androcles wanted to distribute it among the councilmen, perhaps with a view to putting 500 fellow citizens under a debt of gratitude to himself.

In the end, the dispute went to arbitration, by a court consisting, like every Athenian court, of ordinary citizens chosen by lot, and making all decisions of fact and law by majority vote. The arbitrators rejected both claims. Instead, in true democratic spirit, they awarded the 100 minae to the slave Andromachus, and the 1,000 drachmae to the foreigner Teucer. Presumably Andromachus was now government property, having been confiscated along with the rest of Alcibiades' possessions. Perhaps he spent part of his reward on buying himself from the people, to become a free man.

As for Andocides, he was allowed to live, but the people passed a special decree, by which anyone who dishonored a god or goddess and admitted it was barred from entering the Agora or any temple. This was considered to apply to Andocides, perhaps because he had at any rate admitted to having belonged to the Hermes-chopping group; and it had the effect of excluding him from the political, social, and religious life of the community. Rather than live in Athens as a pariah, he went into exile.

Finally there was the business of identifying, seizing, and selling the confiscated property of more than fifty convicted Hermes-choppers and defilers of the Mysteries. This task was assigned to the Board of Vendors, a group of citizens—once again, chosen by lot—who were in charge of the sale of government property. Their assignment was a complex one, and it probably took them a couple of years. When they had completed it, the records of the confiscations and sales were carved in stone for permanent display in the Eleusinium, the Athenian temple of the Two Goddesses.

Fragments of these records, unearthed in recent years by archaeologists, indicate that the troublesome operation was well worthwhile. Many of those condemned had been wealthy men, and the total proceeds may have amounted to as much as thirty tons of silver, the equivalent of a year's tribute from the subject states. For Alcibiades, one of the main items recorded in the documents was four dining tables and twelve couches for guests to recline on as they ate, manufactured in Miletus, a city renowned for its fine furniture. It was a very suitable item to confiscate, from a man whose after-dinner activities had gotten him into so much trouble.

As for Alcibiades himself, he had made his way from Italy to the Peloponnesian state of Argos, where he had friends. Following his condemnation, the Athenians demanded his extradition. He then disappeared from Argos, and eventually surfaced in a place that was beyond the reach even of the Athenians: Sparta.

When the news arrived in Argos that his fellow citizens had condemned Alcibiades to death, he is supposed to have said: "I'll show them that I'm alive!" He spent the rest of his life making good on this promise, first of all doing great damage to the community that had rejected him, and then doing his best to save it, as it entered a period of crisis and disaster that very nearly destroyed it.

5
"I'LL SHOW THEM THAT I'M ALIVE"

Considering what hap-
dozen years that followed
herms, one is tempted to
ans who thought that it
pened to Athens in the
the mutilation of the
agree with those Atheni-
was an omen. Just as the
sacred images were smashed almost beyond repair, so, between 415 and
404 B.C., the Athenians all but lost everything that a century of bold
achievement had brought them: their empire, their position as a "great
power," and democracy itself.

All these disasters began with the failure of the great stroke that was
supposed to make the Athenians the masters of the Greek world: the
Sicilian expedition. The expedition was weakened by indecisive leadership on the part of Nicias, and met with unexpectedly strong resistance
from the Syracusans, stiffened by help from Sparta and its allies. The
result was total defeat. Of the armada of 415 B.C., and another sent out
two years later to reinforce it, hardly a man ever saw Athens again. The
destruction of two Athenian fleets encouraged the previously outnum-
bered and outclassed navies of the Spartans and their allies to carry the
war to the Aegean, with financial help from Athens's old and still powerful adversary, Persia. All of a sudden, the Athenians found themselves
engaged in a desperate struggle for survival, in which their enemies
were benefiting from the advice of the man who had been their boldest
commander; for both Sparta's assistance to Syracuse, and its offensive
naval strategy, had been undertaken at Alcibiades' urging.

The defeat in Sicily not only crippled Athenian power, but it also
destabilized Athenian democracy. Exploiting the panic and loss of self-
confidence in Athens, in 411 B.C. a group of antidemocratic politicians
took over power. They introduced oligarchy—that is, the rule of a small
elite—intimidated their opponents with gangs of "fine and noble"
young thugs of the same type as the Hermes-choppers, and attempted
to make peace with the Spartans. After a few months, however, they fell
from power, thanks mainly to the citizen-sailors of the one remaining
Athenian fleet, stationed at the Aegean island of Samos, who refused to
accept their authority. The successful resistance of the sailors was

largely due to the resourceful leadership of a new commander who had put himself at their head: Alcibiades.

It is not clear whether Alcibiades had always meant to defect and then redefect, or whether he was making his moves from day to day. What is certain, however, is that he accompanied the Peloponnesian fleet to the Aegean, and once there, started a whole series of brilliant intrigues with the Persians, the Athenian oligarchs, and the sailors at Samos. He told the Persians that they should not let Athens be totally destroyed, for fear of Sparta becoming all-powerful; he told both the oligarchs and the sailors that they should deal with him, because he alone could turn the Persians against the Spartans; and finally, sensing the weakness of the oligarchs, he came down on the side of the sailors. He had finished with being a traitor. From now on he would be the savior of Athenian democracy and Athenian power.

In the next few years, Alcibiades almost succeeded in this role. After the fall of the oligarchs, he led the fleet to victories that for a time brought the Aegean back under Athenian control. In 407 B.C., he returned to Athens itself. The people elected him general, and voted him an estate to replace his confiscated property. The priests and priestesses revoked the curse on him, and the bronze pillar recording his crimes was thrown into the sea. So popular had he become that according to the Athenian historian Xenophon, "No one spoke in opposition [to his exoneration], because the Assembly would not have tolerated it." And in the fall of that year, when the great procession made its way from Athens to Eleusis for the celebration of the Mysteries, Alcibiades was its leader.

It was an extraordinary comeback, but in the end it led nowhere. All the old doubts about Alcibiades among the people, and all the old hatreds he had aroused among the politicians, still persisted. In 406 B.C., taking advantage of his relative lack of success in the naval fighting of that year, a group of politicians led by the "friend of the people" Cleophon got him relieved of his command. In fear of his life he left Athens, and thereafter watched helplessly as the Athenians stumbled through a series of disastrously wrong political and military decisions, ending in total defeat.

In 405 B.C., the one and only remaining Athenian fleet was surprised and destroyed by the Spartans at Aegospotami in the northern Aegean. Blockaded by land and sea, in the following year the Athenians were forced to surrender. They lost their empire, their city fortifications, and their navy, and became a satellite state of Sparta. At the behest of the Spartans, democracy was again abolished, and the government was put into the hands of a tiny group. The Thirty, as they were called, were so alienated from the community they ruled, and so hated by it, that even with Spartan backing they could only stay in power by means of an out-and-out reign of terror.

As for Alcibiades, he was dead. How it happened is a mystery, about which there cluster many legends. The likeliest story is that he was murdered by a Persian satrap (provincial governor) in Asia Minor, with whom he had taken refuge. Probably the satrap was acting in response to the request of a Spartan naval commander, made at the urging of the Thirty in Athens, who felt unsafe in power so long as Alcibiades lived. Even as a refugee, he was a man to be afraid of.

As complete as the defeat of Athenian power and Athenian democracy had been, it was not final. It took only a couple of years for the Spartans to decide that Athens would be less troublesome as a stable democracy than under a hated tyranny, requiring continual intervention to support it. In 403, they permitted the Thirty to be overthrown. Moreover, hardly had Athens surrendered than the fears and suspicions of the other Greek states, formerly directed against it, found a new target in overmighty Sparta. Taking advantage of this, the Athenians were able early in the fourth century B.C. to reestablish themselves as a "great power," though they were never again so dominant and self-confident as in the fifth century. As for democracy, now that the alternatives had been tried and failed, it was more firmly based than ever before. When it finally perished, in 322 B.C., what brought it down was no internal challenge, but the outside power of the northern Greek kingdom of Macedon, which led the Greeks on to universal empire at the price of destroying the traditional world of the city-states. The great scandal of 415 B.C., far from being a portent of destruction, had been simply an episode in the turbulent history of the world's first successful experiment in democratic government.

Twenty-four centuries later, what gives this episode its enduring interest is the way in which it shows the Athenian democracy in action. Under the stress of the crisis, the institutions and procedures of the democracy were tested in such a way as to reveal both their strengths and their weaknesses. Precisely because the crisis involved a scandal, that is, a major breach of community values, it also reveals much of the traditions and attitudes on which Athenian democracy was based—both those that we still share today, and those that are alien to us.

One impression that is left by the story of the scandal is that of the speed and effectiveness of the institutions and procedures of the democracy. Here was a system where a few thousand ordinary, inexpert citizens, or a few hundred selected from the rest by blind chance, could perform complex operations of government. They could take decisions rapidly; they could set on foot emergency measures that altered the normal functioning of the state; they could discover and punish large numbers of conspirators; and when everything was over, they could return to their normal constitutional procedures. The Athenians had found a way to put the government under the control of ordinary citizens, while permitting speedy decision making and maintaining the effectiveness of state power. True, they were helped by the small size of their state, but even so this was a notable feat. History's other most famous city-states—Uruk at the dawn of civilization, ancient Rome and Carthage, medieval Florence and Venice—all took the easier course of ensuring the effectiveness of the state by limiting the power of ordinary citizens, or doing away with it altogether.

Furthermore, in this particular crisis, much of the Athenian decision making was probably correct. Confronted with a sudden and massive act of violence against a god whom the community loved, the Athenians would have been irresponsible not to have assumed that this was in some way an act against the community that loved him, and not to have taken action accordingly. It is also probable that the actions the Athenians took did in fact lead to the discovery of the culprits. Thucydides, it is true, doubted this. He reports that there were those in Athens who did not believe Andocides' story, and declares that "it was uncertain whether those who suffered had not been punished unjustly." But he gives no evidence for this view; and no other writer at the time, including those such as the philosopher Plato and the historian Xenophon, who were usually eager to report the democracy's miscarriages of justice, ever took up Thucydides' surmise. Most likely, then, Euphiletus and his gang were the real Hermes-choppers.

But what exactly did they intend to achieve? For us today, that is the greatest unsolved mystery of the scandal. All we know for certain is that the mutilation of the herms was supposed to be a "pledge" among the members of the gang. But it is also known that among the Greeks, one of the things that made a dreadful deed suitable as a pledge was that it should have some kind of destructive political consequences. Thus it is likely that one or other of the scenarios that the Athenians debated at the time was in fact correct.

This is not to say that the Athenians got to the bottom of the business. Did it really take only twenty-two men to smash what seems to have been a great many herms in a single night? Was there really no established upper-class politician pulling the strings? But even if there were things that remained undiscovered, the main point is that the Hermes-choppers probably were political conspirators, and that their conspiracy was frustrated. Thus the Athenian democracy possessed the will and the means to defend itself against threats.

Likewise, it seems that the condemnation of Alcibiades, for all its political overtones, was based on facts. True, a few years later the Athenians quashed their own verdict. But Xenophon's description of how this was done makes it sound as if, in his view, it was the exoneration of Alcibiades, not his original conviction, that was the miscarriage of justice. So far as can be seen, in 415 B.C. there really was some kind of fad among Athenians of the upper class for mocking the Mysteries—no doubt as a way of expressing their contempt for the promises and hopes of Eleusis, and for the ignorant masses who believed in them—and Alcibiades seems, as always, to have been a leader of fashion. Given the beliefs and traditions of the Athenians, it was the correct decision for them to withdraw their confidence from Alcibiades, and to treat him as a deadly threat to the community that must be eliminated.

But in other respects, the decision making of the Athenian democracy, and the institutions and procedures that helped produce the decisions, do not show up so well. The system acted speedily to crush a real threat; but it moved just as fast against a false one, and its very speed of operation nearly destroyed many innocent men denounced by Dioclides. This happened because of the mood of political suspicion and religious dread that had seized the people, and because under the Athenian constitution, there was nothing to insulate the judicial process from the people's moods. On the contrary, the suspicion and dread were fanned to the point of witch-hunting hysteria by the politicians and their circles of friends, in their eagerness to destroy Alcibiades. In this particular case, there were no disastrous results; but in other cases—the best known being the celebrated trial and conviction of Socrates—the combination of manipulative politicians and witch-hunting hysteria did indeed lead to miscarriages of justice, as well as to political and military defeats.

Of course, the suspicion and dread were in themselves a natural reaction to extremely menacing deeds. The rivalries of politicians, and the circles of friends who acted as levers to extend their power, were essential to the functioning of Athenian democracy, just as competition among parties, and the leverage provided by patronage and influence, are to the democracy of the present day. And Athenian democracy was no more liable to wrong decision making than any other form of government. But the system certainly tempted politicians to abuse their functions as leaders, and gave free rein to the people's moods. Thus democratic processes were far from guaranteeing infallibility to the decisions of the Athenian state.

As with the decision making of any type of government, that of the Athenians only makes sense if one bears in mind the values on which it was based. One of these—perhaps the most admirable from our point of view—was unapologetic pride in democracy as a good in itself, unyielding attachment to it as a way of life, and a willingness to defend it against any threat.

But in many other ways, the values of Athenian democracy were very different from those that inspire the democracy of today. Without guilt or doubt, the Athenians excluded female citizens and resident aliens from their democracy, and practiced slavery on a massive scale. The purpose of their democracy was not just to ensure popular control of decision making, or to guarantee a free way of life, but to harness the energies of every last citizen in the service of the community's will to power and domination. In addition, as the story of the scandal very clearly illustrates, Athenian democracy knew nothing of the separation of church and state, but was held together by all-pervading religious traditions that were protected by the law.

These religious traditions, too, combine things that are familiar to us with things that are alien. Here was a highly civilized society that revered the male genitals, and displayed them prominently at every street corner, intending thereby to win prosperity and protection for the community, and to celebrate values and personal qualities on which its greatness was built. To the Athenians, an object that in our world counts as obscene or superstitious was public, respectable, and official, and an attack on it was an attack against the community, worthy of the death penalty. So far as they harbored beliefs of this kind, the Athenians lived very much in the traditional world of pagan religion: a world of mysterious and powerful beings who could be made present, visible, and friendly through image and ritual; and of elemental magic forces that could be harnessed to human purposes through spells and symbols.

Yet the Athenians also practiced religious rituals that were designed to purify believers, and expose them to a power that would change them morally and give them everlasting life; and they believed that this power emanated from events that had happened in a particular place. The purification of the pilgrims to Eleusis was not unlike baptism; the Mysteries themselves in some ways served the same purpose as the Eucharist; and Eleusis itself was a kind of Bethlehem. The belief in an afterlife to be attained by the righteous, and the practice of secret rituals to bring believers into contact with divine beings, were certainly not unique to the Greeks among ancient peoples, but the way these beliefs and practices were acted out at Eleusis does seem to have had features all its own. Within the traditional pagan religion of the Greeks, there had grown up rituals and patterns of behavior that foreshadowed those of Christianity.

In fact, this combination of old and new was in many ways typical of Greek civilization as a whole. The Greeks are often, and rightly, thought of as the greatest of innovators, who were responsible for new ideas and ways of thinking that still influence us today. But to do this, they had partly to build upon, and in some ways radically to alter and reject, the inheritance of their own past and of older civilizations, which was still very much alive for them. Athenian democracy had to deal with this situation on the level of politics, institutions, and everyday life. It did not enjoy the advantage of having been created by a group of founding fathers in a new country that was relatively isolated from the rest of the world. Instead, it evolved out of an old-established society, inheriting its beliefs and values, and even its political elite, from the past; it was surrounded by competing city-states; and not far over the horizon there brooded the menacing power of Persia.

It is therefore hardly surprising that the Athenians were themselves a predatory community and one that was prone to bitter internal conflicts, or that they found it hard to adjust to new religious, philosophical, and scientific ideas.* More to be wondered at are the facts that in spite of terrible mistakes and disasters, Athenian democracy did finally become a stable and accepted form of government; that within this democratic environment, historic cultural achievements that were sponsored by the elite could also be accepted and encouraged by the people; and that Athens was even able to nurture critics of traditional religion, and of democracy itself, of the stature of Plato and Aristotle. Standing as it did, like Greek civilization as a whole, between the past and the future, Athenian democracy played a worthy part in the Greek achievement.

---

*On predatory behavior and the glorification of violence in other ancient civilizations, see Case Study 1, "Uruk: The Rise of a Sumerian City," pp. 38–40, and Case Study 3, "Egypt, Greece, Europe: The Rosetta Stone and Three Civilizations, Part 1, Two Civilizations in One Land," pp. 151–52.

FURTHER READING

Athenian democracy, with its historic military and cultural achievements and its politics and government that seem at once so familiar and so strange, is a subject that never loses its fascination. There are many readable and up-to-date accounts of its various features, and the main contemporary accounts of the events of 415 B.C. are all available in translation.

Andocides. "On the Mysteries." One of the earliest surviving examples of the art of public oratory, this law-court speech is also an eyewitness account by one of the victims of the scandal of 415 B.C. It is translated, with an introduction that assesses how far it can be trusted, in A. N. W. Saunders, *Greek Political Oratory* (Harmondsworth, 1970).

Easterly, P. E., and J. V. Muir, eds. *Greek Religion and Society* (Cambridge, 1985). A brief and readable series of essays by experts, covering the main religious, social, and political features of Greek paganism, as well as of doubt and unbelief.

Jones, A. H. M. *Athenian Democracy* (Baltimore, 1986). Essays by a distinguished scholar dealing briefly and clearly with various social, economic, and political aspects. All the essays contribute to a powerful portrayal of Athenian democracy as a rational and effective system of government.

Plutarch. "Alcibiades." From the celebrated biographer's most famous work, the *Lives of the Noble Greeks and Romans*, composed about A.D. 100. A brief and vivid portrayal of the Athenian leader, full of colorful details. Gives a good deal of information on the events of 415 B.C., mostly taken from near-contemporary writers. In *The Rise and Fall of Athens*, translated by Ian Scott-Kilvert (Harmondsworth, 1960).

Roberts, J. N. *City of Sokrates: An Introduction to Classical Athens* (London, 1984). An up-to-date account for the general reader of all aspects of Athenian life about the time of the scandal of 415 B.C.

Stockton, David. *The Classical Athenian Democracy* (Oxford, 1990). Introduction to the development, institutions, procedures, and political life of the Athenian democracy. Up-to-date, brief, and easy to follow.

Thucydides. *History of the Peloponnesian War,* translated by Rex Warner (rev. ed., Harmondsworth, 1970). Does not go into the details of the events of 415 B.C., but shrewdly assesses the motives of Alcibiades' opponents. Thucydides' history is also the main source for the political and military background of the events of 415 B.C. and after. His accounts of the Assembly meeting that decided on the Syracuse expedition, and of Alcibiades' activities as a fugitive in Sparta, are among the finest examples of his art of combining deep analysis with lifelike depiction of events, while also revealing the character and motives of individuals.

SOURCES

This case study is based on three types of sources. First, there are the works of ancient authors who dealt with the events of 415 B.C., together with commentaries on these works by modern scholars—that is, detailed explanations of the ancient works, assessing the accuracy and truthfulness of what they report. In addition, there are works by modern scholars analyzing the events of 415 B.C., and dealing with the various features of Athenian life that the story of the scandal illustrates.

Allen, Ruth E. "The Mutilation of the Herms: A Study in Athenian Politics." Ph.D. dissertation, University of Cincinnati, 1951.

Andocides. *Discours* [Speeches]. Edited and translated into French by Georges Dalmeyda. Paris, 1960.

———. *On the Mysteries.* Edited by Douglas MacDowell. Oxford, 1962.

Aurenche, Olivier. *Les groupes d'Andocide, de Léogoras, et de Teucros: Remarques sur la vie politique athénienne en 415 avant J.-C.* [The groups of Andocides, Leogoras, and Teucer: remarks on Athenian political life in 415 B.C.]. Paris, 1974.

Burkert, Walter. *Greek Religion.* Translated by John Raffan. Cambridge, MA, 1985.

Connor, W. Robert. *The New Politicians of Fifth-Century Athens.* Princeton, NJ, 1971.

Crome, Johann Friedrich. *"HIPPARKHEIOI HERMAI"* [The Herms of Hipparchus]. *Mitteilungen des Deutschen Archäologischen Instituts, Athener Abteilung* [Bulletin of the German Archaeological Institute, Athens section] 60–61 (1935–36): 300–313.

Decharme, Paul. *La critique des traditions religieuses chez les Grecs, des origines aux temps de Plutarque* [Criticism of religious traditions among the Greeks, from the beginning to the time of Plutarch]. Paris, 1904.

Ehrenberg, Victor. *From Solon to Socrates: Greek History and Civilization during the Sixth and Fifth Centuries B.C.* 2d ed. London, 1973.

Gomme, A. W., A. A. Andrewes, and K. J. Dover. *A Historical Commentary on Thucydides*, vol. 4. Oxford, 1976.

Hatzfeld, Jean. *Alcibiade: Etude sur l'histoire d'Athènes à la fin du Ve siècle* [Alcibiades: a study in the history of Athens at the end of the fifth century]. Paris, 1940.

Jones, A. H. M. *Athenian Democracy.* Baltimore, 1986.

Lullies, Reinhard. *Typen der griechischen Herme* [Types of the Greek herm]. Königsberg, 1931.

Mylonas, George. *Eleusis and the Eleusinian Mysteries.* Princeton, NJ, 1961.

Nilsson, Martin P. *Geschichte der griechischen Religion*, Bd. 1: *Die Religion Griechenlands bis auf die griechische Weltherrschaft* [A history of Greek religion, vol. 1: the religion of Greece up to the time of the Greek universal empire]. 2d ed., Munich, 1955.

———. *Greek Popular Religion.* New York, 1947.

Plutarch. *Plutarch's Nicias and Alcibiades.* Edited and translated by Bernadotte Perrin. New York, 1912.

Realenzykopädie des klassischen Altertums [Encyclopedia of classical antiquity]. Articles "Hermes," "Phallos."

Thucydides. *History of the Peloponnesian War.* Translated by Rex Warner. Rev. ed., Harmondsworth, 1970.

Wycherley, R. E. *The Stones of Athens.* Princeton, NJ, 1978.

EGYPT, GREECE, EUROPE

THE ROSETTA STONE AND
THREE CIVILIZATIONS

PART
ONE   TWO CIVILIZATIONS
          IN ONE LAND

333–196 B.C.

CONTENTS

ILLUSTRATIONS

MAP

INTRODUCTION

One morning in July of the year 1799, a party of soldiers marched out from their encampment near the port town of Rosetta in the delta of the river Nile, armed not with muskets but with pickaxes and spades. They belonged to the army of General Napoleon Bonaparte, which had been sent from France the year before to conquer Egypt from the empire of Turkey, and a Turkish army had just landed a couple of days' march along the coast, in order to drive them out. The soldiers, therefore, faced a hard day's digging in the steamy heat of the Delta, rebuilding an old fortress that stood where this particular branch of the river met the sea, in case the enemy should decide to move on the town.*

Sometime during the day, however, there came an interruption. There are different accounts of how it happened. Perhaps someone's pick banged against an unusual piece of masonry that was part of a wall, or perhaps someone's spade stubbed against something hard beneath the earth. In any case, the soldiers dug down to the object or pried it loose, until finally there it lay in the mud and muck of the riverbank. It was a small slab of black stone, jaggedly broken off at one end and missing a corner at the other. What was left was about four feet long, two-and-a-half across, and a foot thick; and one face had been polished smooth and carved with many close-packed lines of writing.

In the land of the Nile, it was an everyday occurrence for diggers to unearth carved stones from the distant past. But clearly there was something special about this one, for the writing on it was in three different scripts. At the top of the stone it was in what the lieutenant in charge of the working party was able to recognize as hieroglyphs, the mysterious sacred writing of ancient Egypt. Then came a section in an even more enigmatic script, which no one had seen before. Most remarkable of all, these two sections were followed by a third, in a much more familiar script and language: it was in Greek. This, the lieutenant decided, was a relic worth saving.

For the soldiers, the work of recovering the stone, loading it onto a cart, and trundling it off no doubt provided a welcome change of pace from wall breaking and trench digging. Bonaparte's expedition, however,

---

*The locations of all places mentioned in this case study are shown in Map 1.

1. THE ROSETTA STONE

included not only soldiers but also a delegation of *savants*, "men of knowledge," as the French called them; and those among these scholars and scientists who had the opportunity to examine the stone over the next few months soon found out the import of the discovery. Knowledge of Egyptian writing had died out, with the civilization that had used it, 1,300 years before, and the language itself was no longer spoken. Greek, however, was a language well known to educated Europeans. It did not take long for the savants to learn that the stone recorded a decree passed by an assembly of Egyptian priests, meeting at the city of Memphis in 196 B.C.; that the decree began by praising a Greek king of Egypt, Ptolemy V, for his piety toward the Egyptian gods and his generosity to their temples, as well as for his prowess in fighting down a rebellion; and that it proceeded to lay down in detail how the king himself was to be venerated as a god.

Most intriguing of all, it appeared that the stone had been carved on the orders of the priests themselves, in what the inscription described as "sacred and native and Greek characters." The first two sections of the stone, then, were in alternative forms of Egyptian writing, the hieroglyphs for ceremonial and the other presumably for everyday use; and both of them said exactly the same things as the Greek. The implications of this fact were exciting indeed. Even before the savants had completed their study of the Greek inscription, the bulletin of the French Army of Egypt announced to the world: "This stone is of great interest for the study of the hieroglyphic characters; perhaps it will even provide the key to them."

In fact, to turn the key in the lock was no easy matter. It was nearly twenty-five years before the hieroglyphic writing could be read, and even longer before the second script—the demotic ("popular") writing, as it is called today—was satisfactorily understood. To perform these feats of decipherment took a great deal more than simply poring over the inscriptions on the Rosetta Stone. It took the accumulated knowledge of oriental languages and non-European writing systems built up by several earlier generations of savants. It took the study and comparison of many other ancient Egyptian documents. It took a difficult break with many centuries of preconceived ideas about how the Egyptian writing system worked. And it took one man, Jean-François Champollion, who alone among the savants at work on the problem had the persistence to master the necessary knowledge, the insight to see what it all might mean, and the boldness to break with accepted ideas.

But in all this enormously complex effort, the Rosetta Stone provided the essential leads to solving the secret of Egyptian writing, as well as a vital means of checking results obtained from other documents. And once the key was turned, it opened the door to an astonishing past. The deeds of the pharaohs of Egypt, the skills and knowledge of its officials and architects and engineers, the myths and rituals and religious ideas of its priests, the tales of its storytellers, even the private business and personal dealings of its people—all of these, recovered from the temples, monuments, and tombs of the Nile, could be read again after thousands of years. As Champollion put it himself, the decipherment made it possible "to rebuild the edifice of the oldest of human societies."

The decipherment of Egyptian writing was therefore a feat of discovery comparable with those of the most famous scientists, inventors, and explorers. Like all such feats, its accomplishment was a fact of momentous import in the history of civilization. When Columbus sailed, the result was that, for good or ill, the Old World made contact across the ocean with the New. Likewise, when Champollion read the hieroglyphs, he enabled modern European civilization to make contact across the centuries with its ancestor of the distant past.

The story of the Rosetta Stone, however, does not begin with the European savants who deciphered it. On the contrary, that is only the second half of a story that begins 2,000 years before, with the Egyptian priests who, in consultation with the Greek officials of the king, had the stone carved in the first place. Why the stone came to be carved, what it actually says, and how the writings on it worked are just as important a part of the story as how it was finally deciphered.

The Rosetta Stone, in fact, is first of all a document of Egyptian civilization. It testifies to beliefs and institutions that nourished that civilization for 3,000 years: to mighty gods and goddesses, Isis and Osiris, Horus and Seth, Amen-Ra and Ptah, as well as to their powerful priests and wealthy temples; and to the pharaoh, both god and man, on whom not just the prosperity of Egypt but the right order of the whole universe was deemed to depend. It gives evidence of the power struggles that swirled around these so solid-seeming beliefs and institutions: the pitting of gods and goddesses against each other in political disputes among their worshipers; the complex relationship of cooperation and rivalry between pharaohs and priests; and the 3,000-year-old problem of knitting together a powerful state out of hundreds of self-contained communities, each with its fierce local loyalties and its passionately worshiped local gods, that made up Egypt. Last but not least, the Rosetta Stone was the product of the uneasy relationship between two nations, each with its own civilization, that lived in Egypt at the time the stone was carved: the Egyptians themselves, and the Greeks.

For the Rosetta Stone is also a document of Greek civilization. It dates from a period, the Hellenistic Age, when the Greeks had become a nation of conquerors, dominating many lands with other and older civilizations than their own, including Egypt. The making of the stone resulted in part from the needs and policies of the Greek kings of Egypt, whose wealth and power dwarfed those of the traditional city-states of the homeland, and whom the Greeks themselves now venerated as gods; who competed with rival Greek rulers of foreign lands in loyalty to the religion and culture of the homeland; but who also, to gain acceptance from their Egyptian subjects, must find a niche in their civilization too, ruling not as foreign conquerors but as native pharaohs. And the needs and policies of the kings arose, in turn, out of the fact that they ruled a land where two civilizations lived side by side, often rejecting and ignoring each other, but forced by circumstances to co-operate with and influence each other in important ways. It was this conflict and cooperation between rival civilizations, in fact, that ultimately produced the Rosetta Stone.

Like the story of the Rosetta Stone, this case study is divided into two halves. The first part, which may be read independently of the second, deals with why the stone was carved, what it says, and the various writings on it. These are themes that reveal much about the enduring features of Egyptian civilization; about the spread of some of the skills of civilization from Egypt to foreign lands, including Greece; about the internationally dominant Greek civilization of the Hellenistic period; and about something that is relevant to any era, not least our own, namely the coexistence within the same space of different nations, religions, languages, and cultures.

The second part of the case study, which requires knowledge of the first, describes how Egyptian civilization died out, remained forgotten for many centuries, and was finally rediscovered by its European descendant. It is a story of vast upheavals—the rise of new religions, repeated invasions by seemingly all-conquering nations, the extinction of languages and writing systems; of the threads of continuity that nevertheless survived the upheavals; and of the decipherers of modern times who followed those threads to regain knowledge of an entire civilization. It is highly relevant to the study of ancient civilizations to understand both the breaks that separate them from and the continuities that link them with the dominant Western civilization of the present day. And the story also helps us understand a unique feature of Western civilization in recent centuries, namely its double attitude to other civilizations of both the past and the present: on the one hand, the predatory drive for domination and destruction; and, on the other, the sympathetic urge for exact knowledge and understanding.

One of the defining features of civilization is the use of writing, and, in all civilizations, those who are expert in reading and writing produce records that are used by their colleagues of future generations to gain knowledge of the past. What makes the Rosetta Stone extraordinary among written records is that it took the experts of two civilizations to produce it, and that the ones who used it were their colleagues of yet a third civilization. Taken as a whole, the story of the Rosetta Stone is that of three civilizations, Egypt, Greece, and Europe; and of how the first two combined to forge the key that enabled the third to unlock the door to the past.

I
EGYPTIANS AND GREEKS

At the time that the Rosetta Stone was carved, Egyptian civilization had existed for nearly 3,000 years, and its most famous monuments, the pyramids of King Cheops and other early pharaohs, were already older than the stone itself is today. The civilization of classical Greece, on the other hand, dated back at most 600 years, and its best-known monument, the Parthenon, had stood on the Acropolis of Athens for hardly more than a couple of centuries. During the vast extent of Egypt's history it had enjoyed thousands of years of glory but then sunk in the world, leaving an ideal of greatness that the Egyptians were unwilling to forgo. Over the very much shorter period of Greece's history, it had risen to an international supremacy that the Greeks considered theirs by right. What had driven forward both the decline of Egypt and the rise of Greece was one and the same process, in which both nations had played an important part: the ever wider spread of civilized society.

At the beginning of their known history, about 3000 B.C., the people of the Nile, like those of the Euphrates and Tigris, had used the flood-born fertility and wealth of their river valley to leap forward to civilization more or less on their own.* For many centuries thereafter, no neighboring nation had been able to match Egypt in wealth, culture, and military power. In the first great age of their civilization, the Old Kingdom (2700–2200 B.C.), the Egyptians had looked down upon these foreigners with indifference and contempt. When it was necessary to mention them, in inscriptions in temple, monument, and tomb, they were usually described with a word that meant, approximately, "vile" or "miserable," "wretched" or "contemptible." Between these second-class humans and real "people"—a word that at this period the Egyptians reserved for themselves—there was not much in common, and by and large they were not even worth the trouble of conquering.

---

*On river valley agriculture and the rise of civilization in Mesopotamia, see Case Study 1 in this volume, "Uruk: The Rise of a Sumerian City," pp. 12–13, 17–19. Sumerian civilization probably developed slightly ahead of Egyptian, and influenced it in some ways, but still Egyptian civilization was basically a native product.

Even when the outside world finally began to catch up with Egypt, the Egyptians maintained this attitude of superiority to foreigners. Under the Middle Kingdom (2000–1700 B.C.) and the New Kingdom (1600–1100 B.C.), Egypt became one of a belt of civilized states that stretched right through northeastern Africa and southwestern Asia. However, the warlord pharaohs of those centuries made sure that in this newly competitive world their country stayed ahead. The pharaohs of the New Kingdom were especially notable for what they liked to call "treading on" foreign nations. Their Egypt was no longer an insular civilization, confined to the valley of the Nile. It was a predatory superpower, with a superpower's triumphant arrogance.

As the centuries continued to roll, however, the outside world eventually came to surpass Egypt. More and more nations learned the skills of civilization, and even those that had not yet done so grew in numbers and military might. The game of power politics and warfare grew ever larger in scale, and a player that lost a round was liable never to recover. That was what happened to Egypt after the end of the New Kingdom about 1100 B.C. Over the thousand years that followed, the country was overrun at different times by the "vile Libyans," a herding people living to the west of the Delta, and the "miserable Nubians," a black African nation that lived upriver on the Nile. The rulers of these nations set themselves up as pharaohs, and since they assimilated to Egyptian civilization, they were at least able to maintain the country's independence for fairly long periods. At other times, however, Egypt fell under the domination of new superpowers of Mesopotamian-based civilization that formed among the "wretched Asiatics" of the Middle East: Assyria and above all Persia. For more than a hundred years, between 525 and 403 B.C., and again briefly from 341 to 333 B.C., the country formed a mere province of the Persian Empire, which covered the Middle East and many surrounding regions. As the Assyrian and Persian superpowers faltered in their turn, and lost their winnings in the game of power politics and warfare, Egypt continued to enjoy periods of independence. But this made no difference to the fact that from being a treader upon nations, Egypt had joined the ranks of the trodden.

Even so, the ideal of Egypt's supremacy among the nations obstinately persisted, and sustained the country in its decline. It helped Egyptian civilization to absorb Libyans and Nubians, to throw off Assyrian and Persian domination when possible, and to survive and even flourish under their rule when this had to be. Now, the same ideal would help Egyptian civilization to survive and flourish under the rule of a recently civilized nation from among the "contemptible Northerners" across the Mediterranean Sea: the Greeks.

As with all internationally dominant civilizations, the rise of Greece to this position was the direct result of its excellence in warfare. In the early days of their civilization, the Greeks had lived in hundreds of small and quarrelsome city-states, scattered across the northwestern fringe of the civilized world, and poor and primitive in comparison with the superpowers of the Middle East. Precisely because of their small size and frequent wars, however, the city-states had developed relatively free and participatory forms of government that mobilized and energized their citizens for warfare, and methods of fighting that other civilized nations for long found it impossible to cope with.* From their poverty, their liberty, and their victories, the Greeks had developed an image of themselves as hardy, vigorous, and free, and of other civilized nations as soft-living, cowardly slaves. The conclusion to be drawn from this notion was obvious. Already before 400 B.C., Euripides put it into the mouth of a character in one of his tragedies: "It is a right thing that Greeks rule foreigners, and not foreigners Greeks. . . . And why? They are bondsmen and slaves, and we . . . are Greeks and free."

Eighty years later, the northern Greek country of Macedon, not a city-state but a hereditary tribal kingdom that had adopted and improved upon their fighting methods, won a temporary supremacy in the Greek struggle for power. Then, between 334 and 323 B.C., the youthful King Alexander of Macedon put Euripides' idea into practice, when he led the Greeks against the Persian superpower, destroyed it, and took over its dominion—including Egypt.

In many decades of bitter warfare that followed Alexander's death in 323 B.C., the Greeks lost their brief unity. His own family did not survive the wars, and, instead, most of his empire came into the possession of the families of three of his leading generals: Antigonus, whose descendants ruled Macedon; Seleucus, who ended in control of most of the Middle East; and Ptolemy, who took over Egypt. Subsequent generations of the Antigonid, Seleucid, and Ptolemaic dynasties struggled mightily to preserve and extend their inheritances of what they frankly called "spear-won land." Endlessly they feuded and disputed, made and broke alliances, and intermarried and went to war. Countless lesser rulers, both Greek and non-Greek, jostled for control of scraps of territory that the new superpowers had neglected to swallow. By playing off the various kings and kinglets against one another, the traditional city-states of the homeland were even able to recover a good deal of

---

*On the workings of the best-known Greek form of government, Athenian democracy, and the way in which it enhanced the war-making power of that city-state, see Case Study 2 in this volume, "A Political Scandal in Democratic Athens," pp. 77–79.

independence, and resumed their own quarrels as best they could. The power struggle among the Greeks, instead of ending, continued on a larger scale than ever before.

Even so, Alexander had given the Greeks an international supremacy that they had never previously enjoyed. The Greek world now stretched from the southern coast of present-day France to the northern plains of what is today Afghanistan. In much of this vast territory, Greeks ruled over foreign nations with civilizations more ancient than theirs. In Egypt in particular, the result of Greek conquest was that two nations now confronted each other in one land, each with its distinctive tradition of civilization and a strong belief in its own superiority.

True, the haughtiness of each nation was tempered by more generous-minded traditions. Ever since the New Kingdom—a period that in spite of its superpower arrogance, or perhaps because of its superpower self-confidence, had been open to foreign cultural influences—there had been Egyptian thinkers who proclaimed that the gods of their country held worldwide power, which they wielded, without favoritism, to the benefit of the entire human race. The Greeks, for their part, were well aware that they had learned the skills of civilization from foreigners, including the Egyptians, and had a tradition of curiosity about other nations and openness to their influence. Still, the Egyptians were now under the rule of the dominant Greeks, and the Greeks lived as a minority among a large majority of Egyptians. The main priority of each nation was to cultivate its own traditions and hold on to its own identity against the threat presented by the other.

> Countless lands and tribes of men without number
> Raise crops that ripen under Zeus' beneficent rain,
> But no land is as fertile as the lowland of Egypt,
> Where the Nile, overflowing, soaks and breaks up the clods.
> Nor is there a country with so many cities of men skilled in
>   labor . . .
> And Ptolemy rules as king over them all.

These lines, written by the internationally successful poet Theocritus in praise of King Ptolemy II (285–246 B.C.) at a time when the Ptolemaic dynasty was at its height, express the basic attitude of the Greeks to Egypt: whatever their feelings about the country's ancient civilization, what they were mainly interested in was its Nile-born wealth. In fact, of all the kingdoms carved out of Alexander's empire by

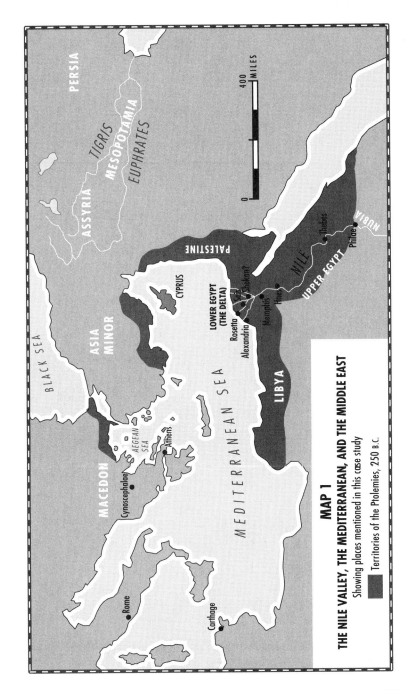

MAP 1
THE NILE VALLEY, THE MEDITERRANEAN, AND THE MIDDLE EAST

Showing places mentioned in this case study

Territories of the Ptolemies, 250 B.C.

his generals, none had the same combination of massive and easily available resources as the kingdom of the Ptolemies (all of whom bore the same name as the dynasty's founder). About 250 B.C. their territories ran right around the eastern Mediterranean, from Libya through Palestine to Cyprus, southern Asia Minor, and various islands and coastlands of the Aegean Sea. But the core of their kingdom was Egypt. As inheritors of spear-won land, the Ptolemies were more than the country's rulers: they actually owned it, as income-producing family property. Taxes in money and foodstuffs, monopolies on a variety of industries, and above all the profits of selling the surplus harvests of grain-rich Egypt to the grain-poor countries on the northern shores of the Mediterranean made their wealth, in the words of Theocritus, "outweigh the riches of all other kings." In fact, their wealth was literally reckoned by weight—in talents, or sixty-pound bags of silver coin. Rough estimates indicate that around 250 B.C. the cash income of the Ptolemies amounted to about 15,000 talents or 450 tons of silver a year. That was fifteen times the state revenues of Athens when it had been the greatest of Greek city-states a century and a half before.

Sole owners of Egypt though the Ptolemies might be, their position as rulers also depended on attracting large numbers of Greeks to their service, and the only way to do that was to share the country's wealth with them. The royal "friends"—the Greek courtiers, ministers, and generals who provided the advice, expertise, and leadership that the rulers needed to hold their own against rival dynasties—received lavish gifts of money and land. The Greek soldiers who formed the first line of the royal army were given substantial farmsteads that in practice became their personal property. Greek officials and bankers who supervised local administration and revenue collection lined their own pockets more or less lavishly in the process. Traders and artisans and schoolmasters and clerks made a good living supplying the needs of their fellow Greeks. Attracted by all these opportunities, for more than a century Greeks emigrated in masses from their poor and overcrowded homeland to the Egyptian El Dorado. By 200 B.C. they formed a community of several hundred thousand people, living among perhaps 5 or 6 million Egyptians.*

The result of this immigration was that much of the wealth of the Nile, which had created Egyptian civilization in the first place and

---

*Alexandria also harbored a large community of Jews, emigrants from another poor and overpopulated homeland. But they assimilated to the Greeks in most areas except that of religion.

nourished it for 3,000 years, now went to nourish the civilization of the Greeks. The kings, above all, used their enormous revenues not only for frequent large-scale warfare against other Greek rulers, but also to compete with them in magnificent patronage of their national religious and cultural traditions. In a world where the Greeks were united across 4,000 miles and three continents only by their common traditions, this was an important matter of policy.

Alexandria, the new international metropolis to the west of the Delta, at once bustling seaport and magnificent capital city, benefited most of all from the lavish spending of the Ptolemies. Its temples of Greek deities and its rituals in their honor were among the most splendid in the world. In many fields of thought and learning, it outshone even Athens. Its library, founded by Ptolemy II, was the largest in the world, with more than 100,000 books. The library's most famous director, the great Eratosthenes of Cyrene, was coming to the end of his career at the time that the Rosetta Stone was carved. His fame has lasted down to the present day as the discoverer of the size of the earth, and in his own time he was internationally renowned as one of the first scientific geographers and an expert on the literature of fifth-century B.C. Athens. He also wrote on Egyptian history and geography, but this was only a small part of his activities as universal cultural leader of his own nation. For him, the main point of being in Alexandria must have been that as director of the library, he had a comfortable salary, plenty of time to read and write, and the run of the stacks. Yet what made the library of the Ptolemies possible, just like the pyramids of the pharaohs, was ultimately the wealth of the Nile.

What was true of the great kings and the internationally famous scholars and scientists was also true of thousands of lesser Greeks who lived in the "countryside," as they called, without distinction, the cities, towns, and villages of "Egyptian" Egypt. Scattered in clumps and islands among what they persistently called the "natives," they clung all the more fiercely to their culture and way of life, and took particular care to pass these on to their children. Even small Greek communities, which in the homeland would never have bothered to found schools, hired teachers and built gymnasia—Greek-style educational institutions for male youth. Here the schoolboys studied the traditional grammar, rhetoric, music, and mathematics that made up the basic culture of their nation, and did the traditional athletic exercises and arms drill on which its prowess in warfare was founded. The language, literature, and writing of Egypt, however, were not part of the curriculum. Along the edge of the school area stood the traditional herms—images of Hermes, the god, among other things, of Greek manly virtue, bearing the traditional symbol of that kind of virtue, the phallus.* But among their many powers and functions, Hermes and the phallus were also the god and the symbol of boundaries; and, in this case, the boundary the images marked was between the Greek world of the gymnasium and the Egyptian world outside.

In this way, the Greeks succeeded in living the life of the homeland by the banks of the Nile, and avoided being assimilated by the nation they ruled over. They thereby faced the Egyptians with the greatest challenge of preserving their own way of life that they had confronted in all their 3,000-year history.

> *You distinguished me before millions,*
> *When you turned your back on Egypt.*
> *You put love of me in the heart of Asia's ruler,*
> *His courtiers praised god for me . . .*
> *You protected me in the combat of the Greeks,*
> *When you repulsed those of Asia.*
> *They slew a million at my sides,*
> *And no one raised his arms against me.*

Not long after the Greeks marched into Egypt, the priest Somtutefnakht of the city of Hnes, about 200 miles up the Nile from the sea, composed this prayer to the city's god, Harsaphes, thanking the god for enabling him to make a successful career in very difficult times. A few years earlier, he had been a courtier of Egypt's last native pharaoh, King Nectanebo II. Then the Persians had reconquered Egypt, and Somtutefnakht had managed to become a trusted adviser of their king, Darius III ("Asia's ruler")—only to witness the "combat of the Greeks," in which Alexander had destroyed the Persian superpower. Even so, Somtutefnakht was able to return to Egypt under Greek rule and become a prominent man in his town, with enough influence to arrange a memorial to himself in the god's temple, on which his prayer was carved.

But in spite of all Somtutefnakht's survival skills, he also had his ultimate loyalties and his fundamental beliefs about Egypt's place in the world, and he made no secret of these before his god. The hour of his country's latest loss of independence was a tragic one, "when you turned

---

*On the herms, see Case Study 2, "A Political Scandal in Fifth-Century Athens," pp. 60–64.

your back on Egypt." Yet that very same god, known only to the Egyptians, had worldwide power, playing the rulers and nations of the world like puppets on a string: it was the god, acting through the Greeks, who had "repulsed" the Persians, and it was the god who had let the Persians into Egypt in the first place, by turning his back on the country. (Somtutefnakht did not explain why the god should have done such a thing, but most likely he believed, as another priest of Hnes put it in a collection of prophecies written a century later, that Nectanebo and other recent pharaohs had brought divine punishment on themselves by "departing from the law" and "not walking in the path of god.") Confronted with the grim facts of defeat and conquest, Somtutefnakht successfully adapted his outward life accordingly. But in his heart, he kept the ideal of Egypt and its people as having a unique place in the worldwide order of things decreed by the god. That was his contemporary version of the ancient ideal of Egypt's supremacy among the nations.

The rule of the Greeks was to test this ideal as never before, for of all the nations that had conquered the country, none made its domination so deeply felt in Egyptian daily life. In one way or another, the Greek presence hurt the interests and pride of every important class of "natives." The priests, whose wealth and power as "servants of the gods" dated back 2,000 years to the last centuries of the New Kingdom, found their use of that wealth and power strictly controlled and supervised by royal overseers in each temple; in addition, priests from each shrine had to make a yearly "downstream journey" to Alexandria, presumably to render account of their dealings to the royal "friends." The "warriors," farmer-soldiers of Libyan origin who had settled in the Delta and become in effect native Egyptians, found themselves treated as second-line troops, with their farmsteads set at smaller sizes than those of the Greek mercenaries who now did the real fighting in the rulers' wars. The peasants, whose surplus production ultimately paid for the good life of the Greeks in Egypt as well as the wars and libraries of the rulers, were under a heavy burden of labor service, crop deliveries, taxation, and the accompanying corruption and extortion of officials. "Absconding up-country" became a regular item in the reports of tax collectors and estate managers, as peasants left their farms to disappear into the swamps of the Delta or the deserts on either side of the upper valley of the Nile—only to reappear sooner or later as rioters or bandits.*

---

*On the use of peasant-produced wealth by the upper classes and the state in agrarian societies of the past, see Case Study 17 in Volume 5 of this series, "Peasant and Emperor: An Enlightened Despot Plows a Field."

2. TEMPLE OF ISIS, PHILAE   Located on an island about 700 miles up the Nile, this is one of the most spectacularly beautiful of Egyptian temples. It was mostly constructed under Ptolemy II (283–245 B.C.) and Ptolemy IV (221–205 B.C.), and remained a major center of Egyptian religion for 700 years. This early nineteenth-century view shows the temple as it used to be before it was moved in the 1970s above the waters of Lake Nasser, impounded by the Aswan Dam.

Instead of surrendering to the influence of the dominant foreigners, however, the Egyptians grouped themselves defensively around the traditions of their own religion and culture, and worked hard and successfully to keep these alive. Some of the finest temples still to be seen in Egypt today were built under the rule, not of native pharaohs, but of the Ptolemies. They housed gods and goddesses whose worship went back to the very beginning of Egypt's history, and was connected with myths and beliefs that glorified the Egyptian state and its rulers: Hathor, the cow goddess who nurtured the land; Horus, the falcon god of light and victory and the upholder of order against chaos throughout the universe; his mother Isis, queen of the dead and protectress of the wellbeing of all the living. Though these great buildings were actually younger than the Parthenon, none of them showed the slightest trace of Greek influence. On the contrary, to stress the purity and Egyptian correctness of their design, inscriptions on their walls proclaimed that they had been built according to plans and proportions found in sacred books originally composed by the recorder of the divine decrees and their interpreter to the human race, none other than the god Thoth himself.

Within these and other shrines, the "Houses of Life"—a combination of school, archives, and writing department—became the main centers for preserving and handing on the traditions of Egypt: the language, literature, and writing of Greece were not on the curriculum. If any of the students learned Greek on the side, it was for the utilitarian purpose of communicating with the rulers, and making a good career as intermediaries between them and the mass of non-Greek-speaking "natives." As for the priests who served the gods in the temples and staffed their Houses of Life, marrying and begetting children and forming deeply rooted dynasties that wielded power in each shrine, they became the principal guardians not only of religion, but also of every other aspect of Egyptian civilization.

Thus, from behind the gates of their temples, the Egyptians peered suspiciously out at the Greeks, while from between the herms that lined their gymnasia, the Greeks squinted warily back. But that did not mean that the Greeks were out to destroy Egyptian civilization, or that the Egyptians wanted to maintain a total boycott of the Greeks. Even if most Greeks knew nothing of what went on inside the Egyptian temples, still, they believed that the gods and goddesses who dwelt there were as real and powerful as their own—indeed, that they were the same as their own, under different names and in different guises that must be respected. Even if the Egyptian language and writing were not taught in the gymnasia, still, the Greeks made no effort to have their own language and writing introduced as compulsory subjects in the Houses of Life. On the contrary, the government itself operated in both languages, and the few Egyptians who learned Greek had plenty of work furnishing reports and petitions with translations and summaries for the benefit of non-Egyptian-speaking higher bureaucrats, and writing out double copies of government announcements on whitewashed boards, to be posted up in offices "in the Greek and the native languages." And as sure in their hearts as the Egyptians might be of their own uniqueness among the nations, they were also, like Somtutefnakht, astute survivors who could adapt their outward lives to outward realities. All this made it possible for a middle ground to grow up between the civilizations, in which Greeks and Egyptians practiced mutual cooperation in their own best interests.

2
PTOLEMIES AND PRIESTS

Even those Greeks and Egyptians who ventured into the middle ground did not usually assimilate to their partners' way of life. On the contrary, when they cooperated with each other, it was normally on condition of each side maintaining its national identity. Among the two nations, those who most fully understood and practiced this kind of cooperation were their leaders: the Ptolemies and their "friends" on the Greek side and, on the Egyptian side, the priests. There was, in fact, a kind of unspoken bargain between the dynasty and the priests, the terms of which were more or less as follows. The priests would recognize the Ptolemies as true pharaohs—that is, as Egyptian god-kings to whom was due utmost loyalty and obedience—while for the most part being free to ignore the rulers' Greekness. The rulers, for their part, would fulfill the traditional pharaonic duty to "do good to the temples"—that is, to cooperate in building them, and to uphold the wealth, status, and power of their priests—while otherwise not having to behave as Egyptians.

For the most part, the bargain seems to have worked very effectively. So far as is known, the rulers only rarely carried out any ritual functions of pharaohs, and several of them were probably not even crowned; perhaps the ceremonies seemed to them too outlandish. But that did not really matter. What counted was that they upheld the wealth and power of the priests, even if under strict supervision; that they used their power to appoint the more important priests so as to foster friendly dynasties in each shrine; and that they gave their cooperation and support to the massive, long-continued undertaking of building the new temples. Within these temples, designed as they were according to the plans of Thoth, there were endless depictions of traditional Egyptian pharaohs performing traditional Egyptian rituals before traditional Egyptian gods and goddesses; but next to each depiction of the pharaoh, the hieroglyphs that gave his name all said "Ptolemy." That was enough to make the Greek rulers into Egyptian god-kings.

Just by carving "Ptolemy" on the walls of their temples, the priests were doing a large part of what the dynasty required of them. In addition, they would from time to time assemble from all over Egypt in the presence of the king, so as to show their loyalty. If he had recently won a victory, they would exultantly celebrate it; if it was his birthday, they would joyfully congratulate him; if one of his family had died, they would solemnly mourn the deceased. As a clinching token of their devotion, they would usually also decree special rituals, to be observed in every temple, in honor of the king and his queen as Egyptian god and goddess; and the decree would then be published, in both the Greek and the Egyptian languages.

Of course, the bilingual decrees of priests were not written in ink on whitewashed boards, like government announcements, to be posted up on the walls of offices. Instead, they were inscribed on stone slabs, to be placed in temple forecourts throughout the land. The Egyptian part, moreover, appeared not only in the everyday demotic script, as was the case with more ordinary documents. Instead, as befitted such solemn religious pronouncements, it was also carved in the ceremonial hieroglyphic writing. It was in this way that the custom grew up of reinforcing the cooperation between the Ptolemies and the priests by carving it in stone.

True, for a long time it was the priests who were the junior partners in this cooperation. It was they whose temple administration was supervised by the kings, and who had to make the yearly "downstream journey" to Alexandria. But eventually, after more than a century of Ptolemaic rule, the balance of power between Ptolemies and priests began to shift. In the midst of a lengthy crisis of war and rebellion, the dynasty was obliged to buy one of the customary declarations of priestly loyalty with concessions that had the effect of revising its partnership with the priests. Of course, that only made it more important to carve this particular transaction in stone, "in sacred and native and Greek characters."

Toward the end of the third century B.C., the Greeks, like so many dominant nations before them, began to lose their spear-won international supremacy. Partly the reason was their own continuing struggle for power, which had become excessively costly in lives and resources. The homeland itself was continually at war, and the outward flood of emigrants was drying up. Throughout the Greek-dominated world, the rulers were finding it harder than before to raise the necessary hundreds of tons of silver. All the same, kings, kinglets, and city-states persisted in fighting each other fiercely and competing lavishly for cultural prestige as if nothing had changed. As a result, they also had to cope with widespread discontent leading to uprisings both in Greece itself and among the subject nations.

In addition, the continuing spread of civilization had brought new players into the game of power politics and warfare with resources that the older ones could not match. At the western end of the Greek world, two non-Greek city-states, Carthage and Rome, were nearing the climax of a fifty-year struggle for supremacy, the winner of which would control the territories and populations of Italy, Spain, and northwestern Africa. One of the two contenders might well become the world's next unbeatable superpower, and the Greek rulers were already speculating on the likely winner, with a view to getting its help against each other.

In Egypt, the waning of Greek dominance led to a thirty-year crisis, which began about 318 B.C. and reached its height early in the second century B.C. By that time, no less than two "native" rebellions were under way. In the north, discontented "warriors" of the Delta were in arms against the government; in the south, the still-powerful upriver state of Nubia was sponsoring a rival dynasty of pharaohs (themselves probably Nubians) in the historic city of Thebes. Both uprisings took the form of grinding, brutal guerrilla insurgencies. Probably they were not allies, and they may even have been enemies, but between them, they undermined the power of the Ptolemies throughout much of Egypt. Outside the country, the dynasty's Greek rivals, the Antigonid king of Macedon and the Seleucid king of the Middle East, had taken advantage of its problems to conquer all its territories in Palestine, Asia Minor, and the Aegean—possessions that the dynasty would never regain. As for the ruler who faced these overwhelming problems, he was a boy not yet in his teens, King Ptolemy V (205–183 B.C.)—and as generally happened with boy-kings, there swirled around him a cutthroat struggle among the royal "friends," each wanting to rule in his name.*
The Ptolemaic dynasty, it seemed, was on the brink of utter destruction.

For all its weakness, however, the dynasty still had assets that would enable it to survive. The first of these lay outside Egypt: it was the power of Rome. In 202 B.C. Rome won its duel with Carthage, and gained control of the lands and resources of almost the entire western Mediterranean. Then it turned on the Antigonid king, who had wrongly speculated on Carthage as the winner. In 197 B.C., at the battle of Cynoscephalae in northern Greece, the Roman legions crushed the army of Macedon—the first time in recent centuries that non-Greek

---

*The story of the intrigues around another boy-king, the sixth-century A.D. Childebert II of the Franks, is told in Case Study 7, in Volume 2 of this series, "A Germanic Ruler in a Roman Land: Brunhild, Queen of the Franks."

soldiers had won a major battle against Greeks. Clearly, the world's next superpower intended to have a say in the affairs of the Greek-ruled east, and, as it happened, several generations of Ptolemies had been wise or lucky enough to make a point of befriending Rome.

The result was that the Ptolemaic dynasty gained a badly needed breathing space. The Seleucid king, seeing which way the wind was blowing, began to wind down his war against Ptolemy V. As this threat became less urgent, Ptolemy's forces were able to make progress against the Egyptian rebels. In addition, the government became more purposeful and effective with the victory of one faction in the infighting around the king.

But in themselves, all these successes were not enough to bring the dynasty clear of danger. Like most guerrilla insurgencies, those that were troubling Egypt were not to be defeated by military force alone, but also by winning over those who could be persuaded to side with the government. To do so, the dynasty would have to bring its second major asset into play: its partnership with the priests. The time had come for yet another spectacular demonstration of loyalty.

The priests, or at least a large and powerful faction among them, seem to have been willing to oblige. Partly, perhaps, this was because they were trapped by their own past history of cooperation with the Ptolemies: they had everything to fear from a victory of rebels who would probably make a point of killing leading "collaborators." But many priests who favored the Ptolemies were not, in fact, collaborators. On the contrary, they were motivated by ancient, purely Egyptian rivalries—above all, between the deities they served and the great god of Thebes, Amen-Ra.

By Egyptian standards, Amen-Ra was something of an upstart, having been worshiped for only about 1,800 years. The founders of the Middle Kingdom, warlords from Thebes who had conquered the downstream lands, had inaugurated his cult by combining their local wind god, Amen, with the national sun god, Ra, and declaring the resulting deity to be "King of the Gods." In Egyptian religion, this was a perfectly acceptable procedure. Amen-Ra had indeed become the greatest of Egyptian gods, and his priests were for many centuries the most powerful and wealthiest in the land. But the priests of older-established gods and goddesses seem always to have tried to limit the kingship of Amen-Ra; and in this they had been supported by many pharaohs, who had grown anxious to prevent his kingship—and the power of his priests—from overshadowing their own. Whether there were rivalries of the same kind between priests and Delta rebels is not known; but certainly, there was no betrayal of Egypt in the servants of older deities opposing a victory of Nubian-led Thebans fanatically loyal to the "new"-fangled god.

This, then, was why many Egyptian priests wanted the Greek king to win, and were ready to help him do so. But of course, the king and his "friends" were weak and in serious trouble. This was an opportunity that was too good to miss. Rather than giving their support for free, the priests must sell it at a high price—namely, the revision of those features of Greek rule that they and other Egyptians found irksome.

The result was that the dynasty came up with a whole series of concessions, not only to the priests but to all those Egyptian groups whose interests or pride had been hurt by Greek rule. "Warriors" who changed sides were pardoned, welcomed back into the royal forces, and guaranteed the possession of their farmsteads. Some of the most oppressive methods of extracting wealth from the peasants were reformed: tax rates were cut, unpaid taxes forgiven, and those held in prison for nonpayment released. Of course, the priests did not miss out. For their benefit, there was a sudden surge of "doing good to the temples": new construction, gifts of money, tax cuts, even the abolition of the "downstream journey."

In return for these concessions, the priests cooperated in two spectacular gestures that were clearly intended to win for Ptolemy acceptance and legitimacy as an Egyptian pharaoh. The first was the crowning of the Greek ruler according to Egyptian rites. In March 196 B.C., the young king went from Alexandria to the city of Memphis, a few miles upstream from where the Nile branched out into the Delta. At the dawn of Egyptian civilization, the earliest pharaohs had founded and cherished the city as the "Balance of the Two Lands" of Upper and Lower Egypt (the Nile Valley and the Delta), and its very existence was a symbol of the country's enduring unity. The great god of Memphis, Ptah, was one of the oldest-established of Egyptian deities, having been worshiped 2,500 years before by the craftsmen who built the pyramids that still loomed in the desert to the west of the city. The high priests of Ptah had traditionally been rivals and counterweights to those of Thebes, and the current dynasty of "Chiefs of Craftsmen," as they were called, had for four generations worked hand in hand with the Ptolemies.

Here, then, in the "Mansion of the Soul of Ptah," Ptolemy underwent the ceremonies that caused him to "arise," like the sun, as pharaoh. From now on, in addition to the diadem (a simple head-ribbon) of a Macedonian king, he was entitled to wear the "Two Mighty Ones," the Double Crown of Egypt. This was no ordinary piece of headgear, for into each of its constituent crowns, the White and the Red, there had entered a fierce goddess who had become one with the crown: the White was Nekhbet, the vulture goddess of Upper Egypt, and the Red was Wadjet, the cobra goddess of Lower Egypt. From now on, in Ptolemy's dealings with Egyptian rebels, what would count would be not the diadem, but the Double Crown with its vengeful goddesses. They would spew fire and poison upon the evildoers who had risen against him, and on the "miserable Nubians" who had set themselves up as his rivals; and he would tread, pharaoh-like, upon them, with never a hint of the Greek ruler suppressing "native" revolts.

The day after the coronation, the priests met in solemn assembly to make yet another spectacular acknowledgment of Ptolemy's Egyptian legitimacy. By formal decree, they set up elaborate arrangements for him to be venerated in every Egyptian shrine, alongside its regular deities, as a "temple-sharing god."* In this way, the pharaoh would be not merely a far-off potentate in the foreign city of Alexandria, but an Egyptian divine being, ever present throughout the Two Lands.

Like earlier demonstrations of loyalty from priestly assemblies, this one was also to be inscribed in two languages and three scripts, for public display in temple forecourts. Once carved in stone in many copies, it would be not only a religious but also a highly political document, serving two important purposes: to record the deeds by which the partnership between the Ptolemies and the priests had been revised, and to be an effective piece of propaganda in persuading Egyptians to support the dynasty. Of course, no one at the time could foresee that in a vastly distant future, the document would serve a third purpose, even more important than the first two. But those who drafted it were certainly well aware that it must be a document of two civilizations. It must embody and appeal to the 3,000-year-old traditions of Egypt, while also conforming to the younger but equally compelling traditions of Greece.

---

*It is possible that the priests were reaffirming a decree passed at some earlier time.

3
"On This Day Have Decreed the High Priests . . ."

Like the deeds that it recorded, the actual wording of the decree was most likely the result of bargaining between the dynasty and the priests. But probably the two sides were in basic agreement about how the document should reflect the traditions of their respective civilizations. First of all, as the record of a decree of an assembly, it must be a public document of a kind that was typically Greek. The whole idea of assemblies meeting to pass decrees was a Greek one, descended from the participatory government of the city-states and imposed by the Ptolemies on the priests at a time when the rulers had been the senior partners. The system had proven useful to both sides, however, and there was no reason to change it now that the priests had grown stronger.

But this meant that the document must be put together in exactly the same way as if the decree that it recorded, instead of being that of the assembled priests of Egypt, had been voted by the assembled people of democratic Athens. It must begin by giving the date of the decree and identifying the group that had passed it; then must come the reasons for passing it, contained in a preamble, as the introduction to an official document is called; and only then, the decree itself. Last of all, as was customary with decrees of assemblies that were intended for public display, the arrangements must be specified as to how this was to be done.

Though the form of the decree must be traditionally Greek, the actual content and wording would have to be mostly Egyptian. True, the drafting process produced various important passages that expressed the Greek viewpoint and way of thinking. But after all, both sides intended to produce a document that would be aimed mainly at Egyptians. The decree must announce the many concessions that the Greek ruler had made to them, and present him as a true Egyptian god-king who was worthy of full, traditional veneration. These were things that could only be done in the Egyptian manner.

Both of them were in fact done in various ways throughout the document. But the presentation of Ptolemy to his subjects as a god-king was accomplished most solemnly and impressively at the very beginning, in what today would be regarded as the most routine introductory part, to be gotten over with as quickly as possible: the giving of the date.

"Ptolemy Living Forever, Beloved of Ptah"

The Egyptian calendar, like those in use at the present day, was able to identify precisely any day of the year by dividing the year into months and numbering each day of the month. Unlike present-day calendars, however, that of the Egyptians had no single event, like the birth of Jesus, the departure of Muhammad from Mecca, or the date of creation according to Jewish tradition, from which to number the year itself. Instead, the Egyptians numbered years from a recurring event, which to them amounted to a kind of re-creation of the world as well as the reappearance of a god: the coming to the throne of the reigning pharaoh. In this case, the decree of the priests, passed on March 27, 196 B.C., according to the Christian calendar, was dated to day 18 of the second month of winter* in year 9 of Ptolemy.

With a particularly solemn document such as this one, however, it was not enough to identify the pharaoh simply by the personal name that he had been given at birth. Instead, he must be identified by all five of his "great names," which he had been given on coming to the throne.† The decree must be dated to the ninth year

> under the majesty of
> Horus: The Youth who has arisen as king on the throne of his father;
> Him of the Two Ladies: Who is great in might, who has established Egypt and made it perfect, whose heart seeks to do good to the gods;
> Him Who Is over His Enemy: Who has made perfect the life of men, lord of jubilees like Ptah-Tanen, prince like Ra;
> Him of Sedge and Bee: Son of the Gods Who Love Their Father, Chosen of Ptah, Strong in the Power of Ra, Living Image of Amen;

---

*"Winter" came in March because owing to the method of reckoning, the calendar was not synchronized with the actual seasons.

†The great names are presented here in their hieroglyphic version, which is lost on the Rosetta Stone but known from other documents. Unless otherwise indicated, all other quotations are from the demotic text on the stone.

The Son of Ra: Ptolemy Living Forever, Beloved of
Ptah, the God Who Appears, the Possessor of Goodness . . .

In each of the great names, the opening words expressed one or
other of the main Egyptian beliefs about the pharaohs in general as
god-kings; hence, this part of the name was the same for every ruler.
The subsequent words expressed the individuality of the god-king—
how he, in particular, embodied the aspect of his divine or human nature expressed in the opening words—and hence were different for each
pharaoh. Thus, only by naming all five names could the priests fill their
decree with all the commanding power of Ptolemy, both as god himself
and as human being given authority by the gods.

To us today, it may seem strange or even wicked that the Egyptians
should have regarded their ruler as a god. How could they have imagined that an ordinary mortal, who might be weak and evil in all sorts of
ways, could also be divine?

To the Egyptians, however, this idea made good sense, because it fitted in with their general way of thinking about gods and humans. The
gods and goddesses, they believed, were fundamentally mysterious beings—ultimately unknowable divine forces, to any of which could be
applied the 1,800-year-old saying about the wind god, Amen: "'Hidden'
is his name." Such a hidden force might make itself perceptible to humans by "becoming" some familiar thing, for example, a cobra or a vulture. It might also become a less familiar combination of things, like
Horus, who was depicted with the head of a falcon and the body of a
man. That was why the Egyptians venerated cobras, vultures, falcons,
and many other living and nonliving things as divine—and if all these,
why not also a man?

So normal and natural did this seem to the Egyptians that they were
not afraid to address each other, or even describe themselves, as gods,
by way of everyday flattery or boasting. "High Steward, my lord, you
are Ra, lord of sky, with his courtiers. . . . You are Hapy who makes
green the fields, revives the wastelands." That was how, in a tale that
dated back at least fourteen centuries, a peasant spoke to a high official
from whom he needed a favor. Much more recently—only 700 years
before—a priest who had held office at the court of several pharaohs
and wanted to emphasize in an inscription in his tomb how generous he
had been to his relatives said: "I was thus a god to them." Of course,
the peasant did not really think that the high steward was the sun god
and the Nile god combined in one person, and the priest did not really
believe in his own divinity. But their words expressed the same way of

thinking that lay behind the veneration of the pharaoh as an actual god: that in a person who is important and powerful, and uses that importance and power to uphold the life of others, there is a divine force at work.

In the person of the pharaoh, the Egyptians truly believed that such a divine force was actually present—one that had been working to uphold the universe ever since the "Time of the Ancestors." In that distant age, which followed immediately upon the "First Occasion" or moment of creation, the gods had ruled as pharaohs—among them mighty Osiris. But Osiris fell out with his brother Seth, who murdered him; and it took the united efforts of his sister-wife Isis and his son Horus, as well as a great battle of the gods in the Delta, to bring Osiris back. From then on, Osiris ruled as pharaoh among the dead, while Horus succeeded him among the living.

Like similar myths among other ancient peoples, this one celebrated, among other things, the victory of the ordered life of the community and of the universe as a whole—*maat*, as the Egyptians called it—over *isfet*, the hostile forces of disintegration and chaos.* For that reason, ever since human pharaohs had reigned in Egypt, they had reenacted the myth in their own deaths and lives. The death of a pharaoh was in a way a moment of fulfillment, when he closed one phase in the eternal cycle of the myth by "becoming" Osiris. But it was also a moment of great danger, when the forces of *isfet*, under their dreadful leader Seth, could walk abroad to undermine creation. With the accession of a new pharaoh, the danger was past, for the hidden, divine power that was Horus had entered into and "become" him. The god had reappeared in triumph, and once again, in his latest human guise, he would uphold and defend *maat*. The peasants would work diligently in the fields, and the judges would try cases fairly in the courtrooms; the stars would follow their proper courses in the heavens, and the Nile would flood the land in due season. Meanwhile, the forces of *isfet* would flee to their lairs among the vile foreigners. That was why, in his great names, the pharaoh was not only "Horus" but also "He Who Is over His Enemy"—that is, Horus triumphant over Seth.

But like the high steward in the story, the pharaoh was actually two gods. As well as being Horus, he was also the Son of Ra, begotten by the sun god coming in the form of his royal father to the

---

*For the similar myths of Inanna and Dumuzi among the Sumerians, and Demeter and Persephone among the Greeks, see Case Studies 1 and 2, "Uruk: The Rise of a Sumerian City," pp. 22–23, and "A Political Scandal in Democratic Athens," pp. 91–93.

bed of his royal mother. The reason was that the great names had come into use one by one, as the status of gods and goddesses had shifted in the first 1,000 years of Egyptian civilization. Originally, the pharaohs had had only a name as Horus; then, as the sun god became more prominent, they had acquired a name as Son of Ra as well. But the double godhead of the pharaoh also fitted in well with Egyptian ways of thinking about gods and goddesses. There was something formless about these hidden, divine forces, which enabled them, at least as perceived by humans, both to exist individually, yet also to merge together. That was why the Egyptians worshiped Amen and Ra both individually and as a combined god, Amen-Ra. And if the "King of the Gods" could be two gods in one, why not also the king of the humans?

But among gods as among humans, there was a hierarchy, and the pharaoh's name as Son of Ra showed a more humble aspect of his nature than his name as Horus. The difference was clearly expressed in words that, 1,200 years before, the greatest of warlord pharaohs, Ramses II, claimed to have addressed to the god his father, when endangered in the thick of battle:

> *Is it right for a father to ignore his son?*
> *Are my deeds a matter for you to ignore?*
> *Did I not walk and stand at your command?*
> *I have not neglected an order you gave.*

Like any son, the pharaoh needed his father's protection because he was weaker. Like any son in need of protection, he claimed himself worthy of it because he had been obedient. In this divine sonship of the pharaoh, there was already something human.

In fact, the Egyptians thought of the pharaoh as being as much human as divine. His great names as "He of the Two Ladies" and "He of Sedge and Bee" said nothing about his being a god. In the first of these names, the pharaoh was the bearer of the pent-up power of the cobra and vulture goddesses; in the second, he was linked with the plant (a kind of reed) and the animal that symbolized Lower and Upper Egypt. Thus, these two names expressed different aspects of the pharaoh as uniting, in his person, the two halves of the human community he ruled. Indeed, he was thought of as representing, before the gods, the human race as a whole. Strictly speaking, he alone could perform the holy rituals that kept the gods and goddesses in their temples. The priests, in celebrating these rites, had no independent ritual power, but acted only in his name.

The Egyptian understanding of the pharaoh as human went even further than that. They thought of him as being "perfect god" (one of his titles) and ritual representative of the human race only in his public and official role; and they were perfectly well aware that he also had a personal and private character, in which he shared in the human condition just like everyone else.* They loved to invent tales about pharaohs who were grotesquely wicked or got comically humiliated. There was the pharaoh who was so short of money that he sent his daughter to a whorehouse so that her earnings could help refill the treasury; or the pharaoh who was magically hijacked to Nubia overnight and given a good beating in the presence of a large crowd of onlookers headed by the Nubian king. In this way, the Egyptians not only venerated their rulers as gods, but also did more than justice to their all-too-human side.

On a more serious level, the Egyptians believed that it was the duty of a pharaoh, in his personal and private character, to demonstrate the virtues that would enable him to be worthy of his public and official position. He must have the sense of right and wrong to harshly punish wickedness and vice, the insight and prudence to recognize trustworthy servants and reward them spectacularly, the skill and courage to tread on foreigners, the generosity and piety to do good to the temples. If he failed in these things, the gods would turn their backs on Egypt; and as for himself, he could tremble in fear of the day when, like every other mortal, he would face the terrible Weighing of the Soul in the afterlife. In the words of a book of advice from a pharaoh to his successor written 2,000 years before, "The court that judges the wretch, you know they are not lenient." "The wretch" meant any subject whom the pharaoh might have oppressed, and who would rise to accuse him before the court of the gods; as for the one to whom the court would not be lenient, that was the pharaoh himself.†

---

*A similar distinction, between the sacred official authority of the pope as Vicar of Christ and his personal and private character, is discussed in Case Study 11, in Volume 3 of this series, "The Last Crusader: The Career and the Failure of Pope Pius II."

†The advice was attributed to Merikare, who reigned about 2000 B.C., but was probably written at the court of a slightly later pharaoh. Even so, it represents the actual thinking of a pharaoh about his position and duties.

This "Instruction of Merikare" is the first known example of a "political testament," or document of advice from a ruler to his or her successors. For another example dating from about 4,000 years later, the "Motherly Instructions " of Empress Maria Theresa of Austria to her descendants (c. A.D. 1750), see Case Study 17, "Peasant and Emperor: An Enlightened Despot Plows a Field."

In this way, the Egyptians exalted the pharaoh to the level of a god, without pretending that he was above human weakness and wickedness, or that he was free from natural human duties and restraints in dealing with his subjects. Of course, the belief in the pharaoh as an all-powerful god-king was useful to him as a wielder of authority. It called upon the Egyptians to give him total loyalty and obedience, and was largely responsible for the age-long stability of their institutions. But to be politically useful for centuries on end, a belief must be compellingly believable; and what made this one so believable was that it was such a natural part—in fact, the central part—of the whole Egyptian idea of how the universe worked. Needless to say, without the all-powerful god-king, the Nile would, in fact, continue to flood the land, and the stars would not move an inch from their courses; but Egyptian civilization, deprived of this central belief, would fall apart. In that respect at least, the pharaoh really was the upholder of *maat*.

While the opening words of the great names expressed timeless Egyptian beliefs about the pharaoh as god and man, the subsequent, individual part of each name was not only a religious statement; but it was also highly relevant to the political situation of the pharaoh who bore it. Thus Ptolemy's name as Horus, "The Youth who has arisen as king on the throne of his father," was not just a ceremonious way of introducing him as a boy-king. "The Youth" was the customary way of referring to Horus, in his role of restorer of Osiris—and it so happened that the two Nubian pharaohs who had so far reigned in Thebes had also been making propaganda for themselves in this same mythic role. Both sides in this conflict, the Greek and the Nubian, were laying claim to be the restorers of *maat* and trying to cast the other in the role of Seth and his vile foreigners. It was essential, therefore, that in his great names, Ptolemy emphatically stake his claim to be the true Egyptian Horus.

The great names also stressed the Egyptianness of the Greek ruler by linking him with other nationally worshiped gods besides Horus: that was why his name as He of Sedge and Bee mentioned Ptah, Amen, and Ra (though discreetly omitting to combine the last two). But among gods and goddesses, it was customary for the pharaoh to single out one as his "patron deity," so to speak, whose name would appear close beside his own, in the last of the great names. In this case, the choice was obvious—"The Son of Ra: Ptolemy Living Forever, Beloved of Ptah." The name was a clear rallying call to every Egyptian who supported the claims of Memphis against the pretensions of Thebes. Presumably to make sure that everyone heard the call, Ptolemy's name was from time to time followed by these solemn words in the body of the decree, when it seemed appropriate to mention the ruler with particular ceremony.

Ptolemy's great names took account of political needs in another way as well. In the midst of proclaiming his Egyptian divinity, they reminded his subjects that he was also another kind of god—a Greek one. In his name as "He of Sedge and Bee," he was "Son of the Gods Who Love Their Father"; as Son of Ra, he was "the God Who Appears, the Possessor of Goodness." Both of these were Egyptian translations of Greek titles of Ptolemy V and his parents. But that was not the only way in which the pharaoh revealed his Greekness. Having dated their decree in the Egyptian manner, the priests now, as was customary, dated it all over again, using the Macedonian system of days, months, and years. In this way they formally acknowledged the ruler not only as an Egyptian, but also as a Greek god-king.

"The God Who Reveals Himself, the Doer of Good"

Although the Greek kingdoms and city-states had many different calendars, most of them identified years by the names of important religious officials, who in the absence of a professional priesthood were usually prominent citizens chosen for an annual term of office. In Egypt, these officials were the leading dignitaries of the Sema, the temple in Alexandria that was the center of the Greek royal cult. The Greek dating of the decree therefore began with Aetus son of Aetus, who bore the impressive title of "Priest of Alexander, of the Savior God and Goddess, of the Brother and Sister God and Goddess, of the Benefactor and Benefactress God and Goddess, of the Father-Loving God and Goddess, and of the God Who Reveals Himself, the Doer of Good." These were the divine names of the conqueror himself, and of all the Ptolemaic kings and queens who had followed him, down to Ptolemy V. Then came the names of highborn Alexandrian ladies who also held important positions in the royal cult, such as Areia the Basket-Bearer of Arsinoe the Brother-Loving, or Pyrrha the Torchbearer of Berenice the Benefactress.[*]

The cult of living rulers as gods was not nearly such an essential part of Greek civilization as it was of Egyptian. It had appeared only recently: the first Greek to be venerated in this way had been Alexander.

---

[*]The quotation and the titles are from the Greek text on the Rosetta Stone.

3. One Ptolemy, Two God-Kings   Left, a gold coin of Ptolemy V, wearing the Macedonian royal diadem or head-ribbon, and carrying a warrior's javelin; from his head spring rays of light and ears of grain, Greek emblems of divinity. Right, a wall carving from the temple of Isis at Philae, also depicting Ptolemy V. As pharaoh, he wears the "War-Cry Crown," topped by sun-disks and dripping with cobras, both Egyptian emblems of divinity. The hieroglyphs say: "Ptolemy Living Forever, Beloved of Ptah."

Many Greeks, including rulers themselves, could never get used to the idea of treating mere humans as divine. A third-century B.C. Macedonian king was supposed to have said, when it was proposed to do him that honor: "The man who empties my chamber-pot doesn't think I'm a god!"

Still, there was nothing in Greek beliefs about gods and humans that made the practice unthinkable. "There is one race of men, one race of gods," their famous fifth-century B.C. poet Pindar had written, "but we both have breath of life from one mother," the earth; and he went on to praise an athlete whose prowess as a wrestler seemed to lift him from the human level almost to that of those related beings, the gods. In this way, the Greeks came to the same idea as the Egyptians—that exceptional achievement or exceptional power was something godlike. They, too, found this so natural that they expressed it in everyday speech. When they heard of some outstanding example of the powerful helping out the weak, they would turn to each other and say, "Man is a god to man!"*

---

*Seventeen hundred years later, a leading scholar of the European Renaissance, Erasmus of Rotterdam, would include this saying in his best-selling collection of ancient proverbs, the *Adages*, together with an explanatory essay that tried to make sense, from a Christian point of view, of the practice of venerating humans as gods. See Case Study 12, in Volume 4 of this series, "Library without Walls: A Humanist Classic Gets into Print."

In accordance with this way of thinking, the Greeks had never had any inhibitions about venerating men of exceptional prowess, once they were dead, as minor divine beings or "heroes."

From beliefs and customs like these, it was not such a big step to the belief that the most powerful and exceptional of all humans, namely kings, should be honored as divine during their lifetimes. From the time of Alexander onward, the Greek world expanded and the individual came to seem small and helpless; the traditional gods and goddesses of the city-states grew distant and shadowy; and the unheard-of power and magnificence of the kings made them seem godlike indeed. It was then that the Greeks took that step.

In Egypt, where the survival of the Greeks as a separate and privileged nation depended directly on the rulers, and the survival of the rulers depended directly on the heartfelt loyalty of the Greeks, the royal cult seems to have flourished. Many of the kings claimed to be incarnations of Dionysus, whose rites, filling worshipers with the intoxicating frenzy of the divine presence, were among the most vigorous remaining features of Greek religion. Not only were the Ptolemies god-kings, but their queens were also goddesses—and often their sisters as well, for had not Zeus wed his sister Hera? Their divine names suggested both family-mindedness and benevolence toward the human race. That of Ptolemy V, "The God Who Reveals Himself, the Doer of Good," given him in 197 B.C., also hinted at prowess in war, for gods were supposed to reveal themselves by superhuman and preferably warlike deeds. The rulers were a close-knit family of gods and goddesses just like those of Olympus, they seemed to be saying, that was here to stay and could be counted on to be helpful.

The Greeks seem to have taken this idea seriously enough, dedicating tablets in public shrines in which they thanked the rulers for miraculously helping them out of danger, and keeping cheap mass-produced images of them in their homes. But like the Egyptians, the Greeks also recognized the humanness of their rulers. They often dedicated offerings to the Olympian gods and goddesses "for the well-being" of the rulers, as if these stood in human need of divine protection. And in later times, King Ptolemy VII (145–116 B.C.), "The Benefactor God," was also known to his Greek subjects, evidently in tribute to his most impressive human feature, as "Potbelly."

Thus, in combination with the solemn Egyptian dating, the solemn Greek dating asserted the ruler's claim to double-divine status, as both Egyptian and Greek god-king. But in the dating of the document as in the rest of what it said, it was the Egyptian god-king who came first.

With the lengthy date giving completed, the next order of business was for those who had passed the decree to identify themselves. "On this day have decreed the High Priests and Prophets, and the priests who enter the sanctuary to conduct the Robing of the Gods, and the Scribes of the Sacred Books, and the Scribes of the House of Life, and the other priests, having come from the temples of Egypt to Memphis . . ." It was a roll call of the religious elite of Egypt, which gave the impression, true or false, of solemn priestly unity behind the ruler. Now it was time for the high priests, prophets, and all the others to explain why they intended to set up Ptolemy as a temple-sharing god.

"Being the Likeness of Horus, Son of Isis and Osiris"

In every Greek-style decree conferring honors on a person, including those of veneration as a god or goddess, the preamble naturally listed as reasons for the decree everything that the person had done to deserve the honors. This, then, was the right place for the priests to mention all the concessions that the government had made to themselves, the "warriors," and the peasants—giving credit for everything, of course, to the boy-king personally.

> Of the dues and taxes existing in Egypt some he has cut and others he has abolished completely, to cause the army and all the people to be happy in his time as Pharaoh (Life! Prosperity! Health!). . . . He has ordered also regarding those of the warriors and the remainder of the men who had been on the other side of the rebellion which occurred in Egypt, to let them return to their homes and their property belong to them again. . . . He has given gold, silver, and grain in plenty and other things for the temple of the Apis;* he has had the new construction completed in exceedingly beautiful work. . . .

One after another, the priests listed more than a dozen of the ruler's good deeds. By doing so, of course, they were not in fact just giving the

---

*The Apis was a sacred bull, believed to be the incarnation of Ptah, that was kept during its lifetime in Ptah's temple in Memphis, and buried after its death in a special temple in the desert to the west of the city. The cult of the Apis was one of the most popular in Ptolemaic Egypt, and gifts to the cult were one of the best ways for rulers to broaden their own popularity.

reasons for honoring him. They were also recording in writing the altered terms of their partnership with the dynasty, and influencing and rallying all Egyptians who might favor the Ptolemies.

Furthermore, the priests presented Ptolemy's concessions not just as a sign of his wisdom or goodness of heart, but much more portentously, as the traditional deeds of an Egyptian god-king doing his duty of restoring *maat*. "Everything which had lost its order for time untold he has restored to its proper condition," they said; and he had done this "being god, son of god and goddess, being the likeness of Horus, son of Isis and Osiris, who has protected his father Osiris." Once again, it was important to leave no doubt as to who was the real Horus, and who was, so to speak, Seth in Horus's clothing.

That was also how the priests presented another, very important side of Ptolemy's pharaonic nature, his prowess as a warrior. To demonstrate this, they described at length a recent victory: the capture of a stronghold of the "warrior" insurgency, the Delta town of Shekan. They gave many technical details of how the besiegers had dammed up the canals that supplied and protected the city, in spite of exceptionally high water on the Nile—a feat "the like of which no former pharaohs (Life! Prosperity! Health!) had been able to do." This outdoing of his predecessors was itself a sign that Ptolemy was a true pharaoh. Successful, or even not so successful, pharaohs had always claimed, in the 1,100-year-old words of Tutankhamun—another youthful restorer of *maat*, following the reign of the "heretic" pharaoh Akhenaton—to have "added to what was done in former times" and "surpassed that done since the Time of the Ancestors."

In addition, as the priests told it, Ptolemy showed his true pharaonic nature not only by capturing the city but also through what happened afterward: the massacre of the defenders.

Far from concealing this, the priests singled it out as a reenactment of the great battle against Seth in the age that followed the First Occasion: ". . . he prevailed over the enemies and gave them over to slaughter as did Ra and Horus son of Isis to those who were hostile to them in the said places formerly." For the pharaoh to slaughter his enemies and boast of it afterward was among the oldest of Egyptian traditions. Nearly 3,000 years before, an early ruler, King Narmer, had also won a victory in the Delta. Then he held a parade, in which enemy prisoners also took part—lying on the ground in neat rows, with their chopped-off heads between their legs. Finally he had the scene depicted, with the nurturing cow goddess Hathor presiding over the slaughter, on a ceremonial palette for mixing eye paint that he presented to a temple of the

4. KING NARMER'S PARADE   Scene from a palette for mixing eye paint, commemorating a victory of King Narmer over enemies in the Delta, about 3000 B.C. On the left is the king, wearing the Red Crown of Lower Egypt and surrounded by high officials. In the middle are soldiers bearing nome (district) standards. At right, bound enemy soldiers have been laid out with their heads between their legs, as trophies. The human faces with cows' horns and ears at top are depictions of the goddess Hathor; between them, in a diagram of a royal palace, are hieroglyphs saying "Narmer."

goddess in Upper Egypt. Now, the priests were expressing in words the very same belief, that bloody deeds were a sign of the god-given power of the pharaoh, that one of the founders of the Egyptian state had once expressed in pictures. Probably the priests knew nothing of Narmer's deed, but they certainly did intend to say that the massacre at Shekan was yet another proof that Ptolemy was the true Horus, triumphant over Seth.

"A STATUE OF THE CITY GOD"

Having listed all the deeds that showed Ptolemy to be a traditional god-king, the priests now came to the decree itself, establishing the veneration of him as a temple-sharing god. The two most important provisions came right at the beginning.

> With good fortune [the standard opening of the actual provisions of a Greek-style decree] it entered the hearts of the priests of all the temples of Egypt to set up a

statue of Pharaoh (Life! Prosperity! Health!) Ptolemy, . . .
which is to be called "Ptolemy Protector of Egypt," . . .
with a statue of the city god giving him a sword of victory,
in the temple, in the most conspicuous place in the temple, in each and every temple, made in the style of the
Egyptians' work. . . .
    [The priests] are to cause to appear the divine image
of Pharaoh (Life! Prosperity! Health!) Ptolemy, . . . with
the gold shrine, in each and every temple, and they are to
set it up in the sanctuary with the other gold shrines.

Along with these there were many other arrangements. The rituals with
which the statues and images were to be tended, which were to be exactly the same as those for the principal gods and goddesses of each
temple; the decoration of the shrines that were to contain the royal images; the monthly celebration of the days of Ptolemy's accession and
birth; the veneration of the king by private persons outside the temples,
so that "it shall be known that those who are in Egypt honor the God
Who Appears, Whose Goodness Is Perfect, as it is right to do": all these
things were laid down in every detail.

But the key to the whole idea of the temple-sharing cult lay in the
first two provisions. Every Egyptian temple had its forecourt, where the
people were permitted to assemble, and its sanctuary, a tiny chamber
that only the priests might enter in order to tend the images of the gods
in their shrines, which were themselves small enough so that several
could fit into the chamber. If the provisions were carried out, the effect
would be that in every temple, in its most public and visible and its
most secret and mystical place, Ptolemy would be one among the local
gods. The veneration of him as a traditional Egyptian god-king would
become part of the daily routine of the temple, and the daily life of
the people, in every community throughout the Two Lands.

This was a matter of vital importance to anyone who wanted to rule
Egypt. In spite of the monolithic appearance and pretensions of
pharaonic rule, the country had never been an easy one to unite. It was
not one land, or even two; rather, it consisted of hundreds of separate
communities, strung out along the Nile or nestling in the swamps of the
Delta. Throughout the centuries of their civilization, the loyalty of
Egyptians to city, town, or nome—the name of the districts into which
the country was traditionally divided—had been at least as strong as
their loyalty to their rulers or, for that matter, of the Greeks to their
city-states. Even the mightiest pharaohs had had to take this into

account. A thousand years before the priests passed their decree, none other than the triumphant Ramses II had understood very well what kind of loyalties inspired the soldiers of his superpower armies. In an inscription that appeared on a whole series of battle monuments that he built up and down Egypt, he asked: "Does not a man act to be acclaimed in his town, when he returns as one brave before his lord?" To be acclaimed in his town, in other words, the soldier must fight bravely for his pharaoh; but to fight bravely for his pharaoh, he must have the hope of acclaim in his town. In this way, Ramses II had recognized that loyalty to himself and loyalty to the local community were two sides of the same coin, and that the second kind of loyalty was something he must work with and not against.

In accordance with this rule of statecraft, successful pharaohs had generally tried to take account of local interests and loyalties, which meant above all "doing good to the temples" of local gods and goddesses, and linking themselves with these by the practice of temple sharing. This had become even more important in the troubled centuries of Egypt's decline. A book of "wisdom," that is, of religious and moral instruction, written in Ptolemaic times had a whole section devoted to "The Teaching Not to Abandon the Place in Which You Can Live," with mottos like: "The god who is in the city is the one by whose command are the life and death of the people. . . . The impious man who leaves the way of his town, its gods are the ones who hate him. . . . He who worships his god in the morning in his town will live. . . ." More than ever, it seems, Egyptians were looking to their local communities, and the gods and goddesses who presided over them, as the main resource of their lives.

It was probably in order to appeal to this feeling that priestly decrees under the Ptolemies had already promoted the practice of temple sharing more systematically than ever before. Now, if the provisions of this decree were carried out, in the forecourt of every temple the local people would see Ptolemy V being congratulated on his prowess as "Protector of Egypt" by their very own god or goddess, by whose command they lived and died. Surely they would come to see Ptolemy as the protector, not just of Egypt as a whole but of their very own city, town, or nome, so that if they worshiped him in the morning they would live.

The decree was now almost at an end. The priests had presented Ptolemy to his subjects as an Egyptian god-king. They had explained why his deeds were both kingly and godlike in the Egyptian tradition. They had made arrangements intended to anchor the veneration of him as a god and loyalty to him as a king in every community of Egypt. That left only one more item, seemingly the most routine but in fact the most momentous: the details of how the decree was to be publicly displayed.

4
"THEY SHALL WRITE THIS DECREE ON A SLAB OF HARD STONE . . ."

Over the fifty years or so in which Egyptian priests had been passing decrees in honor of the Ptolemies, the procedure for publishing the decrees had become more or less standardized. In this case, the procedure was spelled out most specifically in the hieroglyphic version:

> [They shall write] this decree on a slab of hard stone, in the writing of the words of god, the writing of documents, and the letters of the Northerners, and set it up in all the temples of first, second, and third rank, beside the statue of Him of Sedge and Bee: Ptolemy Living Forever, Beloved of Ptah, the God Who Appears, the Possessor of Goodness.*

The publication of the decree, in fact, would be part of the whole business of setting up the ruler as a temple-sharing god. In each temple, the image and the shrine and the statue and the stone would all go up together.

Of course, it was easy enough for the priests to issue these orders, but actually to carry them out was something else again. For any individual temple, just to manufacture all the paraphernalia of the cult of the ruler would be a big undertaking. How long it would take would depend on the temple's wealth, the skill of its craftsmen, and the enthusiasm of its priests—not to mention the local balance of power between loyalists and rebels. To get even a noticeable proportion of the hundreds of Egyptian temples to do what was necessary would take years of pushing by the government and its leading friends among the priests.

In at least one temple, however, the priests were prompt in setting up the cult of the ruler. The location of this trendsetting shrine is not

---

*The words in brackets are missing from the hieroglyphic text of the Rosetta Stone, but it is clear from the demotic and Greek versions that they must have been there. Ptolemy's name as Son of Ra was probably given, against the rules, as his Sedge and Bee name so as to stress both his connection with Ptah and his role in uniting war-torn Egypt.

known for certain, but it must have been an important one, somewhere in the western Delta not far from the sea. Most likely it was the temple of the war goddess Neith in the city of Sais, which had been the capital of many pharaohs in recent periods of Egyptian independence. One can imagine the priests, prophets, and scribes of the "Mansion of Neith" returning from Memphis with a clean copy of the decree written out on papyrus, the Egyptian paper made from the beaten stems of reeds, by their colleagues of the Mansion of the Soul of Ptah; the high priest of Neith perhaps urging quick action, to set an example that would get the nationwide cult of the ruler off to a good start, and win the gratitude of the court for the goddess and her servants; the temple woodworkers, metalworkers, and stonecarvers hard at work for several months; and finally, secret ceremonies in the sanctuary to consecrate image and shrine, and public celebrations in the forecourt to inaugurate statues and stone.

So far as the stone was concerned, the local priests had followed the provisions of the decree, one might say, to the letter. Just as instructed, they had had it carved in all three writings—not straggling over the sides of the monument as sometimes happened, but all clearly readable on the front face of a five-by-two-and-a-half-by-one-foot stone slab. Just as instructed, the stone of which the slab was made was hard—black basalt, a volcanic rock that was difficult to carve but extremely durable. There the stone stood in the temple forecourt, probably against a wall, so that the back did not have to be finished; probably a few feet off the ground, so that the middle of it, the part with the demotic writing which literate Egyptians could most easily read, was at eye level; and probably capped, as was customary, by another curved piece of stone, showing Ptolemy doing harm to a captured enemy while gods and goddesses looked on approvingly. It must have been a handsome monument, which could be expected to remain readable for many centuries.

As for the writings on the stone, apart from what they actually said, they also reflected much of the 3,000-year-old story of the rise of Egyptian civilization, its fortunes over the centuries, and its influence on other civilizations. The "writing of the words of god" was one of the most notable achievements of the original upsurge of Egypt. The "writing of documents" was an outcome of the changes that had overtaken the country as the centuries had rolled on. And the "letters of the Northerners" were a product of improvements in the art of writing made by several foreign nations, as the skills and knowledge of Egypt had spread through the Middle East and finally on to Greece.

"In the Writing of the Words of God . . ."

The hieroglyphic writing system had come into being quite suddenly in the burgeoning time of Egyptian civilization about 3000 B.C., when the world of the Nile Valley was rapidly growing and changing, and a host of newly arisen needs was calling forth a host of new skills. The appearance of this particular skill may have been inspired by the example of Mesopotamia, where another youthful civilization was already in the midst of a much longer process of experimentation that would eventually produce cuneiform writing.* But Egyptian writing was different, both in the way it worked and in terms of the need that called it into existence. True, in Egypt as in Mesopotamia, the holders of power used writing to keep track of the otherwise unmanageable amounts of goods that were being produced and consumed by the newly wealthy society that they ruled. But they also used writing for another purpose, which was probably more important to them than mere administration. The builders of the Egyptian state, on their way to becoming universal god-kings of the Two Lands, needed writing above all in temple, monument, and tomb, as an instrument of their religious and magical power.

Probably with this requirement in mind, the inventors of Egyptian writing endowed it from the start with a feature that made it unique among scripts for its strange and solemn beauty. Every sign in the system was designed to be a picture of a real or mythical object, depicted with the utmost truthfulness, according to the standards of truthfulness that were being developed about the same time by Egyptian sculptors and painters. In fact, the art and the writing arose together, and served the same purpose. To depict a thing, or to utter its name, the Egyptians believed, was to bring it into actual being. The sculptors and painters, by depicting a pharaoh killing a prisoner or enjoying the pleasures of the afterlife, could make those things actually happen, in a timeless, magical world more real than that of everyday life. And the scribes could help them happen, by naming them in writing that formed part of the depicted scenes, and that was designed on the same principles of truthfulness in depiction.

But the hieroglyphs were far from being mere inexpressive "picture writing." Any individual hieroglyph could in principle be used to "depict" three things: either the object it portrayed; or an idea that was somehow associated with that object; or one or more sounds of speech,

---

*On the beginning of cuneiform writing, see Case Study 1, "Uruk: The Rise of a Sumerian City," pp. 26–30.

in the Egyptian name of the object.* As a result, the hieroglyphs could be used to write down anything that could be thought or said, while also being charged with the magical power to make that thing come to pass. It was by the use of these 3,000-year-old principles, for instance, that the carver of the black stone slab in the temple forecourt could both express and make a reality of such a complex idea as "Ptolemy Living Forever, Beloved of Ptah."

To express this idea, the stonecarver—having first of all marked up the stone with the hieroglyphs, carefully following the papyrus copy of the decree—would begin by cutting what the Egyptians called the "circle":† a protective loop of rope that surrounded the name and title of the king. (That this was the procedure is known from cases where stonecarvers, having made the circle, for one reason or another never filled it in with the name.) On this particular slab, where many hieroglyphs had to be carved in miniature into one of the hardest of stones, the carver was allowed to cut corners on realistic depiction. Instead of showing the details of the rope, with the twists of the knot and the two free ends, as was done with larger hieroglyphs, he simply chipped out an oval line with a vertical stroke on the left:

Even so, the carver had accomplished two important aims. The first was a magical one: by depicting a knotted loop of rope, he had caused an actual one to be present on the stone. This was an important matter,

---

*Technically, when a hieroglyph stands for the object that it portrays it is said to be a *pictogram* (picture-sign), and its method of portrayal is *pictographic;* when it stands for an associated idea, it is an *ideogram* (idea-sign; *ideographic*); and when it stands for a sound it is a *phonogram* (sound-sign; *phonetic*).

The distinction between pictograms and ideograms is often hard to make in practice, and both types can also be said to stand for the words that are used to express objects and ideas. Many experts therefore prefer to classify both together as *logograms* (word-signs; *logographic*). But the pictogram-ideogram distinction is helpful in explaining how Egyptian writing arose historically, and was used by all the decipherers including Champollion (p. 227), so it is adopted here.

†Present-day Egyptologists call it the "cartouche." For the origin and meaning of this name, see below, p. 199.

for the carver was about to cause Ptolemy himself to be present on the stone by uttering his name in writing, and it would never do for the king to be present, even for an instant, without the loop to protect him against evil magical influences. Even where the king's name was unaccompanied by his title, it was always within its own shorter circle. The second purpose was the more humdrum one of conveying meaning: the presence of the circle conveyed the fact that the name and title within it were those of a king.

So far, the carver had operated the writing system, so to speak, in object-depicting mode. Now that it was safe to cause the king to appear on the stone, the system had to be switched into sound-depicting mode so as to portray, one by one, the sounds that made up his Greek name: *Ptolemaios.*

To portray the first sound of the name of the king, the carver positioned his chisel at the right-hand end of the circle, since the writing usually ran from right to left. (The hieroglyphs could also run in the opposite direction, appearing as mirror images of their right-to-left versions, or even vertically from top to bottom, if either seemed necessary so as to ensure their magical power or fit them into a cramped space, but that was not the case here.) At the chosen starting point, the carver

chipped out a small rectangle: . Again, this was only a sim-

plified version of the original hieroglyph. In thousand-year-old royal tombs, the same hieroglyph was painted in luminously colored detail, though intended to remain in darkness, doing its work of magic unseen by human eye, for all eternity. It was a mat such as might be used to cover the seat of some high personage, made of fresh green reed stems bound together with yellow thongs.

In fact, in object-depicting mode, the sign meant "seat." But some pioneering scribe in the early days of Egyptian civilization had decreed that it should also portray the single consonantal sound that, in combination with perhaps one or two vowels, made up the Egyptian word for "seat," namely *p*. From that time on, the sign could be used to bring that sound into being in any word whatever—including, now, the name of Egypt's foreign king.

Likewise, in order to portray the second sound of Ptolemy, the stonecarver chipped out a semicircle, ▲ —a sideways view of a loaf of bread, in the Egyptian word for which there was also a single consonantal sound, *t*. As it happened, the *t* sound also appeared, no doubt accompanied by a different vowel or vowels, in the word for "hand,"

, and this hieroglyph, too, could be used in sound-depicting mode for *t*. Over the centuries, in fact, most of the sounds of Egyptian speech had come to be portrayed by several different signs, and, as a result, the spelling of words often varied. But in this case, the choice was "bread."

Since the "seat" and the "bread" hieroglyphs were smaller than the average, however, the carver put the second sign not to the left of the

first but beneath it, —a standard practice, so as to fill out the space neatly and create the impression of a regular procession of hieroglyphs marching across the stone.

Proceeding sound by sound in this way, the carver had signs available accurately to depict all the consonantal sounds of *Ptolemaios*. But the name was also thickly sown with what, in the Egyptian writing system, were dangerous pitfalls: vowels.

The reason that the vowels were pitfalls probably had to do with the fact that in the Egyptian language they served entirely different purposes from consonants in forming words. In English, families of words are usually built up by adding on endings and beginnings to some basic word, which is made up of both vowels and consonants: "love," "loving," "lovable," "lovely," "beloved," for instance. In Egyptian, on the

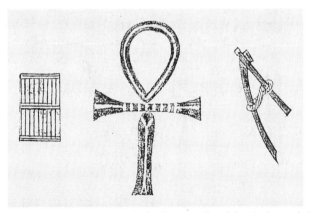

5. "Picture Writing" Hieroglyphs from tombs of the Eighteenth Dynasty period (about 1550–1300 B.C.), showing detailed depictions of objects that were also "depictions" of sounds. Left to right: reed mat used as seat covering (yellow ocher, red, and green), *p*; knotted thong (blue and grey), *'nḫ* (the *ankh* sign); hoe (brown, white, and red), *mr*.

other hand, families of words were formed by making vowels appear, disappear, or change among groups of consonants that always stayed the same. Most likely, to the early scribes, the consonants seemed to form the essence of a word. Once they had been portrayed, the word had been truthfully depicted, and the vowels, being mere temporary features, were not worth bothering with. At any rate, in devising their system of sound depiction, the scribes had passed over the vowels entirely.

From today's point of view, this is a serious disadvantage, for it means that no one now knows how most Egyptian words were actually pronounced.* For speakers of Egyptian at the time the system was devised, on the other hand, the consonants alone would have been enough to suggest the pronunciation of a word. But as the centuries passed and Egypt came into closer contact with foreigners, the scribes found themselves more and more often having to write down foreign words and names whose pronunciation they did not automatically know. For this purpose, at least, they felt they needed vowels, so they set about adapting existing consonantal hieroglyphs to capture these more fleeting sounds. Not surprisingly, the results were never entirely satisfactory. Still, the result was that the stonecarver had signs available, adapted 1,500 years before to suggest the vowel sounds of Middle Eastern nations that Egypt had been treading on at the time, which could also vaguely approximate the vowels in the language of the country's Greek conquerors.

One by one, then, following the ▮ and the ▲ , the carver cut depictions of a lasso, ⟨glyph⟩ , w, used in foreign words for o; a resting lion, ⟨glyph⟩ , for l; an unknown object, ⟨glyph⟩ , for m; the feathery tops of two reeds, ⟨glyph⟩ , the y sound in "yellow," used in foreign words for ai; and finally, a folded cloth, ⟨glyph⟩ , for s. The king was now fully present on the stone, and fully protected by the circle:

---

*Most present-day versions of Egyptian words—*maat, isfet,* Amen-Ra—are not authentic, but have been devised by inserting vowels so as to make the consonants pronounceable. (The name of the god Ptah is one of the few authentic versions.) Many of the best-known "Egyptian" names are in fact Greek versions of the originals: Isis, Osiris, and Horus; Cheops and Ramses; Memphis and Thebes.

True, he was present in an Egyptian guise that was noticeably different from his Greek one: from *Ptolemaios*, he had become *Ptolmais*. But after all, presenting the Greek ruler in Egyptian guise was what the stone was all about.

Having finished with "Ptolemy," the stonecarver must now go on to "Living Forever, Beloved of Ptah." These solemn words must appear in the 2,000-year-old "classical" Egyptian of the Middle Kingdom, and they must be portrayed, without adaptations, in the traditional Egyptian way. From now on, the carver would chisel out consonants only. Some words he would cause to appear sound by sound, as he had done with *Ptolemaios*, only omitting the vowels. Others, however, he would portray with signs that depicted two or even three consonants at once. And one sign he would use not in sound-depicting, but in idea-depicting, mode.

Thus, to make the entire Egyptian word for "Living," the carver needed to use only a single sound-depicting hieroglyph. The word itself contained three consonants. The first was a throaty and rasping sound, which is not met with in English and which Egyptologists transcribe with an opening quote mark, '; the second was *n*; and the third was the *ch* sound in Scottish "loch," which is transcribed as *ḫ*. There were separate hieroglyphs available to depict each of these consonants, but it so happened that the same combination of them, *'nḫ*, also occurred in the word for the leather thong of a sandal; and the early scribes had decreed that the object-depicting sign for that item of footwear, ☥ , should be used to portray that particular group of consonants wherever it might be spoken, including in the words for "living," "to live," and "life."

Like every other sign in the system, this one was credited with the power to bring about what it portrayed. Since what it portrayed was so precious to most people, it was among the most revered and beloved of hieroglyphs. In temple, monument, and tomb, gods and goddesses carried it about and handed it to each other, to pharaohs, or to less prominent tomb dwellers, holding it by the loop at the top like a kind of oversized key. Ordinary people kept three-dimensional versions of it in their homes, or hung them around their necks. Even today it counts as a lucky charm, under the name of the *"ankh* sign." So the three-consonant hieroglyph had great power, as well as solemn meaning, when the carver used it to make the word "Living."

To make "Forever," on the other hand, the carver returned to one-consonant hieroglyphs: he chiseled out a wriggling cobra, *d* (the first sound of "John" or "George"), and beneath it the "bread" sign,

to form the word ◖▬ , *dt*. But this word, though Egyptian, also

contained a pitfall. There were several others in the language that were also made up of the consonants *d* and *t*, and which, there-fore, whatever the vowels that might be wrapped around the conso-nants, all looked the same in writing. How was the reader to know

whether this particular ◖▬ stood for *dt*, "eternity" or "forever,"

dt, "body" or "self," or *dt*, "male genitals"? To clarify this, the carver added an extra, explanatory sign, ▬ , which depicted a flat stretch of "land," and hence also the associated idea of "extension" or "length." The sign was not intended to be pronounced, but simply to help the reader determine which of the various *dt*s this was

supposed to be. In this way, the combination ◖▬ was clearly recognizable as "forever."

This practice of using hieroglyphs to help out their neighboring signs, explaining and clarifying their meaning, was a regular feature of Egyptian writing. It was necessary not only because of the uncertainty created by the missing vowels, but also because it was often unclear whether a particular hieroglyph was being used to depict an object, an idea, or a sound. When a reader saw the hieroglyph ◯ , for instance, was it supposed to depict an object, *r'*, the "sun," or an associated idea, *hrw*, "day"? If, next to the sign, there was a depiction of a reed-built hut, ◖▢ , *h*, the first consonant of the word for "day," then without actually being pronounced, the "hut" sign confirmed that the neigh-boring hieroglyph meant "day." Or how was the reader to know

whether the hieroglyph ⦚ depicted a "bunch of foxes' skins"—an

important item of ceremonial clothing—or the first two consonants of the single Egyptian word for that item, *ms?* If, next to the foxes' skins, there appeared the folded cloth, *s,* then—again, without being pronounced—it signaled that the bunch of foxes' skins here meant the sounds *ms,* which happened also to be those of the word for "birth." Thus elsewhere on the stone, where the decree dealt with the various anniversary rituals in honor of Ptolemy the god-king, the carver put all

four signs together to make the word "birthday": .

After "Forever" came yet another pitfall—not a technical one of portraying sound or clarifying meaning, this time, but a religious and magical one, of not dishonoring a god. In the course of the following words, it would be necessary to utter in writing the name of Ptah, and thereby make him, too, present on the stone. But if the carver were to follow the natural order of Egyptian speech, which in this case was the same as in English, then Ptah would bring up the rear of the procession of hieroglyphs within the "circle"—an impossibly humiliating position for a deity. There was only one way to avoid this blasphemy. In accordance with a rule of writing that no one ever dared to violate, the carver must forget about the natural order of speech and put "Ptah" before "Beloved."

The name itself was not much trouble to carve: just the "seat" and the "bread," as in the *p* and *t* of Ptolemy, and a wick of twisted flax, *ḥ*

(a strong and breathy *ḥ* sound), to make *Ptḥ:* . And the reversal of

words may have spared the carver some additional trouble. Perhaps because it left the word for "of" or "by" floating in midair, so to speak, the carver dealt with the word in a way that was also standard in religious formulas of this kind: he left it out.

That left only "Beloved," which took a hoe, *mr,* and two reed tops, *y,* to

make , *mry.* The circle was now full. With eighteen pictures of

objects as varied as a lion and a lasso, a snake and a sandal strap, the carver had brought into being the words and sounds, the idea and the reality, of "Ptolemy Living Forever, Beloved of Ptah," *Ptolmais 'nḫ ḏt mry Ptḥ:*

To make the eighteen pictures mean those words and ideas had been no easy matter. With its lack of vowel signs and its excess of single-, double-, and triple-consonant signs, its habit of using the same sign to mean several things and several signs to mean the same thing, and its total of 700 signs that needed to be known for normal writing purposes, the hieroglyphic writing system was hard to learn and complicated to use. Yet evidently its users were content with it. For 3,000 years, in spite of important changes like the adaptation to foreign vowel sounds, the basic principles of how hieroglyphs were used to depict objects, ideas, and sounds had stayed the same.

Partly, no doubt, this was because the hieroglyphs were more than just a means of communicating information. How could one change a system that was charged with such religious and magical power, and which had been invented, it was said, by Thoth himself, in his role as scribe of the gods?

But even apart from that, the scribes were satisfied with their writing system, for they did not confine its use to temple, monument, and tomb. Out of the hieroglyphs they had developed another script, which could be rapidly written for the humdrum information-communicating purposes of everyday life, but otherwise worked in the same way. It was perhaps at the insistence of the Greeks—who of course used their alphabet for both everyday and ceremonial purposes—that the priests had adopted the practice of recording their decrees concerning the rulers also in this second script. Consequently, the demotic writing, which was normally only applied with an ink-filled brush to papyrus, whitewashed board, or broken pieces of pottery, had now to be carved in stone as well.

"And the Writing of Documents . . ."

The demotic script was the end product of nearly 3,000 years of tinkering with the hieroglyphs so as to make them easy to write. Although its basic principles were exactly the same as those of the original system, over the centuries the details of how these were applied had come to be very different. The mix of object-, idea-, and sound-depicting signs; the spelling of words when sound-depicting signs were used; even the words themselves, which were those of the contemporary rather than the "classical" language: all these things varied very much from the hieroglyphs. In addition, the crabbed demotic characters for the most part looked nothing like the stately originals from which they were descended. Thus when the time again came to cut into the stone the

words "Ptolemy Living Forever, Beloved of Ptah," the carver now had
to chip out the following collection of signs for *Ptolemaios:*

The first, ⟩ , and last signs, ⟨ —running from right to left,
as demotic writing always did—were all that was left of the circle. It
was too much trouble, now, to make the circle stretch all the way from
Ptolemy to Ptah. Even the king was left, one would think, with gap-
toothed protection that any passing demon would only laugh at. But in
this everyday script, magical protection counted for far less than the
simple information-communicating task of identifying the name of a
king, and the remains of the circle were still good enough for that.

The second sign from the right, ⟨ , was a single-consonant,
sound-depicting sign, just as in the hieroglyphs, that stood for *p*. It was,
in fact, the direct though remote descendant of the hieroglyphic sign.
Its pedigree stretched back 3,000 years, to a detailed version of the
"seat" hieroglyph, ⊞ . The pioneering scribes had no sooner invented this sign than they had set about devising a "shorthand" version
of it—urged on, no doubt, by the builders of the Egyptian state, who
must have sensed that their new instrument of religious and magical
power would also come in very useful for the daily running of the country. What the scribes came up with was a sign that suggested the details
of the original with only four strokes of a brush: ⊔⊔ .

For a thousand years, through the Old and Middle Kingdoms,
this version—and hundreds of similar "shorthand" versions of the
hieroglyphs—was speedy enough to satisfy the scribes and their masters. But the scribes of the New Kingdom, perhaps even busier than
their forerunners now that Egypt was a superpower, replaced the sign
with a new version that could be made with only one stroke and a
squiggle: ⌣ . The four-stroke version and its fellow signs continued
to be used, but only in ritual and magical manuscripts, as an alternative
to hieroglyphs. The Greeks, therefore, called this original "shorthand"
the "hieratic" or priestly writing, a name that is still used for it today.

Meanwhile, as Egypt declined but the scribes remained busy, even
the squiggle-and-stroke version became too much trouble to write.

After all, it was still necessary to lift the brush between the squiggle and the stroke. By the time that the Greeks marched into Egypt, the two parts had been run together, 🝡 . It was this and similar characters that the Greeks called "enchorial" (native—as on the stone itself) or "demotic." But even the nonstop squiggle-and-stroke version took a good deal of zigging and zagging of the brush. After a hundred years of Greek rule, with its overworked bureaucracy spewing out floods of documents in the language of the natives as well as the conquerors, even the squiggle had gone, to leave the *p* sign that the carver chipped into the stone: 🝢 .

In exactly the same way, the hieroglyphic loaf of bread, *t*, had changed over the centuries into ⟨ , the lion, *l*, into 𝈐 , and the lasso, *o*, into 𝈘 . Subsequent characters of the king's name were derived from originals alternative to the signs used in the hieroglyphic version of the name, and the problem of the vowels was differently managed. 𝈫 was *m*, ⫴ was *ai*, and ⫷⫸ was *s*. This time, the carver had given the king yet another Egyptian guise. *Ptolemaios*, which the hieroglyphs had turned into *Ptolmais*, was now *Ptlomais*, or sometimes also *Ptlomeos*.

Following the name of the king came the Egyptian words for "Living," "Forever," "Ptah," and "Beloved," in that order and without vowels, just as in the hieroglyphs. To make "Living Forever," the stonecarver could even cut demotic signs that looked recognizably like the originals: 𓏤𓋹 .

With "Ptah," however, the demotic writing once again drifted off on its own. In recent centuries, when many pharaohs had worshiped the god of Memphis more eagerly than his rival of Thebes, the scribes had run together and distorted the signs in Ptah's oft-repeated name, to arrive at a special, super-shorthand version: 𝈝 . Then they had added an explanatory, idea-depicting sign, 𝈙 , meaning "god"—but even so, the whole group was probably quicker to write than with the normal signs.

Thus for *Ptḥ* the carver now had to chip out ⟨figure⟩ —making the *p* and

the *t*, in particular, quite differently from the way he had made them just a short while earlier, at the beginning of the king's name.

That left, once again, "Beloved," a word that in contemporary Egyptian had lost its final *y* to become *mr*. Even so, the carver needed two signs to make it: the demotic version of the hoe, ⟨figure⟩ , and yet another explanatory sign, ⟨figure⟩ , which meant "feeling." The name and title of the king, *Ptlomais 'nḫ ḏt mr Ptḥ*, were once again on the stone:

⟨figure⟩

Again it had taken eighteen characters—far easier to form with an ink-filled brush than the hieroglyphs, it is true, but otherwise operating according to rules that were just as hard to learn and complex to apply.

Since the demotic writing was the only one that most literate Egyptians ever learned, one cannot help wondering why they did not go on to simplify it in other respects besides the actual forming of the characters. Why did they not get rid of the object-depicting and idea-depicting signs, cut down the sound-depicting ones to the twenty-four that each portrayed a single consonant, refine the vowel-portraying ones to make them more "realistic," and use these in Egyptian as well as foreign words? After all, the experts in the Houses of Life could perfectly well have gone on setting down their words of power according to the unchangeable rules of Thoth. Meanwhile, the overworked scribes who did the vast mass of everyday writing would have enjoyed the ease and convenience of an alphabet.

Part of the reason why this did not happen was probably that once an Egyptian scribe had mastered the ins and outs of the system, he could actually write faster with demotic characters than his Greek colleague could using letters. Moreover, in a society where, according to educated modern guesses, not more than 1 percent of Egyptians and 5 percent of Greeks could read and write, mass literacy was not even a dream. The ease and convenience of the alphabet were therefore not such an advantage as they are today.

But there were other and probably more important reasons why the Egyptians did not want to change the way they wrote. Culturally, it would have been an affront to their pride and a disorienting break with the past. From a practical viewpoint, it would have brought confusion by making everything written yesterday unreadable by the readers of tomorrow, from the tales of the pharaohs to the back files in the tax offices. The writing system, one might say, was an example of *maat*. To change it would have been willfully to plunge from *maat* into *isfet*.

In this conservatism about writing, the Egyptians were no different from any other nation. Today's English speakers, for instance, prefer to suffer years of torment in grade school rather than get rid of their "magic 'e's" that turn "cut" into "cute" and "hat" into "hate" without being pronounced, or cut down on their four different ways of depicting the *f* sound, as in "if" and "stiff" and "laugh" and "photograph." The fact is that nations do not make big changes in their writing systems except in time of revolution, when the general level of turmoil is in any case so high that the extra confusion of having to relearn the alphabet no longer seems to matter. And in spite of all the ups and downs of their history, the Egyptians had never yet experienced *isfet* catastrophic enough to detach them from their traditional way of writing.

What could not be done by a nation with an ancient tradition of writing was, however, perfectly possible for nations to which writing was new. It was foreigners, absorbing and adapting cultural influences from Egypt, who had got rid of the object- and idea-depicting signs, cut down on the consonantal ones, and made the vowel-depicting signs more realistic. The end result of this lengthy process of influence and adaptation in foreign lands was the next writing that the carver must cut into the stone: the alphabet of the Greeks.

"And the Letters of the Northerners"

This third and final writing had originated about 1700 B.C., somewhere in the eastern or southeastern coastlands of the Mediterranean Sea. The previously illiterate "vile Asiatics" of these regions, who were growing in wealth and power at the time, had felt in their turn the need of writing, turned to Egypt as a source of this skill, and changed what they learned so drastically as practically to reinvent the system. In subsequent centuries, the new system spread to many peoples of the Middle East, including the Phoenicians of present-day Lebanon, a wide-ranging commercial nation. It was they who, sometime between

1100 and 800 B.C., brought the system to the Greeks—or perhaps it was Greeks themselves, now also in need of writing as their way of life became more advanced and complex, who went to the land of the Phoenicians and brought it home. Either way, the Greeks made further drastic changes in the system to meet the needs of their language. Thus the carver had fifteen centuries of innovation and experimentation behind him when he now proceeded to chisel out, yet again, the sounds of the name of the king.

Since the process of innovation had begun with Egyptian writing, the Greek letters that now portrayed the sounds were themselves remote descendants of hieroglyphs—though not the same ones that the carver had previously cut. The letter that now depicted the first sound of the name of Ptolemy, for instance, had originated in an object-depicting hieroglyph, ⌐, which meant "corner." It had been a pioneering Asiatic scribe, this time, who had decreed that a simplified version of this sign,) , should depict the first sound of the word for "corner" in his language, namely *pi't;* and that it should depict this single sound in any word whatever. Likewise, he or a colleague had also ordained that a hieroglyph depicting two planks fastened together into a cross, ✝ , should henceforth depict the first sound of their word for "cross" or "owner's mark," *taw:* ✝ .

So far, there was nothing revolutionary about what the Asiatics had done. They had simply adapted to their language the sound-depicting procedure of their Egyptian forerunners. In other ways, too, they closely followed the Egyptian example. They wrote their signs from right to left, as the Egyptians usually did. In addition, their language was a Semitic one, akin to Hebrew and Arabic, and forming part of a wider, Afro-Asiatic group of languages that included Egyptian itself. Like Egyptian, the language of the Asiatic scribes formed words by altering vowels amid unchanging consonants. They therefore followed the Egyptians in applying the sound-depicting procedure to consonants only.

The revolution, in fact, came not in what the Asiatics did but in what they did not do. Once they had come up with signs to depict the thirty or so basic consonantal sounds of their language, they stopped inventing signs. With *pi't* and *taw* and their modest platoon of fellow signs, they could depict in writing anything that could be thought or said.

Why, then, recruit and learn the tricky business of maneuvering a battalion of 700?

The Greeks had then enrolled the platoon of thirty in their service—at first so completely unaltered that they even called them by the same names: *pi, tau,* and so on. But it was not long before they decided, so to speak, to change the marching order. Perhaps they found it easier for a right-handed scribe to "pull" a pen made of a piece of reed with the end sharpened and split—their chosen writing instrument—toward him over clean papyrus, than to "push" it away and have to be careful not to smear what had already been written. In any case, by 700 B.C. they were writing their letters from left to right. The letters themselves about-faced, and in the process changed their shapes. ⊃ became ⊂ and then Γ ; ✚ lost its top to become Υ ; and over further centuries, they changed into the Π and Τ that the carver now cut into the stone to depict the first and second sounds of Ptolemy.

Thanks to yet another drastic innovation of the Greeks, the third sound of the name of the king was no longer a pitfall. The sign that the carver now chipped out to depict this sound was also descended from a hieroglyph—in this case ⬭, which in object-depicting mode meant "eye." In their usual fashion, the Asiatic scribes had used this sign to depict the first, throaty and rasping sound of their word for "eye," 'enu—a consonant that their language had in common with Egyptian. Other nations of the Middle East rounded out the eye and eliminated the pupil to make ◐, while still using the sign to depict the same consonantal sound of their Semitic languages.

The language of the Greeks, however, was not Semitic. It belonged to another widespread group of languages, the Indo-European, that also includes present-day English. Like English, Greek lacked the consonant ', and therefore had no use for a sign to depict it. On the other hand, again like English, Greek formed families of words by adding endings and beginnings to basic words made up of both vowels and consonants: *agapē* ("love"), *agapētikos* ("loving"), *agapēteos* ("lovable"), *ēgapēmenos* ("beloved"). Probably for this reason, the Greeks were not content with letters that merely suggested the sound of words. They wanted a realistic portrayal that included all the details—vowels as well as consonants. Accordingly, at the latest by 850 B.C. their scribes reassigned the spare ◐ sign to a new duty. From now on, it would depict the vowel sound *o*.

But even this was not a completely realistic portrayal. The sound *o*, like all vowels, came in two "sizes," which the Greek scribes called "big" and "little" (long and short). How would a reader know which was meant? By 700 B.C. they had taken care of this problem. They bent apart the ● sign at the bottom, 𝛀 , perhaps so that its open-ended shape would suggest the "big *ō*" sound; they kept the original sign just for "little *o*"; and they called each sign by the name of the sound it portrayed, *ōmega* and *omicron*. Thus the stonecarver, in depicting the third sound of Ptolemy, no longer had to use makeshifts that vaguely suggested the sound. He could give an exact rendering, both of the type of sound and of its length.

Furthermore, there was no change of speech-depicting methods as the carver cut his way from "Ptolemy" to "Living Forever, Beloved of Ptah." The name of the god, this time, came at the end where it belonged, because that was the only aim of the writing system—not the magical bringing into being of what words described, but simply the realistic portrayal of the sounds of speech. In one way, however, the carver showed more respect to the god in Greek than in Egyptian writing. To portray the consonants of the god's name, he did not use the ∏ and ⊤ of Ptolemy, but two signs devised by the Greek scribes so as accurately to depict breathier versions of these consonants, ϕ and ⊖ . "Ptah" thus came out as "Phtha"—probably because that, in fact, was how his name was pronounced in northern Egypt at the time.

Finally, then, the name and title of the king were once again on the stone, consonant by consonant and vowel by vowel—*Ptolemaios aiōnobios, ēgapēmenos hupo tou Phtha:**

---

*Literally, the Greek means "Ptolemy Ever-Living, Beloved by the Phtha"—in Greek, proper names unaccompanied by adjectives have a definite article. There was one sound, the *h* of *hupo* ("by"), that the standard Greek alphabet used on the stone could not portray. The reason was that the standard alphabet had been perfected among the Greeks of Asia Minor, whose dialect had no *h* sound; they therefore used their version, **H** , of the Phoenician letter for *h* to stand for the long *ē* sound, *ēta*. Nonstandard Greek alphabets of regions where the *h* sound was spoken kept **H** for that sound, and handed it on to the Latin alphabet.

In the original carving, all the words appear on one line, as part of a much longer line of text.

ΠΤΟΛΕΜΑΙΟΣΛΙΩΝΟΒΙΟΣ

ΗΓΛΠΗΜΕΝ·ΣΥΠΟΤ·ΥϞΘΛ

This time the carver had cut many more signs—thirty-eight, as against eighteen hieroglyphic and demotic ones. That was because the Greek writing divided words into the smallest possible units of sound, and then insisted on reproducing all of them. The fifth-century philosopher Democritus of Abdera had been so impressed by this procedure that he had compared the atoms out of which he believed the world was made to the letters of the alphabet; and in fact, it took only twenty-four such letters to reproduce every "atom" of sound in every word of the entire decree of the priests.

It was this system of writing that the Greeks would hand on to the nations of Europe, and which would accompany the Europeans to the Western hemisphere and elsewhere around the globe. Meanwhile, from other alphabet-using peoples in the Middle East, more or less similar systems of writing would spread far and wide in Africa and Asia. Users of alphabets would never cease to be amazed at how easy those few letters were to learn, yet how they seemed to contain within themselves, so to speak, the entire universe. "I am Alpha and Omega, the beginning and the end, the first and the last"—an early Christian would hear those words from Jesus himself, proclaiming his presence throughout the ages of the world. And twentieth-century English speakers would reassure each other, when an unfamiliar task had to be accomplished, that "It's as easy as ABC!" Printing, mass literacy, the easy filing of unlimited amounts of information—all would become possible thanks to those few letters. But behind the world-conquering alphabets, there would always hover the ghostly forms of the earliest ancestors of all of them, the Egyptian hieroglyphs.

It would have been in this way that the decree of the priests, the outcome of cooperation and conflict between two civilizations in one land, came to be carved in three writings on one piece of stone. The story of how it happened is one that tells a great deal about both the civilizations that combined to produce the document.

Perhaps the most striking impression of Egypt left by the story is that of the extraordinarily contradictory character of the civilization of the

Nile. The Egyptians both adored their pharaoh as one among the gods and goddesses, to be served beside them in their temples with ritual and ceremony, and yet thought of him as an ordinary human being who must render account of his actions to the gods. From Philae to the sea, the people of the Nile all submitted to the same all-powerful central authority, yet felt themselves to belong to city, town, or nome even before they felt themselves to be Egyptians. Their gods and goddesses were awesome beings whose power reached right across the world, yet they joined deities together to form combined ones, and split the combined ones back again into their component beings, as if no god or goddess had any real individuality, and perhaps not even any real existence, but all of them were simply changing human perceptions of some hidden, divine power.

Above all, the Egyptians clung doggedly to an inner ideal (or as they perhaps saw it, an inner reality) of timeless permanence, while endlessly adapting to the outward realities (or as they may well have thought, the outward illusions) of change and circumstance. About 3000 B.C., the scribes had decided that a picture of a reed mat should portray a particular sound of their language, and a victorious king had proved his worthiness to rule by massacring his defeated enemies; for the priests who assembled in 196 B.C., both the reed mat and the massacre of enemies bore exactly the same meanings. But the same reed mat that had survived unchanged in temple, monument, and tomb had changed, in contract, will, and government announcement, into an unrecognizable squiggle; and the pharaoh whose massacre the priests celebrated as proof of his Egyptian legitimacy was an unassimilated Greek.

Yet rather than being torn apart by these contradictions, the Egyptians were able to harmonize them; in fact, it was this harmony of opposites that caused their civilization to survive for more than 3,000 years. The belief in the pharaoh was no megalomaniac fantasy: it exalted his absolute power by making him a god, yet made that power bearable by demanding of him, as a human, that he use his power for good. The pharaoh's government was no all-trampling central authority: rather than forcing his subjects to choose between loyalty to himself and loyalty to city, town, and nome, he expected them to be loyal to both. And the combining and splitting of gods and goddesses had the effect of containing rivalries. In Mesopotamia, the deity of a winner in political and military strife was thought of as defeating and humiliating the deity of the loser; in Egypt, the deities of winner and loser would end by being worshiped as one.

Above all, the ageless stability of Egyptian civilization came from the fact that the Egyptians did not just cling doggedly to the past, but also cannily adapted to the present. The Egyptians themselves sometimes speculated that there could be no permanence without change, no stability without alteration—no eternal harmony of *maat*, indeed, without the energizing turmoil of *isfet*. The history of their own civilization proved that they were right.

As for the Greeks, their story was one that had happened before, and would happen many times again: a nation on the fringes of the civilized world learning from more advanced neighbors, adapting what it learned so as to produce a new type of civilization, and in the process developing skills or exploiting previously untapped resources that enabled it to become internationally dominant. The writings on the stone, with the progression from the religious and magical "words of god" to the efficiently information-communicating "letters of the Northerners," are an example of this learning and adapting process. But it was something that happened in many other fields of religion and culture, technology and economics, government and warfare, so that the Greeks became, for a time, the masters of the world.

As masters of the world, naturally, the Greeks were arrogant, brutal, and greedy. Naturally, too, they diverted the resources of other nations, with different types of civilization, into nurturing their own type of civilization and upholding its supremacy. Nevertheless, one of the most striking features of Greek civilization was its willingness to coexist with other civilizations, even when it was dominant. The whole history of the Ptolemies shows that arrogant, brutal, greedy, and determinedly Greek as they might be, it never entered their heads to assert the superiority of their civilization by "spreading" it, or to consolidate their power by undermining or suppressing the civilization of the Egyptians.* On the contrary, their insistence on being Egyptian as well as Greek god-kings shows that what they wanted was for Egyptian civilization to flourish, and themselves, in their official capacity as rulers, to be part of it. Civilization as a whole owes a good deal to the live-and-let-live ethnocentricity of the Ptolemies, since it was this feature of their rule that led to the three writings being carved on one stone, and thereby enabled the European successors of Egypt and Greece one day to rediscover the civilization of the Nile.

But before the civilization of the Nile could be rediscovered, it first had to die.

---

*For the deliberate suppression of one civilization by another, as seen by someone who belonged to both, see Case Study 13, in Volume 4 of this series, "Garcilaso de la Vega: Spanish Gentleman and Inca Prince."

FURTHER READING

There are countless books for the general reader on every aspect of traditional Egyptian civilization. The following is a selection of some of the most recent ones, written by experts, on aspects discussed in this case study. Perhaps because the Ptolemaic period of Egyptian civilization was until recently regarded as one of unrelieved decline, there are as yet no general-reader books dealing specifically with the period.

Bowman, Alan. *Egypt after the Pharaohs, 332 B.C.–A.D. 642* (Berkeley, 1986). Concise treatment, but with many vivid quotations from sources, of Egypt from Alexander to the Arab conquest, concentrating on Greco-Roman government and civilization.

Davies, W. V. *Egyptian Hieroglyphs* (Berkeley, 1988). Brief but authoritative account of the origins, purposes, and workings of the hieroglyphs, with information on the other scripts as well.

Gardiner, Sir Alan. *Egypt of the Pharaohs* (Oxford, 1966). Authoritative account of Egyptian history up to the Greek conquest, by a distinguished scholar and fine writer.

Healey, John F. *The Early Alphabet* (Berkeley, 1991). Brief and clear account of the origins of alphabetic writing, and its development down to the Latin, Arabic, and Hebrew alphabets.

Lichtheim, Miriam. *Ancient Egyptian Literature*, 3 vols. (Berkeley, 1975–80). This anthology makes a wide range of Egyptian literature accessible in modern English that vividly evokes the original. The third volume includes all types of literature from the Ptolemaic period.

Quirke, Stephen. *Who Were the Pharaohs? A List of Their Names.* (London, 1990). Explains in simple terms the origins, development, and purpose of the great names of the pharaohs, against the background of Egyptian religious and magical beliefs.

———. *Ancient Egyptian Religion* (London, 1993). Clear and up-to-date account, covering every aspect of mythology, ritual, and belief.

Quirke, Stephen, and Carol Andrews. *Rosetta Stone* (New York, 1989). Written by two British Museum experts, this publication includes a concise account of the cultural and historical background of the stone, side-by-side translations of all three texts, and a full-size facsimile of the stone itself.

Zauzich, Karl-Theodor. *Hieroglyphs without Mystery* (Austin, TX, 1992). Easy-to-follow explanation of hieroglyphic writing and the Egyptian language, designed to enable laypeople to read simple Egyptian texts.

Sources

This case study is based partly on the words of contemporaries, both Egyptian and Greek, whether carved in stone or are written on papyrus manuscripts. These are quoted in works by modern scholars, or are available in translations of complete works or collections of excerpts. Detailed, scholarly investigations of the events leading up to the carving of the Rosetta Stone, as well as of relevant aspects of Greek and Egyptian civilization in the Hellenistic period, have been used. In addition, standard works on Egyptian writing have been consulted.

Aldred, Cyril, et al. *L'Egypte du crépuscule* [The twilight of Egypt]. Paris, 1980.

Alliot, Maurice. "La Thébaïde en lutte contre les rois d'Alexandrie sous Philopator et Epiphane" [The struggle of the Thebaid against the Alexandrian kings under Philopator and Epiphanes]. *Revue Belge de Philologie et d'Histoire* [Belgian review of philology and history] 29 (1951): 421–43.

Bagnall, Roger S. "Greeks and Egyptians: Ethnicity, Status, and Culture." In *Cleopatra's Egypt: Age of the Ptolemies*, edited by Robert S. Bianchi. New York, 1988.

Baines, John. "Literacy and Ancient Egyptian Society." *Man*, n.s. 18 (1983): 572–99.

Bennett, John. "The Restoration Inscription of Tutankhamun." *Journal of Egyptian Archaeology* 25 (1939): 8–15.

Bevan, Edwyn. *A History of Egypt under the Ptolemaic Dynasty*. London, 1927.

Budge, E. A. Wallis. *The Decrees of Memphis and Canopus*. 3 vols. London, 1904.

Burstein, Stanley M., ed. and trans. *The Hellenistic Age from the Battle of Ipsos to the Death of Kleopatra VII*. Cambridge, 1985.

Clarysse, Willy. "Notes de prosopographie thébaine, 7: Hurgonaphor et Chaonnophris, les derniers pharaons indigènes" [Notes on Theban prosopography, 7: Hurgonaphor and Chaonnophris, the last native pharaohs]. *Chronique d'Egypte* [Chronicle of Egypt] 53 (1978): 243–53.

Daumas, François. *Les moyens d'expression du grec et de l'égyptien comparés dans les décrets de Canope et de Memphis* [The means of expression of Greek and Egyptian compared in the decrees of Canopus and Memphis]. Cairo, 1952.

Davies, W. H. *Egyptian Hieroglyphs*. Berkeley, 1987.

Derchain, Philippe. "Le rôle du roi d'Egypte dans le maintien de l'ordre cosmique" [The role of the king of Egypt in the maintenance of cosmic order]. In Centre d'Etude des Religions, *Le pouvoir et le sacré* [The state and the sacred]. Brussels, 1962.

Erichsen, W. *Demotische Lesestücke* [Demotic reader]. 2 vols. Leipzig, 1937–39.

————. *Auswahl frühdemotischer Texte* [A selection of early demotic texts]. Copenhagen, 1950.

————. *Demotisches Glossar.* [Demotic glossary]. Copenhagen, 1954.

Fairman, H. W. "The Kingship Rituals of Egypt." In *Myth, Ritual, and Kingship*, edited by S. H. Hooke. Oxford, 1958.

Frankfort, Henri. *Kingship and the Gods.* Chicago, 1978.

Fraser, P. M. *Ptolemaic Alexandria.* 3 vols. Oxford, 1972.

Gardiner, Sir Alan. *Egyptian Grammar: An Introduction to the Study of the Hieroglyphs.* 3d ed. Oxford, 1957.

————. *Egypt of the Pharaohs: An Introduction.* Oxford, 1961.

Goyon, Jean-Claude. "Ptolemaic Egypt: Priests and the Traditional Religion." In *Cleopatra's Egypt: Age of the Ptolemies*, edited by Robert S. Bianchi. New York, 1988.

Grant, Michael. *From Alexander to Cleopatra: The Hellenistic World.* New York, 1982.

Grimal, Nicolas. *A History of Ancient Egypt.* Oxford, 1994.

Haarmann, Harald. *Universalgeschichte der Schrift* [General history of writing]. Frankfurt, 1990.

Habachi, Labib. "Sais and Its Monuments." *Annales du Service des Antiquités de l'Egypte* [Annals of the Egyptian Antiquities Service] 42 (1943): 369–416.

Habicht, Christian. "Die herrschende Gesellschaft in den hellenistischen Monarchien" [The ruling group in the Hellenistic monarchies]. *Vierteljahrschrift für Sozial- und Wirtschaftsgeschichte* [Quarterly journal of social and economic history] 45 (1958): 1–16.

Harris, William V. *Ancient Literacy.* Cambridge, MA, 1989.

Healey, John F. *The Early Alphabet.* London, 1990.

Helck, Wolfgang. "Die Ägypter und die Fremden" [Egyptians and foreigners]. *Saeculum* 15 (1964): 103–14.

Hess, J. J. *Der demotische Teil der dreisprachigen Inschrift von Rosette* [The demotic portion of the trilingual inscription of Rosetta]. Freiburg, 1902.

Holmberg, Maj Sandeman. *The God Ptah.* Lund, 1946.

Johnson, Janet H. *Thus Wrote 'Onchsheshonqy: An Introductory Grammar of Demotic.* Chicago, 1986.

————. "The Demotic Chronicle as a Statement of a Theory of Kingship." *SSEA Journal* 13 (1983): 61–72.

————, ed. *Life in a Multi-Cultural Society: Egypt from Cambyses to Constantine and Beyond.* Chicago, 1992.

————. "The Ptolemaic Bureaucracy from an Egyptian Point of View." In *The Organization of Power: Aspects of Bureaucracy in the Ancient Near East*, edited by McGuire Gibson and Robert D. Biggs. 2d ed. Chicago, 1991.

Koenen, Ludwig. "Die Adaption ägyptischer Königsideologie am Ptolemäerhof" [The adaptation of the Egyptian ideology of kingship at the court of the Ptolemies]. In *Egypt and the Hellenistic World*, edited by E. van't Dack et al. Louvain, 1983.

Kyrieleis, H. "Die Porträtmünzen Ptolemaios' V. und seiner Eltern: Zur Datierung und historischen Interpretation" [The portrait coins of Ptolemy V and his parents: Dating and historical interpretation]. *Jahrbuch des Deutschen Archäologischen Instituts* [Yearbook of the German Archaeological Institute] 88 (1973): 213–46.

Lacau, Pierre. "Un graffito égyptien d'Abydos écrit en lettres grecques" [An Egyptian graffito at Abydos written in Greek letters]. *Etudes de Papyrologie* [Studies in papyrology] 2 (1933): 229–46.

Lewis, Naphthali. *Greeks in Ptolemaic Egypt: Case Studies in the Social History of the Hellenistic World*. Oxford, 1986.

Lexikon der Ägyptologie [Encyclopedia of Egyptology]. Edited by Wolfgang Helck et al. 7 vols. Wiesbaden, 1975–92.

Lichtheim, Miriam, ed. and trans. *Ancient Egyptian Literature*. 3 vols. Berkeley, 1975–80.

Lloyd, Alan B. "Nationalistic Propaganda in Ptolemaic Egypt." *Historia* 31 (1982): 33–55.

————. "The Inscription of Udjahorresnet: A Collaborator's Testament." *Journal of Egyptian Archaeology* 68 (1982):166–80.

Maystre, Charles. *Les prêtres de Ptah à Memphis* [The priests of Ptah at Memphis]. Freiburg, 1992.

Mooren, Leon. "Macht und Nationalität" [Power and nationality]. In *Der ptolemäische Ägypten* [Ptolemaic Egypt], edited by Herwig Maehler and Volcker M. Strocka. Mainz, 1978.

Morenz, Siegfried. *Egyptian Religion*, translated by Ann E. Keep. Ithaca, NY, 1973.

Müller, W. Max. *Egyptological Researches*. Vol. 3: *The Bilingual Decrees of Philae*. Washington, DC, 1920.

Naveh, J. *Early History of the Alphabet*. Jerusalem, 1982.

Nock, Arthur Darby. "Notes on Ruler-Cult." In *Essays on Religion and the Ancient World*, selected and edited by Zephaniah Stewart. Vol. 1. Cambridge, MA, 1972.

————. "*Sunnaios theos*" [Temple-sharing deity]. Ibid.

Onasch, Christian. "Zur Königsideologie der Ptolemäer in den Dekreten von Kanopus und Memphis" [The Ptolemaic ideology of kingship in the decrees of Canopus and Memphis]. *Archiv für Papyrusforschung* [Archive of Papyrology] 24–25 (1976): 137–55.

Otto, Eberhard. "Die Endsituation der ägyptischen Kultur" [The final phase of Egyptian civilization]. *Welt als Geschichte* [World as history] 15 (1951): 203–13.

Peremans, Willy. "Über die Zweisprachigkeit im ptolemäischen Ägypten" [Bilingualism in Ptolemaic Egypt]. In *Studien zur Papyrologie und antiken Wirtschaftsgeschichte* [Studies in papyrology and ancient economic history], edited by Horst Braunert. Bonn, 1964.

———. "Le bilinguisme dans les relations gréco-égyptiennes sous les Lagides" [Bilingualism in Greek-Egyptian relations under the Ptolemies]. In *Egypt and the Hellenistic World*, edited by E van't Dack et al. Louvain, 1983.

———. "Les révolutions égyptiennes sous les Lagides" [Egyptian revolutions under the Ptolemies]. In *Der ptolemäische Ägypten* [Ptolemaic Egypt], edited by Herwig Maehler and Volcker M. Strocka. Mainz, 1978.

Pestman, P. W. "Harmachis et Anchmachis" [Harmachis and Anchmachis]. *Chronique d'Egypte* [Chronicle of Egypt] 40 (1965): 157–70.

Polybius. *The Histories*, translated by W. R. Paton. Vols. 3–6. Cambridge, MA, 1923–27.

Posener, Georges. *De la divinité du pharaon* [The divinity of the pharaoh]. Paris, 1960.

Préaux, Claire. *Le monde hellénistique* [The Hellenistic world]. 2 vols. Paris, 1978.

———. "Politique de race ou politique royale?" [Racial or royal policy?]. *Chronique d'Egypte* [Chronicle of Egypt] 11(1936): 111–38.

———. "Esquisse d'une histoire des révolutions égyptiennes sous les Lagides" [Egyptian revolutions under the Ptolemies: A sketch]. Ibid., 522–52.

Quirke, Stephen. *Who Were the Pharaohs? A History of Their Names with a List of Cartouches*. London, 1990.

Quirke, Stephen, and Carol Andrews. *Rosetta Stone: Facsimile Drawing with an Introduction and Translations*. New York, 1989.

Reymond, E. A. E. *From the Records of a Priestly Family from Memphis*. Wiesbaden, 1981.

Samuel, Alan E. *The Shifting Sands of Time: Interpretations of Ptolemaic Egypt*. Lanham, MD, 1989.

———. *Ptolemaic Chronology*. Munich, 1962.

Sauneron, Serge. *Les prêtres de l'ancienne Egypte* [The priests of ancient Egypt]. Paris, 1957.

Sethe, Kurt. "Zur Geschichte und Erklärung der Rosettana" [The history and interpretation of the Rosetta inscription]. *Nachrichten der Königlichen Gesellschaft der Wissenschaften zu Göttingen*, Philosophisch-Historische Klasse [Bulletin of the Royal Society for the Advancement of Learning, Göttingen, philosophy and history section], 1916.

———. "Die historische Bedeutung des 2. Philä-Dekrets" [The historical significance of the Second Decree of Philae]. *Zeitschrift für ägyptische Sprache* [Journal of Egyptian philology] 53 (1917): 35–49.

Sottas, H., and E. Drioton. *Introduction a l'étude des hiéroglyphes* [Introduction to the study of hieroglyphs]. Paris, 1922.

Spiegelberg, Wilhelm, ed. and trans. *Die sogenannte Demotische Chronik* [The so-called Demotic Chronicle]. Leipzig, 1914.

———. *Der Demotische Text der Priesterdekrete von Kanopus und Memphis (Rosettana) mit den hieroglyphischen und griechischen Fassungen und deutscher Übersetzung nebst demotischem Glossar* [The demotic text of the priestly decrees of Canopus and Memphis (the Rosetta inscription), with the hieroglyphic and Greek versions, German translation, and demotic glossary]. Heidelberg, 1922.

———. *Demotische Grammatik* [Demotic grammar]. Heidelberg, 1925.

Spiegelberg, Wilhelm, and Walter Otto. *Eine neue Urkunde zur Siegesfeier des Ptolemaios IV. und die Frage der ägyptischen Priestersynoden* [A new document on Ptolemy IV's victory celebration and the question of Egyptian priestly synods]. Munich, 1926.

Theocritus. "Encomium to Ptolemy." In *The Idylls of Theocritus: A Verse Translation,* by Thelma Sargent. New York, 1982.

Thissen, Heinz-Josef. *Studien zum Raphiadekret* [Studies on the Decree of Raphia]. Meisenheim/Glan, 1966.

Thompson, Dorothy J. *Memphis under the Ptolemies*. Princeton, NJ, 1988.

———. "The High Priests of Memphis under Ptolemaic Rule." In *Pagan Priests: Religion and Power in the Ancient World,* edited by Mary Beard and John North. London, 1990.

Trigger, B. G., B. J. Kemp, D. O'Connor, and A. B. Lloyd. *Ancient Egypt: A Social History*. Cambridge, 1983.

Walbank, F. W. *A Historical Commentary on Polybius*. 3 vols. Oxford, 1957–75.

———. *The Hellenistic World*. Brighton, Sussex, 1981.

———. "Monarchies and Monarchic Ideas." In *The Cambridge Ancient History* (2d ed.), Vol. 7, pt. 1: *The Hellenistic World.*

Winter, Erich. "Der Herrscherkult in den ägyptischen Ptolemäertempeln" [Ruler cult in the Ptolemaic temples of Egypt]. In *Der ptolemäische Ägypten* [Ptolemaic Egypt], edited by Herwig Maehler and Volcker M. Strocka. Mainz, 1978.

Egypt, Greece, Europe

The Rosetta Stone and Three Civilizations

Part
Two   Death and Rediscovery
of a Civilization

196 B.C.–A.D. 1822

CONTENTS

ILLUSTRATIONS

MAP

5

"WHERE IS PTAH?"

The years passed, the gov-
and once in a while the
peated, with variations, their
Ptolemy spread from tem-
ernment no doubt pushed,
priests reassembled and re-
decree. Slowly, the cult of
ple to temple. With it, there
also multiplied copies of the decree, of which no less than ten are known
today. Generally they were altered and updated in various ways. In particular, they usually covered the latest events that proved Ptolemy, and later
also his queen, the Seleucid princess Cleopatra, to be true god and true
goddess.

The most notable of these events was recorded in 186 B.C., in a copy
of the decree carved into a wall of the distant island temple of Isis, 700
miles up the river at Philae. "There was fighting in the land of the
south, in the territory of Thebes, with the impious foreigner, the enemy
of the gods. . . . They slew his son, . . . together with the chiefs of the
Nubians brought with him. He was led to the place where was His
Majesty, and punished for the crimes which he had committed, with
death." The "impious foreigner" was Ankhwennefer, Ptolemy's Theban
rival. In the struggle between the Greek and the Nubian to decide who
would be the Horus of Egypt, the Greek had won.

In the 150 years that followed, there would be many more such
Greek Horuses and their queens. Six more generations of Ptolemies
and Cleopatras reigned in Egypt, in spite of further revolts, continued
warfare with rival dynasties, and bitter feuding among themselves. So
long as they ruled, the revised partnership between Greeks and Egyptians remained in effect. There were no more spectacular demonstrations of priestly loyalty to the dynasty, but perhaps they were not
necessary anymore: the two sides were now routinely friendly, and still
from time to time commemorated their friendship in stone. About
120 B.C., for instance, the rulers dedicated two red granite obelisks—
traditional Egyptian structures, originating in the cult of the sun god
and consisting of tapering, four-sided shafts—in the temple at Philae.
On the bases of the monuments, the priests later recorded, in Greek,
valuable royal concessions in the matter of supply requisitions by government officials; and on the shafts themselves, hieroglyphs praised the
goddess and the rulers' piety toward her. Within the "circles," there

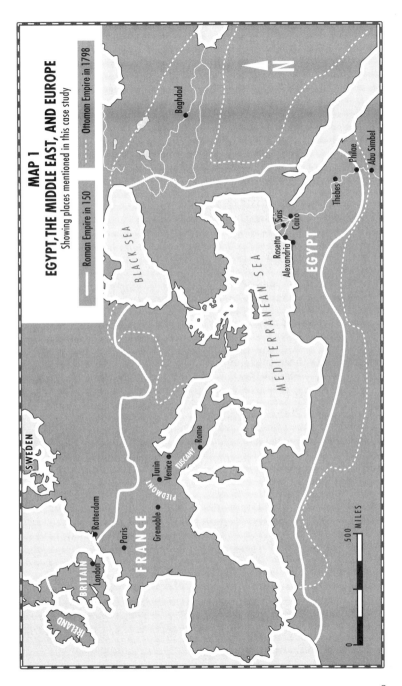

MAP 1

EGYPT, THE MIDDLE EAST, AND EUROPE

Showing places mentioned in this case study

— Roman Empire in 150

---- Ottoman Empire in 1798

appeared, this time, not only the name of the incumbent Ptolemy, but also that of the incumbent Cleopatra of the day.

But the power of the Ptolemies and Cleopatras as god-kings and goddess-queens depended on the greater power of Rome, and as Rome grew ever more ambitious and sure of itself, it turned from upholding them as allies to undermining them as victims. True, the last and most famous of the Cleopatras tried to bring Rome and Egypt into partnership, by linking her destiny with those of two men who briefly held Roman power in their hands, Julius Caesar and then Mark Antony. But they both failed her, and she chose death rather than fall to the mercy of Mark Antony's triumphant rival, Augustus. The land she ruled, however, could not so easily escape that fate. From 30 B.C., when Augustus arrived with his legions, Egypt became the property of the Roman emperors.

In this way, the ever wider spread of civilization, which had made Egypt a subject nation of the Greeks, now made it a province of the Roman Empire. Egyptian civilization, from which this outward spread had partly begun, had become a local one, sharing a corner of a vast new world with the dominant international civilization of Greece and Rome.

This did not mean that Egyptian civilization had lost its importance, or its power to influence foreign nations. From about the time that the partnership between Greeks and Egyptians was revised, the Greeks came more and more under the influence of the civilization of the land that they now called home. They continued to be the dominant foreign element even under Roman rule, and from them, in turn, the influence of Egypt spread through the international world of Greco-Roman civilization.

The Roman emperors, like the Ptolemies, expected to be recognized by the Egyptian priests as pharaohs, and in temple, monument, and tomb there now appeared hieroglyphic versions of Greek versions of their Latin names: Augustus, Caesar, Tiberius, Domitian, and the like. This was no mere concession to "native" feeling. The emperors set up obe-lisks in Rome, shipped all the way from the Nile to the Tiber— some of them pharaonic originals, and others contemporary work, carved by Egyptian experts with authentic hieroglyphs that praised imperial deeds. In this way, the new masters of the world borrowed some of the ancient glory of Egypt to add luster to their upstart power; and Egypt was a visible presence in the very center of the dominant international civilization.

1. **A Roman Obelisk** This obelisk was quarried in Egypt in A.D. 81, carved with authentic hieroglyphs celebrating the "arising" of Domitian as Roman emperor, shipped to Rome, and set up in the city's temple of Isis and Osiris. For many centuries after the empire's fall, it lay broken in pieces. Finally, in 1651, Pope Innocent X had it repaired and reerected in one of modern Rome's most splendid public squares, the Piazza Navona, above a fountain by the greatest sculptor of the time, Giovanni Lorenzo Bernini.

Most of all, however, the presence of Egypt was felt throughout the world in matters of religion. The new international world needed international gods and goddesses, and true to their traditions, the Greeks and Romans produced these by amalgamating their gods and goddesses with foreign ones. But in the mixture, it was often foreign gods and goddesses who predominated—above all the Egyptian triad of Isis, Osiris, and Horus. Unimaginably ancient founders of Egypt yet upholders of order against chaos throughout the world, internationally mighty yet acquainted with grief and death, shrouded in cosmic mystery yet still a family of suffering father, nurturing wife and mother, and triumphant royal son, they claimed the love and reverence of believers even in Britain, far away in the great ocean that now formed the western boundary of the civilized world. "I am Isis, queen of every land," began a Greek hymn to the goddess dating from the first century B.C.; and it ended, "Hail to Egypt, who reared me!" For the worshipers of Isis and her "Holy Family," Egypt was a "Holy Land." Its enigmatic myths and secret rituals, they believed, conveyed unique spiritual experience and intellectual knowledge of the divine powers that ruled the world.

But although much of the international worship of Isis and Osiris was genuinely Egyptian, the god and goddess themselves were depicted in safely familiar Greek guise, looking for all the world like Pluto and Demeter, their Greek equivalents. Like most civilizations confronted with alien partners, that of the Greeks and Romans borrowed from Egypt only what it could "repackage," so to speak, to meet its own religious and cultural needs. As for those items that could not be used in this way, they were not worth bothering about.

In another field, too, Greco-Roman civilization practiced this kind of selective repackaging: that of Egyptian writing. About A.D. 120, Plutarch of Chaeronea, famous Greek essayist, scholar of many fields, and all-round cultural leader of Greco-Roman civilization, wrote a detailed and reverent account, *Of Isis and Osiris*, in which he also had a good deal to say about the hieroglyphs. Among others, he mentioned what was probably the wriggling-cobra sign in "forever" (p. 164).* "The heaven," he declared, "as it is ageless through its eternity, they write with a cobra," because "the cobra does not grow old."

Plutarch also knew that the Egyptians had what he called "twenty-five letters"—no doubt the single-consonant sound-depicting signs

---

*References in the text are to Case Study 3 in this volume, "Egypt, Greece, Europe: The Rosetta Stone and Three Civilizations, Part 1, Two Civilizations in One Land," where features of Egyptian writing that are mentioned here were originally explained.

(pp. 160–61). But it never occurred to him that the wriggling cobra might be one of them, or if it did, that did not interest him. What was exciting about the hieroglyphs, after all, was the fact that they were a sacred writing that used pictures to portray ideas. Surely the ideas must be deep ones, arising out of Egypt's unique experience and knowledge of the divine; and surely the point of using pictures must be to portray the ideas in suitably mysterious form. For the mythically ever-youthful cobra to depict, in riddle-like fashion, the idea of "ageless heaven" was much more solemn and profound—much more Egyptian, one might say—than for it to depict simply the first sound of "John" or "George."

As for other, everyday forms of Egyptian writing, they were not worth discussing at all, beyond the bare mention of the fact that they existed. It was this youthful-cobra idea of Egyptian writing, then, that Plutarch and other Greco-Roman authorities left with their readers— of both their own and many future generations.

For all the continued influence of Egypt in foreign lands, at home the powerful international civilization gradually undermined the native one. Several centuries as a province of the Roman Empire made a mockery of the ideal that had nourished Egyptian civilization—of their country as the center of the world and their god-kings as the linchpin of the universe. It was hard even for Egyptians to cling to this ideal, under the rule of absentee Horuses who sucked dry the riches of the Nile to feed the mobs of Rome and equip legions on distant frontiers, and who, as the empire's problems mounted, had less and less left over with which to "do good to the temples."* Besides, the dominant international civilization was now full of echoes of Egypt. Where was the betrayal in accepting its ways? By about A.D. 250, in the temples, monuments, and tombs of the Nile, "the style of the Egyptians' work" had been replaced by the international style of Greece and Rome—a kind of depiction that it made no sense to supplement with hieroglyphs. By that date, too, Egyptian scribes were already well along with a momentous innovation, though as yet restricted to a highly specialized field. For recording magic spells, where the sound of the words had to be exactly right if a spell was to have the desired effect, they were now writing their language, both consonants and vowels, with Greek letters.

Thus Egypt was already becoming a province of the dominant international civilization and less and less the seat of a local one, at the time

---

*On a Roman legion that spent time on both the European and the Middle Eastern frontiers and also in Egypt, see Case Study 5, in Volume 2 of this series, "The Fifth Legion (The Loyal and True Macedonic): A Unit History."

when both civilizations were overtaken by a great revolution: the triumph of Christianity.

In Egypt, as elsewhere in the Roman Empire, the revolution was a swift one. In A.D. 300, the Christians were a viciously persecuted though rapidly growing minority among both Greeks and Egyptians.* About A.D. 400, St. Shenoute, abbot of the White Monastery near Thebes, could mock triumphantly at the amalgamated pagan gods of both nations: "Where is Cronos, also called Petbe, who chained up his parents and mutilated his father with a scythe? Where is Hephaestus, also called Ptah?" On the way out, was the implication, now that, thanks to the efforts of Christians, whether Greek or Egyptian like himself, fewer and fewer people were worshiping them.

Although the dominant international civilization and the local Egyptian one both underwent the victory of Christianity, their resulting destinies were very different. For Greco-Roman civilization, the rise of the new religion was a drastic change, but it was far from a death blow. The Greeks and Romans, after all, had already strayed far from their ancient pagan myths and rituals. Their art and literature and philosophy and science were at least to some extent independent of traditional religious belief. The Christians could seize upon the treasures that Greco-Roman civilization had heaped up in these realms and use them for their own purposes. It was a seizure that Plutarch's Christian successor as international cultural leader, St. Jerome, compared with the Children of Israel fleeing from the pharaoh, yet, in their exodus, "taking spoils from the Egyptians." For Greco-Roman civilization, the despoiling process was actually one of renewal, enabling it to live on, entwined now with Christianity instead of pagan religion, for many further centuries. With it there also lived on what it knew of Egypt, once Egypt itself was dead.

For Egyptian civilization, unlike that of Greece and Rome, could not survive the triumph of Christianity. In its art and literature and philosophy and science, it had never strayed far from traditional pagan myth and ritual; thus from the actual as opposed to St. Jerome's metaphorical Egypt, there were no spoils that Christians could safely take. With their gods and goddesses, the Egyptians must abandon every other feature of

---

*On the persecution of Christians in the Roman Empire, see Case Study 6, in Volume 2 of this series, "A Hundred Years after Jesus: The Life and Death of St. Justin Martyr."

their 3,500-year-old civilization—including, of course, the "writing of the words of god" and its derivative scripts.

In the revolutionary times of Christian takeover, the anxiety and confusion of changing the writing system must have seemed to the victors a small price to pay for ridding Egypt of pagan worship. As for the vanquished, who had already given up so much of their traditional ways, they were now confronted with blaspheming pharaohs, ransacked temples, and massacred priests. In the face of this terminal *isfet*, what was the point of clinging to the writing system? About A.D. 500, the Alexandrian scholar Horapollo, long a pagan holdout and finally a reluctant Christian convert, wrote a book in Egyptian, *On Hieroglyphics*, which was later translated into Greek. Although he gave the true meaning of thirty or so idea-depicting signs, many more of those he listed were wrong, and his explanation of the system as such was based on the youthful-cobra theory. Even this native Egyptian and sympathizer with the old ways no longer knew how the hieroglyphs worked.

Instead, Christian Egypt now wrote its language with thirty-one letters—twenty-four Greek ones, and seven converted from single-consonant demotic signs. It was an alphabet that could be quickly taught to the shock troops of the Christian takeover, the monks, who were recruited by the thousand from illiterate peasant homes; and it left no doubt about how they should pronounce the words in their prayerbooks. For the first time, every "atom" of Egyptian speech was accurately depicted in writing (p. 174). Most of the words were more or less changed from the days when they had been depicted by hieroglyphs, but often they were still recognizable. The hieroglyphic words *hrw ms*, "birthday" (pp. 164–65), for instance, now revealed themselves as *houmise*. And when St. Shenoute mocked the god of Memphis, he was now able to spell the god's name in full as the stonecarver had done in Greek 600 years before (p. 173)—only in the saint's southern Egyptian dialect, the name came out as *Ptaḥ*.

With this simple and accurate alphabet, Egypt could now express itself in writing as never before. Books of ritual and prayer, lives of saints, and works on disputed theological questions poured from the monasteries. In the international Christendom that between A.D. 400 and 600 replaced the failing Roman Empire, Egypt was in the forefront. It was the headquarters of dissident Christian beliefs that dominated the Middle East and shook the power of the emperors. In spite of religious disagreements, the way of life of its monks was faithfully followed by searchers after holiness as far away as Ireland.* Thus the land of the Nile became the seat of a flourishing new civilization, which was very different from its old one. (To mark the difference, the people of Christian Egypt are known today, from an Arabic word for an Egyptian, as Copts; and their church, language, literature, and art are called Coptic.) Never, indeed, in building a new civilization, had a nation broken so completely with its own past.

Sometime in the turmoil of the Christian takeover, the break with the past would have reached the temple of Neith in the western Delta (pp. 156–57). The buildings would have been looted and abandoned, except, perhaps, for part of them left standing as a church. The temple's devilish monuments would also have been left to fall apart, or perhaps torn down, and the pieces left scattered on the ground.

In 639, Egypt was invaded yet again, by yet another superpower nation that had arisen to dominate the civilized world, the Arabs. With them, they brought yet another religious revolution, that of Islam. For Egypt, that meant yet another break with the past—more gradual than the Christian one, for it took perhaps 400 or 500 years to accomplish, but thorough enough all the same. At the latest by 1100, the people of the Nile had almost entirely given up the language of their ancestors, and had instead come to speak, read, and write the language of their conquerors. By that time, too, the vast majority had come to worship the God and venerate the Prophet of the conquerors, and to despise their Christian as well as their pagan past.

All the same, the Muslim conquest put Egypt yet again in the forefront of a dominant civilization—one that spread, this time, from the tangled forests of West Africa to the endless grasslands of Central Asia. In the intercontinental world of Islam, Egypt's rulers were, so to speak, Muslim Ptolemies, using the wealth of the Nile to win military power and cultural leadership in competition with other rulers. Their capital of Cairo, not far from the ruins of Memphis—for the unchanged, basic geography of the river and its delta meant that Muslim rulers, too, needed a "Balance of the Two Lands"—rivaled Baghdad as the commercial and cultural center of Islam. Around 1200, the city's "House of

---

*An Irish monk, St. Columban of Luxeuil, who lived according to the severe Egyptian pattern and became widely admired and feared in the sixth-century Frankish kingdom on account of his fierce holiness, is discussed in Case Study 7, in Volume 2 of this series, "A Germanic Ruler in a Roman Land: Brunhild, Queen of the Franks."

Wisdom," like the Alexandrian library of old, had over 100,000 books; and its scholars and scientists, like those of Alexandria, were internationally famous. But they knew almost nothing of the pharaonic past of their own country, and the Greek and Roman works that would have told them a little about it were not available to them.

Throughout the centuries of Egypt's Islamic greatness, in fact, it kept only one link with the pharaonic past—apart, of course, from the ever-present ruins of temple, monument, and tomb. That link was maintained, all unawares, by the small Coptic minority. Though they mostly used only Arabic in daily life, they still celebrated the services of the church in the ancient language. Their learned priests and monks studied the language at least enough to know what the words of the services meant. In this way, the Egyptian tongue died out like the hieroglyphs that had depicted it; but unlike them, it was not forgotten.

From 1250 onward, though remaining a basically Arab country, Egypt fell under the rule of a convert nation of Central Asian origin that had come to dominate much of the Muslim world: the Turks. Like the Greeks before them, the Turks were not united as conquerors, and Egypt remained a powerful independent country within Islam, though now governed by a warrior-landowning caste of Turkish origin, the Mamluks. In 1516, another branch of the Turks, the Ottomans, who had built a great empire in Western Asia, Eastern Europe, and the Middle East, successfully invaded Egypt. Even so, the Mamluks remained in day-to-day control of the country, until in 1798 they were overthrown by another conqueror, from among the newest and strongest in the long succession of masters of the world, the Europeans.

Sometime in the early centuries of Muslim rule, the waterways connecting Alexandria with the Delta began to dry up. To maintain Egypt's flourishing trade with both Muslim and Christian countries to the north of the Mediterranean Sea, a new port city sprang up directly at the mouth of the river's westernmost branch. It was called Rashid, a name that the many Italian merchants who visited the city found easier to pronounce as Rosetta. To decorate their fine houses and pave their courtyards, the wealthy citizens of Rosetta quarried stone from the only nearby sources in their land of reeds and mud, the ruined temples of long-forgotten gods and goddesses. It was a time-honored practice, which was followed also by the engineers of the Mamluk Sultan Qaitbay, when in 1479, alarmed at the growing Ottoman menace from beyond the sea, he gave orders to defend Rosetta with a coastal fortress.

In the same centuries during which civilization spread, in Muslim guise, to West Africa and Central Asia, so also, in Christian guise, it spread throughout Europe. Out of the decayed provinces of the Roman Empire and the barbarian warrior nations beyond its former frontier, there gradually emerged a group of powerful, civilized states, intensely predatory and competitive like the Hellenistic monarchies, and not much smaller—only there were many more of them.

Like the Hellenistic monarchies, too, the European states were held together by common religious and cultural traditions. In these traditions, the once-dominant Greco-Roman civilization, thanks to having been despoiled by Christianity, loomed very large. Over the centuries, the Europeans had repackaged some features of Greco-Roman civilization and neglected others, to suit their needs. But always they had been aware of this civilization of the distant past, so different from their own and yet continually a source of inspiration to them. In fact, in the fourteenth century, a couple of hundred years after Italian merchants had begun visiting Rosetta, scholars and artists in their hometowns set to work to strip off the repackaging and recover the reality of what Greco-Roman civilization once had been—a massive cultural enterprise that today is known as the Renaissance.

As the scholars and artists of the Renaissance sifted through the works of ancient writers, it was not long before they came upon what Greece and Rome had known of Egypt. Up to then, most of Europe's information about Egypt had come from the Old Testament—accurate enough, in its resentful "Asiatic" depiction of a powerful, wealthy, and arrogant nation, but with very little to say about the achievements of Egyptian civilization. Now, the scholars and artists learned of a land so ancient and wise that even the revered Greeks and Romans had looked up to the Egyptians as their masters. The gods and goddesses of the Nile were dead and gone, and there was no more need for Christians to be afraid of them. In Rome, when fallen obelisks of the emperors came to light, the popes themselves gave orders to set them up again. It was not enough to revive the civilization of Greece and Rome. The scholars and artists must also revive what they could of Egypt—including its writing.

Accordingly, educated Europeans of the Renaissance developed a fascination with hieroglyphs—which they naturally interpreted by means of the Greco-Roman youthful-cobra theory. Around 1500, for instance, Aldus Manutius, a famous printer in Venice who had dedicated his life to publishing the literature of ancient Greece, adopted as his trademark a picture of a dolphin twisted round an anchor that he

ERASMI ROTERODAMI ADAGIORVM
CHILIADES TRES, AC CENTV-
RIAE FERE TOTIDEM.

ALD·STVDIOSIS·S·

Quis nihil aliud cupio, q̃ prodesse uobis Studiosi. Cum ueniffet in manus meas Erasmi Roterodami, hominis undecunq̃ doctiss. hoc adagiorũ opus eruditum. uarium. plenũ bonæ frugis,
& quod possit uel cum ipsa antiquitate certare, intermissis antiquis autorib. quos pa-
raueram excudendos, illud curauimus imprimendum, rati profuturum uobis
& multitudine ipsa adagiorũ, quæ ex plurimis autorib. tam latinis, quàm
græcis studiose collegit summis certe laborib. summis uigiliis, &
multis locis apud utriusq̃ linguæ autores obiter uel correctis
acute, uel expositis erudite. Docet præterea quot modis
ex hisce adagiis capere utilitatem liceat, puta quẽ-
admodum ad uarios usus accõmodari pos-
sint. Adde, qd̃ circiter decẽ millia uer-
suum ex Homero· Euripide, & cæ
teris Græcis eodẽ metro in
hoc opere fideliter, &
docte tralata ha
bẽtur, præ
ter plu
rima
ex Pla-
tone, De-
mosthene, & id
genus ali
is. An
autem uerus sim,
ἰδοὺ ῥόδος, ἰδοὺ καὶ τὸ πήδημα·
Nam, quod dicitur, αὐτὸς αὐτὸν αὐλῖ·

AL   DVS

Præponitur hisce adagiis duplex index. Alter secundùm literas
alphabeti nostri·nam quæ græca sunt, latinã quoq̃
habentur. Alter per capita rerum.

2. A RENAISSANCE "HIEROGLYPH" The dolphin-and-anchor emblem of the scholar-printer Aldus Manutius, on the title page of the *Adages*, a collection of Greek and Roman proverbs by Erasmus of Rotterdam, which Aldus published in 1507. Aldus had seen the emblem on a Roman coin, and believed it to be a reproduction of an Egyptian hieroglyph: the dolphin depicted the idea of "speed," the anchor that of "steadiness," and together they were a visual form of the saying, "Make haste slowly."

had seen on a Roman coin. The combination of the speedy dolphin with the steadying anchor appealed to him, as a man who was always in a hurry to print the next Greek classic, but must also take his time to make sure that every book met high scholarly standards. Surely the dolphin and anchor must be a hieroglyph, depicting in visual form his favorite Greco-Roman proverb, "Make haste slowly." Aldus's friend Erasmus of Rotterdam, the latest in the line of universal scholars and international cultural leaders, confirmed this "decipherment."[*] After all, did not Plutarch and many other ancient writers, including the native Egyptian Horapollo, state clearly that this was how Egyptian writing worked?

In the three centuries that followed the Renaissance, the predatory and competitive Europeans rose to dominate, not just a region of the world, like every superpower civilization before them, but the entire planet. Like their superpower predecessors, the Europeans brought their ways to the local civilizations they encountered—guns and printing presses, science and Christianity—thereby altering and sometimes destroying the civilizations they encountered.[†] Likewise, they adopted and repackaged items from other civilizations that met their needs—tobacco and chocolate from the New World, styles of art and design from China. In addition, the fashion grew up among wealthy Europeans of acquiring a new kind of "curiosity," or exotic collectable: art objects from the temples, monuments, and tombs of Egypt.

To this encounter with other civilizations, the Europeans also brought a unique feature of their own civilization, derived partly from the Renaissance recovery of the literature and art of Greece and Rome, and partly from the contemporary explosion of scientific knowledge—a passion for exact information, going beyond what they could immediately repackage and use. Of course, it was only a minority of scholars who felt this passion. But the European rulers were Ptolemies in their turn, competing for cultural leadership as well as military power, and they therefore felt bound to help the scholars satisfy their passion. They, too, founded libraries—not just one or two, but dozens of them, as well as museums, learned societies, and many other institutions devoted to the pursuit of knowledge. Along with the institutions, there

---

[*]On Erasmus and Aldus, see Case Study 12, in Volume 4 of this series, "Library without Walls: A Humanist Classic Gets into Print."

[†]On the European destruction of a local civilization, see Case Study 13, in Volume 4 of this series, "Garcilaso de la Vega: Spanish Gentleman and Inca Prince."

grew up a whole class of systematic pursuers of knowledge, many of them full-time professionals—the savants.

As the Europeans spread throughout the world, the savants gained ever more detailed knowledge of non-European civilizations—including their languages and writing systems. Jesuit fathers arrived in Beijing and immersed themselves in the life of China, hoping to convert the emperor and his court; the savants learned of the Chinese characters, a living example of nonalphabetic writing. Italian travelers, wandering out of mere curiosity through the lands under Ottoman rule, came upon the Christian minority in Egypt and the ancient language of their services; the savants studied the vocabulary and grammar of that language, and began to suspect that it might be the same as that spoken by the pharaohs.

In addition, the savants began to study the hieroglyphs attentively, but here, the results were not so encouraging. Egypt's Greco-Roman and Renaissance reputation as the land of ultimate wisdom, and that of the hieroglyphs as visual forms of this wisdom, lasted through the seventeenth century. But eighteenth-century savants, though not disputing the belief that the hieroglyphs depicted ideas, were more sober than their predecessors: they did not see how one could prove, simply by looking at a hieroglyph and with no other evidence to go on, what idea it depicted.

True, there were a few things that could be learned or surmised about the hieroglyphs. By following repetitive sequences of hieroglyphs from one line of text to the next, eighteenth-century savants were able to figure out that the signs were usually to be read from right to left, with individual hieroglyphs facing to the right, but that sometimes the direction of writing was the other way round—with the signs also about-facing—or vertically from top to bottom (p. 160). And then there were the curious stretched-out circles that surrounded certain groups of hieroglyphs (p. 159). These looked vaguely like the "cartouches" or carved surrounds that enclosed the coats of arms of popes on public buildings in Rome. Accordingly, the savants called them by this name, and there were some who suspected that the Egyptian cartouches must also enclose something important, perhaps the names of gods or kings.

But there was no hard evidence to back this or any other theory, and as always when a situation seems hopeless, there were those who began to dream of finding a way out of it through a stroke of fortune. In another situation of this kind, fortune had, in fact, already struck. In the Middle East, inscriptions had been found in the Greek language and alphabet together with other, unknown alphabets. Late eighteenth-century savants were able to decipher these alphabets, and found that they depicted known languages, Aramaic and Persian. Supposing, one day, a carving should turn up that combined Egyptian writing with a language and alphabet that were already understood . . . As the eighteenth century neared its end, there were savants who sighed in print for a "key to the hieroglyphs."

In 1798, in accordance with the predatory and competitive spirit of the new masters of the world, General Napoleon Bonaparte invaded Egypt, intending to turn it from a province of the declining Ottoman Empire into a satellite country of France, and thereby to disrupt the worldwide power of France's deathly rival, Britain. In accordance with the Ptolemaic ambition of European power wielders for cultural leadership through the pursuit of knowledge, Bonaparte took with him a delegation of savants, one of whose assignments was to study systematically the temples, monuments, and tombs of the Nile.

Evidently, even junior officers of the Army of Egypt were sensitized to this particular ambition of their commander in chief. Otherwise, when Lieutenant Pierre-François-Xaver Bouchard, in command of a working party rebuilding the fortress of Rosetta against Turkish attack, came upon a much-damaged black stone slab carved in three writings, he would no doubt have used it to face a wall or roof a cannon hole, instead of keeping the stone as he did, and swiftly reporting the remarkable find to his superior officers.

6
THE SAVANTS AND THE STONE

For two years, the black stone slab stayed in the possession of its French discoverers, while the Army of Egypt held out against Turkish armies and the British fleet. Finally, cut off from reinforcements, abandoned by their commander who had gone home to make himself ruler of France, and defeated by an army newly arrived from Britain itself, the French were forced to surrender. As part of the terms, the British insisted that they yield what had already become a famous trophy, under its new name of the "Rosetta Stone." Eventually, the stone was handed over to London's latter-day counterpart of Alexandria's library and Cairo's House of Wisdom, the British Museum. There it has stayed ever since, its showcase bearing the proud words: "Captured in Egypt by the British Army, 1801."

Even while the French and British contended in Egypt, however, copies of the decree of the priests began to multiply once again—this time, not carved in stone to be displayed in temple forecourts, but printed on paper, to be pored over in libraries and studies. As time went on, masses of other Egyptian documents also appeared in print. Once safely back in France, Bonaparte's savants published their researches into the temples, monuments, and tombs of the Nile in a lavishly produced *Description of Egypt* (1809–28). The multivolume work was full of accurate reproductions, not only of hieroglyphic carvings but also of manuscripts recovered from tombs, bearing sacred texts intended to help the tomb dwellers cope with the ordeals of the afterlife: some of these were written in hieroglyphs, and others in the hieratic script (p. 167). Many originals also arrived in Europe. Egypt's new Muslim ruler, Muhammad Ali, wanted European help so as to turn his ancient land into a modern independent nation. A cheap way to buy this help, he found, was to allow foreign travelers, diplomats, and professional dealers to ship out obelisks and statues, manuscripts and mummies by the ton.

In this way, the words of the decree, so carefully chosen to serve the religious and political purposes of Greek officials and Egyptian priests, now became raw material for the code-breaking efforts of European savants. As usual with the savants, their efforts were both cooperative and competitive, the competition being not only among individuals but also

among the nations to which they belonged. And as so often with notable feats of intellectual discovery, this one was a story of diligent research that found out significant new facts but forced them into a
traditional pattern of ideas; of the old pattern bending and cracking under the strain; and of insight and inspiration that finally broke the pattern, rebuilt it to fit the facts, and thereby achieved understanding.

In their efforts to make sense of the Rosetta Stone, the early would-
be decipherers began with two assumptions about how Egyptian writing worked. The first and most basic of these was that the youthful-
cobra theory of the hieroglyphs, confirmed by the consensus of so many
Greek and Roman writers, as well as the native Egyptian Horapollo,
must be correct. The consensus on this point was proclaimed yet again,
in updated form, by the very first savant to come to grips with the stone,
Antoine Silvestre de Sacy, a Parisian professor and internationally
renowned authority on oriental languages. "The hieroglyphs," said
Sacy in 1802, "being depictions of ideas and not of sounds, belong to no
spoken language."

The second assumption of the savants concerned the demotic writing, and seemed to follow logically from the first. The "Egyptian" or
"intermediate" text of the Rosetta Stone, as they originally called it,
must be written in an alphabet, reproducing every atom of sound, consonant and vowel, just like the alphabet of the Greeks. For had not
Plutarch said that the Egyptians used "twenty-five letters"? And since it
was absolutely certain that the hieroglyphs were "depictions of ideas
and not of sounds," what else could he have meant by "letters," if not
demotic ones? These demotic "letters," then, unlike the hieroglyphs,
must belong to a spoken language—and that language must surely be
Coptic or something like it.

Besides trusting in these assumptions, the savants were also sure they
knew how to go about the actual business of decipherment. They would
use a three-step code-breaking procedure that had already worked well
with Greek-Aramaic and Greek-Persian inscriptions. There seemed no
reason why it should not also work here.

In this belief, the savants were right. The procedure did indeed finally lead on to decipherment—once it was operated on the basis of
correct ideas about how Egyptian writing worked. Even when operated
on the basis of incorrect ideas, it could still guide the savants some way
into the maze of Egyptian writing; but sooner or later it must bring
them up against dead ends.

Step one of the procedure was to match up the Egyptian texts on the stone with the Greek text through which it was hoped to understand them, so as to be able to tell which hieroglyphic and demotic signs, or groups of signs, stood for which Greek words. The way to do this was to begin with the Greek, study it carefully to find a word that was often repeated, and note how far along in the text it appeared each time. Then it would be necessary to go to one or other of the Egyptian texts, and study it even more carefully to find a sign or group of signs that was repeated more or less the same number of times and the same distances along. Once found, the Egyptian sign or group must mean the same thing as the Greek word. In addition, just this one word would serve as a vital initial "landmark." It would enable the Greek and Egyptian texts to be matched up at different points along their lengths, thereby making it easier to find more landmark words and the Egyptian signs that depicted them.

That, at least, was the way step one was supposed to work. But in the case of the hieroglyphic text, the chances of being able to carry it out did not look good, for the broken-off end of the stone had taken with it no less than two-thirds of the "sacred characters" (illustration, p. 119). True, the initial landmark word did seem to be staring the savants in the face. It was a group of eight signs that was repeated several times, sometimes in its own short cartouche and sometimes at the right-hand end of a longer one, in which case it always had the same additional hieroglyphs trailing off to the left:

From the way the signs faced, it was clear that the hieroglyphs on the stone ran from right to left. Surely, then, this group must somehow stand for *Ptolemaios*, with or without *aiōnobios, ēgapēmenos hupo tou Phtha* (p. 173). But what good was this surmise, considering that the rest of the hieroglyphic text consisted of a collection of disconnected lines, with longer and shorter gaps in between, which it would be very hard to match accurately with the Greek text? Yet to make sense of the hieroglyphs, it seemed essential to carry out step one completely. The hieroglyphs, after all, were "depictions of ideas," and how could one know what idea each of them depicted, unless it was correctly matched with the equivalent Greek word?

Thus it seemed to the savants that they would get much quicker results if they concentrated on the demotic text which, like the Greek, had suffered much less damage than the hieroglyphs. Was there in the demotic text, too, an often repeated group, sometimes with and sometimes without an accompanying retinue of signs? Sacy found it in 1802, thereby providing the initial landmark word. Furthermore, in order to find the word at the right distances to match up with the Greek, he had to measure from right to left—a sure sign that the demotic writing, too, ran in that direction.

Already in the same year, however, the professional savant was outdistanced by an amateur, Johann Åkerblad, who had found time amid his duties as a Swedish diplomat to become a scholar of the Coptic tongue. Åkerblad was able to identify more than a dozen additional landmark words, most of them names of people and places, gods and goddesses—proper names, as they are called.

This was a very encouraging success, for it ought to make it possible to move straight on to step two of the decipherment procedure: to figure out what sounds were depicted by the signs that made up the proper names. This, the savants believed, could never be done with the hieroglyphs, "being depictions of ideas and not of sounds"; but it must be doable with the demotic "letters."

To carry out step two, the savants were relying on a general fact about the way languages work—that whatever the differences among them, proper names often sound more or less the same in all of them. Thus an English speaker, wishing to utter the name of the Greek king of Egypt, would say "Ptolemy"; a French speaker would say "Ptolémée"; but neither version was unrecognizably different from the Greek one. Surely the same must also have been true of the Egyptians—and in that case, the demotic signs that had been found to depict the king's name must also portray sounds that made up something not unlike *Ptolemaios*.

But—and this was the trick to getting at the sounds depicted by individual signs—many other proper names on the Rosetta Stone must also have sounded much the same in Egyptian as in Greek; and any of these names that happened to *share some of the same sounds* must also *share some demotic signs*. By comparing the signs in such names, therefore, it ought to be possible to tell which signs depicted which sounds.

Among the names that Åkerblad had located were three that appeared close to that of the king in the opening section of the decree which gave the Greek date: *Alexandros* (Alexander), *Arsinoë* (the name of a queen), and *Pyrrha* the torchbearer (p. 147). Most of the *sounds* of

Ptolemaios were to be found in these names. Did they also have *signs* in common, and did these come in the right places to fit the sounds?

It took a good deal of juggling to get them to fit. Åkerblad had to explain away the sign that always seemed to begin the name of Ptolemy, **⟩** , so as to match up the next sign, **↳** , with the **↳** that also began the name of Pyrrha (p. 167). He had to assume that the Egyptians could not tell the difference between the sounds *d* and *t*, so as to match the third-from-last sign of Alexander's name, **◁** , with the **◁** that came second in Ptolemy's (p. 168). Still, the results seemed convincing enough. The name of the king turned out to have seven signs in common with the others, and one gap: *P, t, l, o, -, e, o, s.* Åkerblad then filled in the gap, crossword-puzzle style, to make *Ptlomeos.* This was not much more different from *Ptolemaios* than "Ptolémée" or "Ptolemy"—and of course, it was also correct (p. 168).

Åkerblad had taken a long second step into the maze of Egyptian writing. Now, it seemed, was the time to move on to the third and decisive step. Armed with his "alphabet" of a dozen "letters" that he had gained from the Greek proper names, he would now venture into the ordinary run of demotic text. Using his letters, he must turn that text into words in the Coptic language that corresponded to those in the Greek.

It was here that Åkerblad suddenly came up against a dead end. True, in a few tantalizing cases he did actually take the third step. For instance, there was another landmark group of signs that seemed to crop up wherever the Greek text said "the kingdom," "the country," or "Egypt." Åkerblad had found all the individual signs in the proper names, and together in this group, they made *Chēme,* exactly the Coptic word for Egypt. But for the most part, what Åkerblad came up with was blank spaces and gibberish. There seemed to be so many more signs in the demotic "alphabet" than Åkerblad's dozen, or even Plutarch's twenty-five—an extraordinarily large number of signs, in fact, for an alphabet. Of course, that did not mean that Plutarch was wrong. No doubt, as Sacy surmised, the extra signs were "capital" and "lowercase" letters, run-together letters and abbreviations. But that did not make them any easier to figure out.

Discouraged by the failure of what seemed to be the only possible decipherment procedure, both Sacy and Åkerblad gave up their efforts. Neither of them forgot about the stone and the strange difficulty of making sense of it; indeed, in an article published in 1811, Sacy actually suggested that at least in a minor way, there might be something wrong with the assumptions on which the decipherment procedure had been operated. Could it be, he wondered, that the hieroglyphs did, in fact, sometimes depict sounds? That was certainly the case with a living non-European writing system that used idea-depicting characters, that of the Chinese.* When the Chinese had to write foreign names, which in their language were mere meaningless collections of sounds expressing no ideas, they temporarily converted some of their characters to depict these sounds. Would not the Egyptians have faced the same problem, and solved it in the same way? If that was so, it followed that the hieroglyphs inside the cartouches on the Rosetta Stone must somehow depict the sounds of *Ptolemaios*. This was only a vague guess, which Sacy himself never followed up, but it was also the first public mention of an idea that in the end would open the way to decipherment.

Meanwhile, however, there were more passageways to be explored in the maze of Egyptian writing, and more dead ends to be bumped up against. Most of this exploration and frustration fell to the lot of a British savant, Thomas Young. Having already built an international reputation as a scientist, and being brilliantly talented in many fields, Young turned his attention in 1811 to Egyptian writing, where he hoped to do something still more notable. The way to do it, he thought—since Sacy and Åkerblad had clearly run out of luck with steps two and three—was to go back to step one, the matching up of the three texts on the Rosetta Stone, and complete it properly. Besides, accurate reproductions of many hieroglyphic and hieratic texts were now beginning to appear in the *Description of Egypt*. Surely, word-for-word matchups of the stone and careful study of other documents would provide enough leads to get around whatever barrier it was that had blocked the progress of the French and Swedish savants.

Young did indeed push a long way further into the maze. In spite of all difficulties, he matched up each broken-off line of hieroglyphs to its corresponding section of Greek text, and was even able to match many Egyptian signs and groups to the exact Greek words they stood for. He carefully studied other hieroglyphic documents, and was occasionally able to make ingenious guesses about the meaning of individual signs. He read over all the ancient writers who claimed to know the meaning of hieroglyphs, and compared their explanations with Egyptian texts. From all these sources, he eventually worked out the correct idea-depicting meaning of about a hundred hieroglyphs.

---

*In fact, Chinese writing, like Egyptian, depicts both ideas and sounds. All the same, Sacy was right about the Chinese method of writing foreign proper names.

In addition, Young noticed an important fact about the way in which the hieroglyphs worked. He found it in manuscripts from tombs, which he could not understand but which often evidently bore the same texts. (In fact, these were standard rituals and spells for the use of the dead.) Poring over identical runs of signs in several different manuscripts, he saw that from time to time there would be a variation: some manuscripts would use one sign, and some would use another. Could it be that the texts were saying different things at these points? But in that case, why did the same pairs of signs always replace each other, and never any additional signs? Another explanation seemed much more likely: that in each pair of hieroglyphs, the two signs were alternatives, meaning the same thing (pp. 160-61).

But Young also pored intently over the demotic text of the Rosetta Stone so as to match it word for word with the Greek, and it was here that he came across an even more surprising fact. It lurked, among other places, in the title of the king (pp. 164, 168). The very first part of the hieroglyphic title, , seemed to match up with *aiōnobios*, and, accordingly, Young identified it as depicting the idea of "Immortality." But did not the group that began the title in the demotic version, and which also matched up with *aiōnobios*, , look startlingly similar? Just by comparing the demotic and hieroglyphic texts on the Rosetta Stone, Young found more than half a dozen such resemblances between signs in the two writings that seemed to match up with the same Greek word.

Then Young began looking at reproductions in the *Description of Egypt* of manuscripts in the hieratic writing. He very soon saw that there were very many hieratic signs that resembled hieroglyphs; and that these hieratic signs very often also resembled demotic ones that did not themselves look like hieroglyphs at all. The hieratic signs were, in fact, a kind of "missing link" between signs in the other two scripts (p. 167).

Young used this fact to push a little further through the maze, by trying to identify sound-depicting hieroglyphs in the one kind of place where, like Sacy, he thought they might be found: non-Egyptian names. So far it had been impossible to check this idea, because nearly all the foreign names in the hieroglyphic text of the Rosetta Stone had been lost with the broken-off end; thus, with the hieroglyphs, there was no way of using the method of comparing names and filling in the gaps. But if demotic signs could be traced to hieroglyphs and vice versa, this offered a way to work out the meaning of both. Sure enough, in the cartouche of Ptolemy, and another that Young had guessed must contain a name common among Ptolemaic queens, Berenice, Young was able to work out the sound-depicting meaning of five signs. Among them were signs number 215 in his published list of hieroglyphs, ▮ , and number 217, ▲ . "The square block and the semicircle," he explained, "answer in all the [hieratic] manuscripts to the P and T of Åkerblad, which are found at the beginning of the enchorial [i.e., demotic] name." In this way, thanks to Young's efforts, the two signs that began the name of the king (pp. 160–61, 167–68) were among the first whose sound-depicting meaning was rescued from the oblivion of the centuries.

Even so, Young in his turn found the passageways closing in and his progress blocked. In spite of all his correct individual hieroglyphs, he had no idea how they combined to form sentences or reproduce speech; owing to inaccurate matchups or incorrect guesses, his explanations of another hundred hieroglyphs were wrong; and for both these reasons, he could not make sense of any Egyptian document other than the Rosetta Stone, where he had the guidance of the Greek.

As for the sound-depicting hieroglyphs, Young himself did not believe that they could lead him through the maze. He was not even sure that they really existed, and when he published them, it was under the tentative heading "Sounds?" If they did exist, he did not believe that they must all be "letters," reproducing individual atoms of sound: besides his five correct ones, there were others that he wrongly guessed to depict whole syllables, or in one case—the *ole* of *Ptolemaios*—two syllables. And besides, the consensus said that there was no chance of the sound-depicting hieroglyphs being used for native Egyptian words— of signs 215 and 217, for instance, depicting *p* and *t* not only in the foreign name of the king, but also when they reappeared among the hieroglyphs trailing off to the left in the long cartouches, as part of a

group, ⯑ , that must depict an Egyptian word in his title (p. 165).

But the most discouraging dead end of all, Young believed, was the fact that the demotic and hieroglyphic scripts were so basically alike. This could only mean that the two scripts did not work differently, as the consensus proclaimed. Instead, they must be different versions of one and the same writing system. This, Young believed, was

very bad news. For was it not certain beyond all doubt that the hieroglyphs themselves, in normal usage, were "depictions of ideas and not
of sounds"? And did it not follow that this must also be true of the demotic writing, with Åkerblad's proven "letters" being a mere exceptional use of idea-depicting signs to depict the sounds of foreign
names? Who was to say, even, that the demotic script depicted such
sounds only by means of "letters"? When Young reproduced Åkerblad's
"letters" in print, it was also under a doubtful heading: "Supposed Enchorial Alphabet." No wonder Åkerblad had been unable to turn the
normal run of demotic text into Coptic words, except in a few cases
that must be flukes. The thing could not be done, for the demotic
signs, like the hieroglyphs, "belonged to no spoken language."

In this way, under the influence of new facts, Young revised the
consensus so far as the demotic writing was concerned, but clung all
the more fiercely to its basic assumption regarding the hieroglyphs.
The consensus was bending and cracking, but it had not broken. In
fact, in its bent and cracked form the consensus now said that there
was no hope of moving to the critical step three of the decipherment procedure with any of the scripts. In 1819, Young published a
lengthy article summarizing the results of his work, in which he
made clear his belief that his partial and tentative interpretations
were about all that would ever be known of Egyptian writing. As for
the Rosetta Stone, he said, "The only monument that has afforded
us any real foundations for reasoning on this subject, is more calculated to repress than to encourage our hopes of ever becoming complete masters of the literature of Egypt." After nearly twenty years
of wandering in the maze of Egyptian writing, it seemed that Sacy,
Åkerblad, and Young had come to a barrier that would never be
passed.

There was, however, another wanderer in the maze, who was also
running from dead end to dead end, but would shortly find a way
through the seemingly impassable barrier: the youthful French savant
Jean-François Champollion.

7
"I'VE GOT TO THE BOTTOM OF IT!"

For Sacy, Åkerblad, and Young, Egyptian writing was one among many scholarly and scientific interests; for Champollion, on the other hand, it was a lifelong obsession. He had an extraordinary gift for languages, studying Hebrew, Arabic, and other Semitic tongues before he was even in his teens; as a schoolboy botanist, he developed a taste for arranging and classifying the plants he found, comparing and drawing the complex details of their shapes; and it seems to have been through reading the reports of Bonaparte's savants, as well as meeting by chance with some of them personally, that he began to focus his talents on one overriding goal. Already as a high-school student in the southern French town of Grenoble, he was known for his habit of carving hieroglyphs into the classroom furniture; and in 1806, at the age of fifteen, he solemnly announced to no less a personage than the mayor, "I wish to devote my life to the knowledge of ancient Egypt."

Even so, Champollion was for many years simply one of the field in the competition to decipher the hieroglyphs. Partly this was because of practical and career problems that got in the way of his work as a savant. He was open in his dislike of kings and priests, and, after 1815, when Bonaparte's fall ended the era of the French Revolution, kings and priests had the upper hand in France; as a result, he had a tendency to lose jobs. Even when he did work, as a professor or librarian, it was in Grenoble, 500 miles from Paris. In an age when the horse was still the fastest means of moving people and information, it was hard for him to keep in touch with other savants, or even to get reliable copies of the Rosetta Stone.

But the real reason that Champollion did not announce any breakthroughs that would have put him in the lead as a decipherer was that he felt he had no breakthroughs to report. He did, in fact, make considerable progress, on the same lines as other savants and often ahead of them. In 1810, a year before Sacy, he surmised that the Egyptians must have used sound-depicting hieroglyphs to portray foreign names. He knew of the resemblances among the scripts at the latest by 1813, two years ahead of Young, and went on to study and compare them

3. JEAN-FRANÇOIS CHAMPOLLION Portrait by Léon Cogniet, dating from 1824, two years after the decipherer made his breakthrough.

more thoroughly than the British savant. By 1818, he had his own word-for-word matchups of the Rosetta Stone, and he knew that the Egyptians often used different signs to mean the same thing. In understanding of the all-important Coptic language, moreover, he excelled every other would-be decipherer.

Yet all this knowledge remained in Champollion's notebooks, because it seemed to him to be going nowhere: it was not leading him to

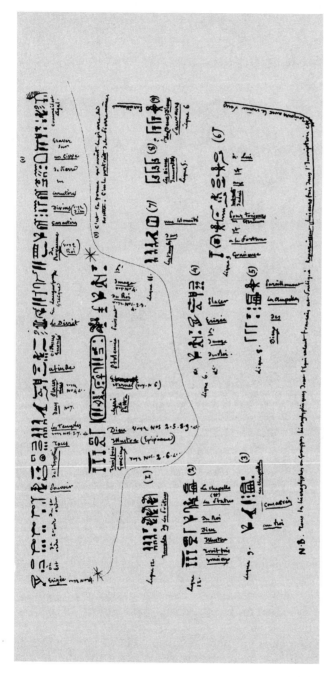

4. CHAMPOLLION AT WORK   On this notebook page dating from 1818, Champollion has copied out the last line of hieroglyphs from the Rosetta Stone, with parts of other lines where some of the signs also appear—the "Forever" group in the cartouche, for instance, reappears in the line of hieroglyphs at bottom right. Underneath each sign or group, Champollion has written what he believes to be its French meaning, evidently from having matched up the hieroglyphic and Greek texts. But he is also trying to move from *what* the hieroglyphs mean to *how* they mean it. At top right, he has written a "(1)" above a sign that means "un cippe" (a slab), and his note (1), just underneath, says: "This was the shape of the Rosetta Stone. It's a *portrait* of the stone itself."

any overall explanation of how Egyptian writing worked. This was not because he could not think of any such explanation. On the contrary, he was constantly thinking of them—each usually contradicting the one before it. In lectures to local societies of savants and would-be savants in Grenoble, or in private letters to his best friend, lifelong mentor, and elder brother Jacques-Joseph, he would regularly announce the latest version of the real truth about Egyptian writing. All the scripts worked in the same way, he would declare—or two of them worked in the same way, while the third was completely different; every last hieroglyph depicted a sound, whether a single atom or a whole syllable—or the hieroglyphs were idea-depicting without exception, down even to those that portrayed the name of Ptolemy. By 1821, he had come around to much the same view as Young's, that the scripts were all basically idea depicting, except when portraying foreign names. But for him, unlike Young, this was simply the latest in a very changeable succession of ideas.

These constant changes of opinion were not mere flightiness. They were the behavior of an impulsive and strong-willed person, confronted with something he could not make up his mind about. Behind Champollion's regular contradictory proclamations of the real truth about Egyptian writing lay a tormenting but fruitful uncertainty. Alone among the savants, Champollion knew, at the bottom of his heart, that he did not know the truth about Egyptian writing. That, of course, was why, alone among the savants, it was he who found it out.

Champollion's final journey from uncertainty to truth began late in the summer of 1821, in the wake of a major upheaval in his life. There had recently been an uprising in Grenoble against the monarchy that at that time ruled France. The uprising had come to nothing, and Champollion was reported to have been involved in it. He had denied everything—truthfully, it seems—but he was, after all, a well-known troublemaker, and the local forces of order were making life more difficult for him than ever. Consequently, it seemed best to leave town for a while. Jacques-Joseph, himself a rising savant who worked in a renowned Parisian knowledge-pursuing institution, the Academy of Inscriptions and Literature, had a good-sized apartment, and in the attic above was a vacant artist's studio that would do very well as a workroom. True, there was no job to go with the accommodation, but perhaps Jacques-Joseph was generous, and in any case Champollion's wife had a dowry. Providence had taken extraordinary care of the would-be decipherer. Thanks to the failed revolutionary uprising, he found himself comfortably settled in the capital, with plenty of time to work, and within easy reach of books and savants—as well as of originals and reproductions of newly discovered Egyptian documents.

It was one such document that first led Champollion in the direction of the truth about Egyptian writing. About the time that he arrived in Paris, the royal collection of "curiosities" had acquired an Egyptian manuscript unlike any other that had so far come to light. This was no hieroglyphic or hieratic text for the use of tomb dwellers, but a legal contract between Egyptians and Greeks, drawn up in the demotic writing—the first example of that script to arrive in Europe since the Rosetta Stone itself. Moreover, in accordance with the policies of the Ptolemies in dealing with the two nations they had ruled over, the contract came with a summary in Greek, giving the names of the parties, as well as of the rulers, and the priests of deceased rulers, under whom the contract had been made. Somewhere in the "native" text, then, must be Greek proper names that could confirm the Egyptian practice of writing such names with demotic "letters."

Sure enough, Champollion was able to find the names. There, among others, was *Ptlomeos*, written exactly as on the Rosetta Stone. There, too, written with the same "letters," was a name that the mother, sister-wife, and daughter of this particular *Ptlomeos* all shared: *Kloptr*, or Cleopatra.

This was welcome confirmation of what Young had begun to doubt, but it also set Champollion's thoughts moving in a direction that no savant had taken before. In a report on his results, published the following year in the form of an open letter to the secretary of the Academy of Inscriptions, he described where his thoughts led him. The demotic writing, he knew, was closely related to the hieratic, and the hieratic to the hieroglyphic. "Once the use of these phonetic characters had been established in the *demotic* writing, I must naturally conclude that . . . the purely *hieroglyphic* writing must also have a certain number of signs endowed with the ability to express sounds—in a word, that there must equally well exist a series of *phonetic hieroglyphs*" that must work exactly like the demotic "letters." And to test this hypothesis, it would only be necessary to be in a position to apply the tried and true method of comparing names and filling in the gaps—"to have before one, written in pure hieroglyphs, two proper names of Greek rulers that were known in advance, and which contained several letters used at the same time in the one and the other, such as *Ptolemy* and *Cleopatra*. . . ."

At the time that Champollion saw the demotic manuscript, he probably knew that a hieroglyphic document had already been discovered, which bore those names. It was a red granite obelisk—one of a pair that had been found in the ruins of the temple of Isis at Philae—which had recently been shipped to England. Among the hieroglyphs on the obelisk were cartouches with the names of Ptolemy and another, unknown ruler. The base of the monument had been left behind, but was said to have been carved with an inscription recording the generosity, regarding requisitions of supplies by government officials, of a Ptolemy and two Cleopatras.* It stood to reason, therefore, that the unknown name was Cleopatra. Young, who had seen a reproduction of the obelisk, certainly thought so, but attached no great importance to the fact. For Champollion, on the other hand, a whole new hypothesis would stand or fall by how the name was depicted, and he passed several anxious months until finally, in January 1822, the reproduction arrived in Paris.

What Champollion saw, as redrawn by himself in later published diagrams, looked like this:

---

*The hieroglyphs, however, mentioned only one of these Cleopatras. See pp. 186–87.

The cartouche on the left, though it was missing the last two signs in the Rosetta Stone cartouches, seemed to say "Ptolemy Living Forever, Beloved of Ptah"—running from top to bottom, this time, so as to fit the slender proportions of the obelisk, though with hieroglyphs on the same level still reading from right to left. In the cartouche on the right, there were a semicircle and an egglike sign at the bottom that often appeared elsewhere, at the end of names standing next to depictions of goddesses. Young had already suggested that they somehow depicted the idea of "female." But what about the other signs? One by one, Champollion compared them with those in the name of Ptolemy.

The first sign of the name of Cleopatra, which depicts a kind of *quarter-circle* and ought to represent *k*, should not be found in the name of Ptolemy; and in fact it is not.

The second, a *lion in repose*, which must represent the *l*, is exactly similar to the fourth sign of the name of Ptolemy, which is also an *l (Ptol)*.

The third character of the name of Cleopatra is a *feather* or *leaf*, which should stand for the short vowel *e*; two similar leaves are also to be seen at the end of the name of Ptolemy, which in view of their position, can only have the value of the diphthong [i.e., double vowel] *ai* in *aios*. . . .

The fifth sign of the name of Cleopatra, which has the form of a rectangle and must represent the *p*, is also the first sign of the hieroglyphic name of Ptolemy. . . .

The seventh character is an *open hand*, representing the *t*; but this hand is not to be found in the word Ptolemy, where the second letter, the *t*, is expressed by a semicircle, which nevertheless is also a *t*, for . . . these two hieroglyphic signs are *homophones* [i.e., they depict the same sound].

In this way, Champollion found that the names in the cartouches had hieroglyphs in common that came in the right places to make *P-lo-ai-* and *-leop----*; he applied his knowledge of the fact that two hieroglyphs could mean the same thing (pp. 160–61), so as to add another letter and make *Ptol-ai-* and *-leop-t--*; and then he filled in the gaps so as to end up with one name that was not too different from the Greek, and another that was exactly the same: *Ptolmais* and *Kleopatra*.

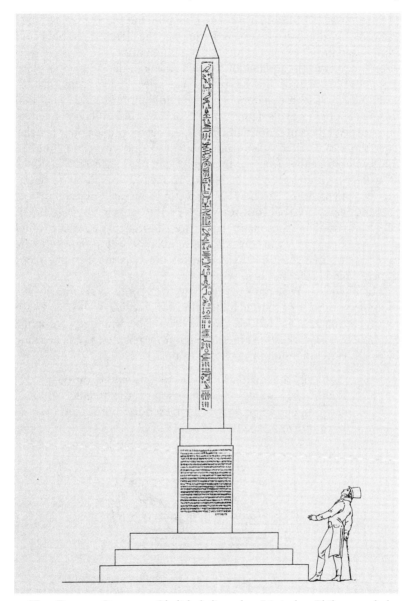

5. THE BANKES OBELISK Obelisk dedicated to Isis in her Philae temple by Ptolemy VII and his niece-wife Cleopatra about 120 B.C., and shipped to England by the traveler and collector William Bankes in A.D. 1821. This is Bankes's own drawing of the obelisk, its base with a Greek carving, and an admiring savant to give the scale, as seen by Champollion early in 1822.

The method of comparing and filling in the gaps, then, seemed to work for the hieroglyphs as it did for the demotic writing; and from his knowledge of Coptic, Champollion was even able to produce a convincing explanation, which was not far from the truth (pp. 160-61), of how the Egyptians had selected idea-depicting hieroglyphs for use in depicting sounds. The lion must have been used to depict *l* because the Coptic for "lion" was *laboi.* The semicircle must depict *t* because, normally, it helped depict the idea of "female" as at the end of Cleopatra's name; and the Coptic word for "the" in the feminine gender (that is, the equivalent of French or Spanish *la* as against *le* or *el)* was *ti* or *te.* Thus, "to form . . . a phonetic script, the Egyptians took hieroglyphs depicting physical objects or expressing ideas . . . the word for which in the spoken language began with the vowel or consonant that it was desired to represent." And since, in Egyptian as in any language, many words began with the same sound, that must be the reason for the homophones: the Coptic for "hand," for instance, was *tot.*

But of course, Ptolemy and Cleopatra were only a preliminary test of the hypothesis of a hieroglyphic "alphabet," which itself would have to be tested; and the test of the test would be whether or not the "alphabet" also worked for other foreign proper names. It was not long before Champollion found a suitable name.

> Among the cartouches collected from the various buildings of Karnak near Thebes [i.e., the temple of Amen-Ra], and published in the Description of Egypt, I noticed one in particular:*

> [It is] composed of signs that are for the most part known from the preceding analysis [of Ptolemy and Cleopatra], and which appear in the following order: the *falcon, a;* the

---

*In the original, the cartouche is shown on a separate illustration page.

lion in repose, l; a *large vase with a handle,* unknown; the *line with a curve, s;* the *single feather, e* or any other short vowel; the sign commonly called the *water sign,* unknown; the *open hand, t;* the *mouth seen from in front, r;* two *horizontal opposed scepters,* also unknown. Putting these letters together, they give us *Al-se-tr-;* and by giving the vase with the handle the value of *k,* the water hieroglyph the value of *n,* and the final sign the value of *s,* we have the word *Alksentrs,* which is written in the same way, letter for letter, in the Rosetta inscription [i.e., the demotic version] and the papyrus in the king's collection, for the Greek name *Alexandros.*

As Champollion looked further through the *Description of Egypt* and copies of Roman obelisks reerected by the popes, other names began to catch his eye, with which his "alphabet" seemed to work. By now, however, he was no longer testing his results, but applying them to get new and certain knowledge. Besides *Alksentrs, Ptolmais,* and *Kleopatra,* there was also *Brnike* (Berenice—in Greek, *Berenikē*). There were *Autokrtr* (*Autokratōr,* the Greek for "emperor"; *Autokrtr Kaisrs* (Emperor Caesar—in Greek, *Kaisaros); Autokrtr Tbris Kaisrs* (Emperor Tiberius Caesar); *Autokrtr Kaisrs Tomitens Sbsts* (Emperor Caesar Domitian Augustus—in Greek, *Domitianos Sebastos).* One by one, the Greek and Roman rulers of Egypt passed before his eyes, and as they did so, he found this strange "alphabet" of beasts and birds, pots and scepters, geometrical shapes and disembodied human limbs ever increasing in number and variety, to depict the different sounds of their names.

In September 1822, in advance of publication of his written report, Champollion presented his results at a meeting of the Academy of Inscriptions, at which the audience included a delighted Sacy and a not so delighted Young. (Åkerblad, whose achievement had made Champollion's possible, was already dead.) For the record, Champollion described his discovery as that of a "phonetic writing, . . . used . . . to transcribe (admittedly in a crude fashion) the proper names of foreign peoples, countries, cities, rulers, and other individuals, in the course of ideographically written texts." But in fact, over the year in which he had deciphered the hieroglyphic writing of foreign names, Champollion had also been undergoing his last and most dramatic change of mind about Egyptian writing as a whole.

The change of mind had probably been under way even before Champollion saw the cartouche of Cleopatra. The first sign of it had come in December 1821, when all of a sudden he had the inspiration to do something that today would be the very first step of a decipherer looking at an unknown script. From his matchups of the Rosetta Stone, Champollion was fairly sure which broken-off lines of hieroglyphs corresponded to which runs of words in the Greek version. Why not count up the number of hieroglyphs, as against the number of Greek words? The answer turned out to be that it took 1,419 hieroglyphs, of 61 different kinds, to express the ideas represented by 486 Greek words. If the hieroglyphs were in fact "depictions of ideas," how come it took 1,419 of them to depict 486 ideas?

In fact, the consensus had an answer to this question. Earlier savants had already noted that there seemed to be less than a thousand different kinds of hieroglyphs altogether, although it stood to reason that the Egyptians must have had many more than a thousand different ideas that they wanted to express. Therefore, the consensus said, individual hieroglyphs depicted only basic ideas, and to depict more complicated ones, the Egyptians simply combined them. Champollion's count certainly did not prove the consensus wrong. All the same, he was very much impressed with the result. Evidently, a hunch was already building in his mind, which also fitted in with his figures: that what the hieroglyphs really combined was not ideas alone, but ideas and sounds.

Then, as Champollion began building up his hieroglyphic "alphabet," he noticed something else. The sound-depicting hieroglyphs that he was now finding in the names of Greek and Roman rulers were already very familiar to him. He had seen them over and over again, in countless carvings and manuscripts, as part of the normal run of Egyptian text—in fact, he estimated that they amounted to no less than two-thirds of the signs used in any native Egyptian document. It seemed very strange that the same signs should be constantly turning up in both Greco-Roman proper names and what must be ordinary Egyptian words, as "depictions of sounds" in the one case yet as "depictions of ideas" in the other.

There was also another, even more curious fact. It involved the pairs of alternative signs in manuscripts from tombs that had revealed to both Young and Champollion that Egyptian writing could use different signs to mean the same thing. Already, based on his knowledge of this fact, Champollion had guessed that the semicircle in *Ptolmais* and the open hand in *Kleopatra* must both depict the sound *t*. But then, with *Alksentrs*, he came upon something truly surprising. Here again, he guessed that two signs—the "line with a curve" in the middle of the name, and the "opposed scepters" at the end—must both depict the same sound, in this case *s*. But in fact, the two signs were already familiar to him as alternatives, for he had several times seen them replacing each other—according to the consensus, as depictions of ideas—in tomb manuscripts. And as he went on to decipher more and more names of Greek and Roman rulers, he found more and more pairs of alternative signs in the manuscripts also turning up as homophones in his "alphabet." Just how usual was it, Champollion wondered, for the same signs to appear as alternatives to each other, both in the names of Greek and Roman rulers and in the normal run of Egyptian text?

> I resolved . . . carefully to compare two hieroglyphic texts with the same content, and to observe and note down any variations of signs that might exist between the one and the other. . . . This comparison *produced a table that was nothing more or less than an actual copy, so to speak a duplicate, of my phonetic alphabet, formed from Greek and Roman proper names*; that is to say, the signs that constantly substitute for each other in the hieroglyphic texts are the very ones that our reading of Greek and Roman proper names has shown to be *homophones*, and which replace each other in the names because they express the same consonant or a similar vowel.

That was how Champollion reported on the comparison in his full account of his discoveries, the *Outline of the Hieroglyphic System of the Ancient Egyptians* (1824). He put the result in italics because in his view, this was a critical test of the consensus theory, and the theory had failed it. It made sense to him that the Egyptians should have used, for instance, both a picture of a hand and a semicircle to depict the sound *t*, given that their word for "hand" and their feminine "the " both began with that sound. But as ideas, "hand" and "female" were totally different—and the same must surely apply to all the other pairs of alternative signs. If these signs regularly replaced each other in native Egyptian texts just as they did in the names of Greek and Roman rulers, it could not possibly be because, in those texts, they depicted the same *ideas*. The only possibility left was that in native Egyptian texts just as in the names of Greek and Roman rulers, they depicted the same *sounds*. And since practically every sound in the names of the rulers was depicted by at least two alternative signs, it followed that every one of these signs must also depict sounds in native Egyptian texts.

It was a compelling deduction, which inevitably pointed Champollion in a new direction: that of looking for sound-depicting hieroglyphs not only in Greek and Roman proper names, but also in native Egyptian words. Exactly when Champollion began moving in this direction is not known, though he would surely have begun the search the instant he had reason to believe that it was likely to be worthwhile. What is certain is that among the places in which he looked was one where a Greek proper name and native Egyptian words stood conveniently side by side: "Ptolemy Living Forever, Beloved of Ptah."

Probably what attracted Champollion to the name and title of the king was the curious repetition, in both the Greek name and the Egyptian title, of the signs ▌ and ▲ (p. 165). In Ptolemy's name, as in those of many other Greek and Roman rulers, the signs obviously depicted the sounds *p* and *t*. But what about when they appeared farther along, together with a third sign, in the group 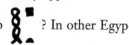 ? In other Egyptian words that Champollion was also looking into, the third sign seemed to depict a breathy *ḥ* sound that was used in Coptic. So the group as a whole, if it depicted sounds, must make *ptḥ*. Could that be a reasonable spelling of the name of the god of Memphis, which the Greeks wrote as *Phtha?*

At this point, Champollion bethought himself of a sentence from a fragment of a sermon by a Christian monk from southern Egypt, which he had seen in a scholarly collection of Coptic texts: "Mē Hēphaistos ete Ptaḥ pe?" "Where is Hephaestus, also called Ptah?" That fitted in perfectly. As he explained in his *Outline*, "The hieroglyphic name of the god . . . reads *Ptḥ*, *Ptaḥ* . . . ; it is letter for letter the Theban Coptic name *Ptaḥ*, . . . apart from the vowel in the middle, which is suppressed in accordance with the usual working of the hieroglyphic system of writing." In this way, by one of history's slow-moving ironies, Shenoute's mockery at the death of Ptah contributed fourteen centuries later to the rediscovery of the civilization that had believed in the god.

Here, at any rate, was the name of one of the greatest of Egyptian gods, written with sound-depicting hieroglyphs. But if this particular group of hieroglyphs meant "Ptah," then it followed that the final

group of hieroglyphs in the title, , must mean something else:
they must match up—out of order, so to speak—(p. 105) with the word
"Beloved." This group, too, included signs that appeared in the name
of the king: the two feathers, as Champollion thought of them, that depicted the *ai* of *Ptolmais*. In other cartouches containing the royal
title, Champollion had seen "the *plow* or *hoe*," , replaced by "the
pedestal," ; and he had seen the pedestal, inturn, regularly used,
in temple and obelisk carvings, to depict the *m* of *Tomitens*, or Domitian.
The hoe and the pedestal, then, were another example of homophones.
They both depicted *m*, and in combination with the feathers, they both
made *mai*—exactly the Coptic word for "to love." "Both these hieroglyphic groups are therefore entirely phonetic; they read . . . *pthmai* . . .
or *Ptahmai* . . . ; and they signify *dear to Phtha, beloved by Phtha, ēgapēmenos hupo tou Phtha*."

Champollion still did not understand how depicted "Living Forever" (pp. 163–64), but that did not matter. What counted was
that all of a sudden, with the title of the king and many other Egyptian
words and phrases, he found himself in a place where the consensus said
he never could be. He was in step three of the decipherment procedure,
using sound-depicting signs derived from Greek and Roman proper
names to form words that made sense in Coptic and corresponded to
the Greek— but he was doing all of this with the hieroglyphs. Surely he
must finally be on the right passageway through the maze.

But even now there was a frustrating dead end. In his report on his
"alphabet" to the secretary of the academy, Champollion explained
what it was that he now found himself up against. Besides the cartouches with names of Greek and Roman rulers from which he had
built up his "alphabet," there were, of course, countless cartouches with
what must be names of native Egyptian pharaohs. These, Champollion
said, "are characterized by their small number of signs, and resist, in
some of their constituent parts, every effort to apply with success the alphabet with which I have acquainted you." In other words, in the summer of 1822, Champollion had been making every effort to apply his
"alphabet" to these cartouches, and form their hieroglyphs into names

that looked like those of pharaohs of whom he knew from ancient authors who had listed the rulers of Egypt. But he had regularly failed, because within the cartouches, alongside hieroglyphs from his "alphabet," were others that he could not get to fit.

At least, Champollion had regularly failed until hardly a week before he signed and dated his report to the secretary of the academy; and since his latest results were so new and unconfirmed, for the moment he was keeping quiet about the fact that he had just discovered the truth about Egyptian writing.

Coming after so many years of bafflement, Champollion's final step out of the maze seems to have been surprisingly easy. From a letter that he wrote a few weeks later to Young, as well as from remarks of his here and there in the *Outline* and memories that were preserved by his brother, it is possible to reconstruct, more or less, how he took the step. So far as can be seen, he did not exactly break through the last barrier. Instead, many things that he already knew suddenly combined, in a single moment of insight, to show him how to slip past it.

It was on the morning of September 14, 1822, in the studio above Jacques-Joseph's apartment. Champollion had just taken delivery of a sheaf of copies of carvings from the famous temple of Abu Simbel, cut into a cliffside overlooking the Nile 700 miles from the sea. When he picked up the top sheet, he saw a name in a cartouche that was evidently that of a native Egyptian pharaoh, for it was "characterized by its small number of signs":

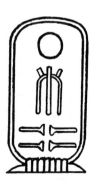

Like the other names of native pharaohs, this one, too, had some constituent parts that "resisted" Champollion's "alphabet"—above all,

its first sign, ◯ . But in this case, the sign was one that he already knew a great deal about. Both he and Young had seen it many times on the Rosetta Stone and elsewhere, in places where it seemed to depict either the "sun," or the associated idea of the sun god. And Champollion also knew the actual name of the sun god, having met it in various forms in works by Coptic and Greek writers. Did it, perhaps, also form the beginning of the name of this particular pharaoh? In that case, the pharaoh's name must start with *Rē-*, *Ri-*, or *Ra-* . . .

The next sign, 𓏠 , was also somewhat resistant, though not so obstinate as the first. Champollion had not seen it in the names of Greek and Roman rulers, but he had come across it elsewhere— including in a group of four on the Rosetta Stone, 𓀀𓎡𓇳 , that matched up with a Greek word, *genethlia* or "birthday" (pp. 164–65). At some point after he had realized that step three of the decipherment procedure would work with the hieroglyphs, he had tried to turn this group into the Coptic word for "birthday," *houmise* (p. 193). In the top two signs, ● 𓎡 , the first he knew from Greek and Roman names to depict the sound *h;* together with the following picture of the "sun," it must somehow make *hou* or "day." In the bottom two signs, 𓀀𓏠 , the second was obviously *s;* therefore, Champollion had guessed, the first must be the other consonant of *mise,* namely *m.* If this guess was right, then in the new cartouche, the first two signs, ◯𓏠 , must together make *Rēm-*, *Rim-*, or *Ram-* . . .

Probably, Champollion could already tell the name that was forming in the cartouche, without even having to look at the last two signs: 𓊂𓊂 . In any case, he had known the signs well, ever since he had identified the "opposed scepters" as depicting the second *s* of *Alksentrs*. With this help from the name of the most famous of world-conquering Greeks, the decipherer certainly had no difficulty in reading through to the end of the name of the mightiest warlord pharaoh of Egypt. Champollion's later scholarly transcription of all four signs would be *Rēmss*. But obviously the name was that of the pharaoh whom the ancient writers called "Ramsse" or "Ramesse," "Ramesses" or "Ramses."

As Champollion looked through more sheets, he came upon the same name repeated over and over again, with many detailed variations in the signs—but every time, he was able convincingly to make out of them "Ramses." And there was another name, too—generally appearing in cartouches together with a title, but itself consisting of only three signs:

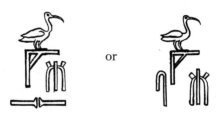

Young had already seen these signs, and had guessed from the top one, an ibis (the sacred bird of the god Thoth), that the whole group must somehow depict the name of another famous pharaoh, Tuthmosis. Now Champollion could see how it did so. The ibis did indeed depict the associated idea of the god—*Thōout*, as he was called in Coptic—which formed part of the pharaoh's name. But the idea-depicting sign was coupled with two sound-depicting ones to make *Thōoutms*—just as the idea-depicting sign of the sun god was coupled with three sound-depicting ones to make *Rēmss*.*

And beyond the names of the pharaohs, Champollion could now finally see the truth about Egyptian writing as a whole. Certainly it was no mere "picture writing," relying simply on the depiction of objects to convey information. Nor did it rely, as the 1,700-year-old consensus of the learned from Plutarch and Horapollo to Erasmus and Sacy had

---

*The names mean "Thoth is born" or "Born of Thoth" and "Ra is born" or "Born of Ra"—a fact that Champollion must certainly have known, but which he does not specifically state in the *Outline*.

insisted, exclusively on the depiction of ideas. It did not even consist only of an "alphabet" of sound-depicting "letters." The truth was rather, as Champollion later proclaimed in his *Outline* (using his preferred names for the three types of depiction), that "the hieroglyphic writing is a complex system: a writing that is at one and the same time figurative, symbolic, and phonetic, in the same text, the same sentence—I would almost say, the same word."

The story goes that when Champollion had finally convinced himself that it was so, he gathered up the papers that had given him the proof, ran across the street to the building where his brother worked, burst into Jacques-Joseph's office, slapped the papers triumphantly down on his desk, and announced: "Je tiens l'affaire!"—"I've got to the bottom of it!" Then, exhausted by weeks of overwork, of raised hopes, chilling disappointments, and the thrill of final success, he slumped to the floor in a dead faint, had to be carried home, and stayed in bed for five days.

When Champollion awoke from his stupor, it was to a new life as a celebrity savant, admired and courted by the highest in many lands. "King Louis XVIII to Monsieur Champollion the Younger, upon the Occasion of His Discovery of the Hieroglyphic Alphabet"—that was the message engraved upon a diamond-encrusted gold box, presented to the decipherer by the monarch whom he had been so recently suspected of trying to overthrow. King Charles Felix of the then independent north Italian kingdom of Piedmont, though he could not bring himself to be so personally gracious as his brother of France, nevertheless permitted his government to dangle before Champollion the prospect of employment as an academic superstar in the Piedmontese capital of Turin, where there was a magnificent Egyptian collection. And when Champollion visited Pope Leo XII in Rome, he managed to stop the admiring pontiff from making him a cardinal—a position whose holders did not have to be ordained priests, but could not be married men either—only by pleading the existence of "two ladies," namely his wife and daughter.

Needless to say, Champollion's feelings toward kings and priests had been softened by success, and in his dealings with these rulers of church and state, he was on his best behavior. Still, it shows how deep was their Ptolemaic respect for the pursuit of knowledge, and how strong their Ptolemaic ambition for cultural prestige, that they should have been so eager to honor this former subversive, simply because he had deciphered the writing of a dead civilization.

But amid the throng of rulers who jostled each other to honor and sponsor him, Champollion took care to give preference to those of his own country, so that the cultural prestige of his discoveries would go to them and to France. In 1826, the king appointed him curator of Egyptian antiquities at France's finest museum, the Louvre, and the government backed him with lavish grants of money, so as to channel into his collection the maximum tonnage of statues, manuscripts, and mummies exported from Egypt. In 1828, he headed an expedition to Egypt, jointly sponsored by the governments of France and Tuscany— another small Italian state, which the French hoped to win over politically by allowing it to share in Champollion's reflected glory. The arduous eighteen-month voyage took him the length of the Nile from Alexandria to Abu Simbel and back, stopping at every temple, monument, and tomb he came to, and finding, to his joy, that time after time he could make sense of their hieroglyphs. At the time that a series of strokes, brought on by relentless overwork, cut short Champollion's life in 1832, he held a specially created chair of "archaeology" at the College of France, a renowned teaching and research institution founded by a French king 300 years before, when the Renaissance had first inspired European rulers to imitate the Ptolemies.

As with every outsider who comes to sudden fame, Champollion's triumph also raised against him a great deal of suspicion and resentment. Partly these feelings emanated from England, where Thomas Young persistently refused to acknowledge that the French savant had done anything more than build on the basic principle of Egyptian phonetic writing which he claimed to have discovered himself.* But Champollion also had antagonists in other countries, including at home: conservatives who could not forgive him his radicalism; believers in the detailed historical accuracy of the Bible who were alarmed because his dating of Egyptian monuments and pharaohs did not square with time reckonings

---

*The relations between the two savants always remained civil, even though each of them felt that the other was trying to take more credit for the decipherment than was his due. But Young's friends and supporters in England, seconded by some of Champollion's French and German enemies, claimed that Champollion had simply stolen Young's results and used them as the basis for his own work. The accusations hinged mainly on the argument that Champollion had got nowhere with his efforts, and the idea that hieroglyphs could depict sounds had not occurred to him, until he read Young's 1819 account of his own results with its list of possible sound-depicting signs.

Yet the idea that hieroglyphs might have been converted to depict the sounds of non-Egyptian foreign names—which was all that Young had ever suspected—had in fact occurred to Champollion in 1810, and had also been suggested in print by Sacy in 1811. So far as is known, both Sacy and Young thought up the idea independently, but of the

derived from the Old Testament; admirers of Greek civilization who were contemptuous of the attention that "barbaric" Egypt was all of a sudden receiving.

There were also cautious doubters who were worried by some of Champollion's procedures and conclusions. In fact, even after Jacques-Joseph published his brother's *Egyptian Grammar* (1836), a systematic analysis of both the ancient language and the hieroglyphic writing, many loose ends remained in the decipherment. Champollion's final version of "Living Forever, Beloved of Ptah," for instance, was *ōnḫ (eneḫ) Phthaḥ-mai*. With its hieroglyphs harnessed to whatever Coptic words Champollion could think of that seemed to make sense, vowels and all, and with its *"(eneḫ)"* (forever) in parentheses because Champollion had never figured out how the wriggling cobra, the semicircle, and the line depicted that word, it still had a long way to go to reach the version of modern Egyptologists: *'nḫḏt mry Ptḥ* (p. 165). And even in Champollion's breakthrough word, *Rēmss*, he mistook the meaning of two of the signs. The second sign did not depict the single sound *m*, as he thought, but the two sounds *ms;* and the third sign, which he believed to depict *s*, actually said: "Reader, be aware that the sign before me depicts the sounds *ms* and not a 'bunch of foxes' skins'!" (pp. 164–65). In fact, Champollion never understood that the sound-depicting hieroglyphs were not really an "alphabet," but a mixture of one-, two-, and three-consonant signs, in which the single-consonant signs were often used to help out the others.

But subsequent scholars tied up the loose ends, copies of other priestly decrees "in sacred and native and Greek characters" were unearthed that confirmed the results obtained from the Rosetta Stone, and suspicion and resentment could not forever outlive the outsider who had inspired them. Today, Champollion's work takes pride of place in a long line of historic decipherments: in the 1850s, the cuneiform writing of Mesopotamia; a century later, the "Linear B" script of the

---

three savants, Young was not the first but the last to do so. Young's particular version of the idea, which permitted hieroglyphs to stand sometimes for single sounds such as *p* and *t*, and sometimes for one or more syllables such as *ole*, was very different from Champollion's "alphabet." And to the day of his death in 1829, Young remained doubtful of Champollion's discovery of sound-depicting hieroglyphs in native Egyptian texts.

This is not to say that Champollion learned nothing from Young. In 1815 the British savant sent Champollion copies of "conjectural translations" of the Egyptian texts of the Rosetta Stone, based on his word-for-word matchups. These may well have been helpful to Champollion in producing his own matchups, though in the arguments of the 1820s over the credit for the decipherment, he was not disposed to say so. But on the main point at issue, the existence, nature, and extent of use of sound-depicting hieroglyphs, there is no doubt that Young was a forerunner, and Champollion the real discoverer.

earliest Greek civilization; and at the present day, the first known writing of ancient Sumer and the Maya glyphs of Central America. Among them, these and many other decipherments have contributed a unique cultural feature to modern civilization: a detailed knowledge of its forerunners of the distant past.

Of all the ways in which scholars investigate the human past, the decipherment of ancient scripts is the one that comes nearest, in its procedures and its spectacular results, to the way in which scientists investigate the world of nature. In this case, the theory that the hieroglyphs were "depictions of ideas" was hallowed by tradition, and it had what seemed like good evidence in its favor—just like the theory that the earth was at the center of the universe. The early would-be decipherers tinkered fruitlessly with the idea-depicting theory to make it decode the writings on the Rosetta Stone—just as the early astronomers vainly tried to fine-tune the earth-centered theory to make it predict the movement of the stars in their courses. Out of a bewildering jumble of signs and scripts, Champollion deduced the simple and beautiful principles of Egyptian writing—just as out of a chaotic mass of observed angles and directions of planets, the sixteenth-century astronomer Johannes Kepler deduced their simple and beautiful orbits.

Of course, Champollion's methods were a combination of logic and guesswork. His count of the hieroglyphs against the Greek words did not really prove anything; and his *ŏnḫ (eneḫ) Phthaḫ-mai*, as well as his *Rēmss*, were inaccurate in all sorts of ways. But the hieroglyph count led to his much more sophisticated and conclusive study of the alternative signs, an elegant "experiment" if ever there was one. And even if his versions of Ptolemy's title and Ramses' name were only approximately true, he was still the first human being in 1,400 years to read and understand them. After all, without hunches leading to hypotheses that are tested by experiment, and without near-enough guesses that lead on to the truth, there would be no progress in science either.

There were also many other factors and motives at work in Champollion's discovery besides the disinterested search for truth. There was the predatory European urge to become the masters of the world, and the intoxicating feeling that non-European civilizations were ripe for conquest, that had taken Bonaparte to Egypt. There was the competition among rulers and nations within Europe itself, which made knowledge and culture into trophies for those who had come out on top in the struggle for territory and power. There was the thirst for fame and recognition of the savants themselves, for whom the discovery of truth was not a satisfaction in itself, but on the contrary, a source of bitter disappointment and frustration, if not rewarded by curatorships, professorships, and diamond-studded knickknacks.

But these factors, too, are not unique to the decipherment of Egyptian writing. As the story of the death and rediscovery of Egypt shows, predatory master nations and killers of civilizations are nothing new. It was the Greeks and Romans who first undermined pagan Egyptian civilization, before Christianity finally destroyed it. It was the Arabs, in turn, who undermined and all but destroyed Egypt's Christian civilization, to build in its place an Islamic one. Likewise, the story of the Rosetta Stone is full of Ptolemies, whether European, Muslim, or genuinely Ptolemaic ones. For better or worse, dominant civilizations acquire wealth, power, and access to knowledge; those who control the wealth and power use culture and knowledge as their status symbols; this leads them to divert some of their wealth into library directorships and special professorships of archaeology; and these, in turn, contribute to the personal fulfillment and satisfaction that an Eratosthenes expects to get from measuring the size of the earth, and a Champollion from reading the hieroglyphs. And after all, the results are not all bad. The size of the earth does get measured; the hieroglyphs do get read.

This, in turn, leads to an important conclusion about the Western civilization that forms the subject of this series. It is common nowadays for the West, being the dominant worldwide civilization of the present day, to be either condemned as the source of all evil in the world and a danger to every non-Western civilization, or praised as the source of all intellectual, cultural, social, and moral progress, as well as a model that every other civilization ought to follow. The fact is that both these things are true. Many predatory civilizations have existed before, which have controlled vast regions and undermined and destroyed other civilizations within their reach; but none have done so on the scale of the West. Many of these dominant civilizations have learned from the other civilizations they encountered on their way to supremacy, but generally they have repackaged what they learned to suit their own beliefs and needs, as Greece and Rome did with Egypt. The West has been the first among civilizations to succeed, at least sometimes, in stripping off the repackaging and confronting the reality of other civilizations of past and present, as Champollion did with the hieroglyphs.

In studying a fact or deed of history, one should not duck the judgment as to whether it was a Good Thing or a Bad Thing. The West has been both, to the fullest possible extent; and the Good and the Bad in it are Siamese twins, so intimately joined that they cannot be separated without killing both.

FURTHER READING

The books by Davies, Gardner, and Quirke and Andrews listed in the first part of this case study all include brief accounts of the decipherment of Egyptian writing. Listed here are longer books on this and related subjects.

Coe, Michael. *Breaking the Maya Code* (New York, 1993). An authoritative and entertaining account, by a participant, of a recent feat of decipherment in the tradition of Champollion. Coe relates the Mayan decipherment to this tradition, stressing the reluctant yielding of a misleading consensus to new insights.

Iversen, Erik. *The Myth of Egypt and Its Hieroglyphs in European Tradition*, 2d ed. (Princeton, NJ, 1993). A standard scholarly work on the "repackaging" of the traditions of Egyptian civilization by Greece, Rome, and Europe, which is also brief, readable, and well illustrated.

Pope, Maurice. *The Story of Archaeological Decipherment* (New York, 1975). Out of print but available in many libraries, Pope's book covers all the major decipherments up to the 1950s, as well as providing much background on early theories of the hieroglyphs and of writing in general. It is brief, clear, and comprehensive, with many diagrams and illustrations.

Sayyid-Marsot, Afaf Lutfi. *A Short History of Modern Egypt* (Cambridge, 1985). Concise account of the history of Egypt from the Coptic period to the present day. Presents the essential facts and weaves them into an appealing narrative.

SOURCES

This case study is based on the works of the early decipherers themselves, as well as on analyses of the process of decipherment by later Egyptologists. Standard works on Europe's cultural inheritance from Egypt and the Greco-Roman world have also been used.

Åkerblad, J. D. *Lettre sur l'inscription égyptienne de Rosette, adressée au C^en Silvestre de Sacy . . .* [Letter on the demotic inscription of Rosetta, addressed to Citizen Silvestre de Sacy]. Paris, 1802.

Bevan, Edwyn. *A History of Egypt under the Ptolemaic Dynasty.* London, 1927.

Bianchi, Robert S. "The Pharaonic Art of Ptolemaic Egypt." In *Cleopatra's Egypt: Age of the Ptolemies*, edited by Robert S. Bianchi. New York, 1988.

Bolgar, R. R. *The Classical Heritage and Its Beneficiaries.* Cambridge, 1954.

Budge, E. A. Wallis. *The Decrees of Memphis and Canopus.* 3 vols. London, 1904.

Burstein, Stanley M., ed. and trans. *The Hellenistic Age from the Battle of Ipsos to the Death of Kleopatra VII.* Cambridge, 1985.

Champollion, Jean-François. *Lettre à M. Dacier relative a l'alphabet des hiéroglyphes phonétiques* . . . [Letter to M. Dacier regarding the alphabet of phonetic hieroglyphs]. Paris, 1822; repr. 1824 and 1828 in the following item.

————. *Précis du système hiéroglyphique des anciens égyptiens* . . . [Outline of the hieroglyphic system of the ancient Egyptians]. 2d ed. Paris, 1828.

————. *Grammaire égyptienne* [Egyptian grammar]. 1836; repr. Paris, 1984.

Dewachter, Michel, and Alain Fouchard, eds. *L'Egypte et les Champollion* [Egypt and the Champollions]. Grenoble, 1994.

Forster, E. M. *Alexandria: A History and a Guide.* Alexandria, 1938.

Grant, Michael. *From Alexander to Cleopatra: The Hellenistic World.* New York, 1982.

Habachi, Labib. "Sais and Its Monuments." *Annales du Service des Antiquités de l'Egypte* [Annals of the Egyptian Antiquities Service] 42 (1943): 369–416.

Hartleben, H. *Champollion: Sein Leben und Werk* [Champollion: His life and work]. 2 vols. Berlin, 1906.

Iversen, Erik. *The Myth of Egypt and Its Hieroglyphs in European Tradition.* 2d ed. Princeton, NJ, 1993.

Lacouture, Jean. *Champollion: Une vie de lumières* [Champollion: An Enlightenment life]. Paris, 1988.

Lagier, Camille. *Autour de la Pierre de Rosette* [Essays on the Rosetta Stone]. Brussels, 1927.

Morenz, Siegfried. *Europas Begegnung mit Ägypten* [Europe's encounter with Egypt]. Berlin, 1968.

Müller, W. Max. *Egyptological Researches.* Vol. 3: *The Bilingual Decrees of Philae.* Washington, DC, 1920.

Phillips, Margaret Mann. *Erasmus on His Times: A Shortened Version of the 'Adages' of Erasmus.* Cambridge, 1967.

Plutarch. *Plutarch's De Iside et Osiride* [Of Isis and Osiris], edited, translated, and commented by J. Gwyn Griffith. Cardiff, 1970.

Pope, Maurice. *The Story of Archaeological Decipherment: From Egyptian Hieroglyphs to Linear B.* New York, 1975.

Renouf, Sir Peter Le Page. "Young and Champollion." In *The Life Work of Sir Peter Le Page Renouf,* 1st ser.: *Egyptological and Philological Essays,* Vol. 1, edited by G. Maspero and W. Harry Rylands. Paris, 1902.

al-Sayyid Marsot, Afaf Lutfi. *A Short History of Modern Egypt.* Cambridge, 1985.

Schenkel, W. "Schrift: Wiederentdeckung und Entzifferung." In *Lexikon der Ägyptologie*, Vol. 5, edited by Wolfgang Helck et al. Wiesbaden, 1984.

Sethe, Kurt. "Die historische Bedeutung des 2. Philä-Dekrets" [The historical significance of the Second Decree of Philae]. *Zeitschrift für Ägyptische Sprache* [Journal of Egyptian philology] 53 (1917): 35–49.

Silvestre de Sacy, A. I. *Lettre au Citoyen Chaptal . . . au sujet de l'inscription égyptienne du monument trouvé a Rosette* [Letter to Citizen Chaptal regarding the demotic inscription on the monument discovered at Rosetta]. 1802; repr. Bad Honnef, 1982.

Sottas, Henri. Preface to centenary edition of Champollion, *Lettre à M. Dacier.* Vienna, 1922.

Sottas, H., and E. Drioton. *Introduction a l'étude des hiéroglyphes* [Introduction to the study of hieroglyphs]. Paris, 1922.

Spiegelberg, Wilhelm, and Walter Otto. *Eine neue Urkunde zu der Siegesfeier des Ptolemaios IV. und die Frage der ägyptischen Priestersynoden* [A new document on Ptolemy IV's victory celebration and the question of synods of Egyptian priests]. Munich, 1926.

Thompson, Dorothy J. *Memphis under the Ptolemies.* Princeton, NJ, 1988.

Young, Thomas. *Miscellaneous Works of the Late Thomas Young, M.D., F.R.S., &c.* Vol. 3: *Hieroglyphical Essays and Correspondence*, edited by John Leitch. 1855; repr. New York, 1972.

Ziegler, Christiane. "Das geheimnis ist gelüftet" [The secret is revealed]. In *Pharaonendämmerung* [Dawn of the pharaohs], volume accompanying exhibition directed by Emmanuel Le Roy Ladurie and Dietrich Wildung. Strasbourg, 1990.